"I laughed all through th̲e̲ have to say goodbye. I enjoyed myself that much."

- Night Owl Reviews

"…not only well-written and entertaining but downright hilarious. I have not laughed so hard while reading in quite a while. And when I mean laugh, I mean I laughed so hard I was screaming. Warning, do not read this book while on the toilet."

- Indie Eclective

"Tony Slater is very gifted at writing comically, and laughter accompanied every page I read at the account of his daily routine looking after animals, birds and reptiles of all shapes and sizes and degrees of ferocity. Despite the tomfoolery of the writing, Tony never forgets the seriousness of the work carried out by the rescue centre, he never forgets to inform us of the beauty and uniqueness of Ecuador, and more importantly, never forgets to reveal not only how much the animals came to mean to him in the short time he was there, but also how much the whole experience touched him. This is one I will read again if I ever need cheering up. It's a guaranteed tonic."

- Kath 'n' Kindle Book Reviews

"Absolutely brilliant book! I loved every bit of it. Tony has such a fun, absorbing way of writing and you can't help but be swept along on his adventure with him. He might be a self-confessed idiot abroad, but he comes across as an extremely likeable idiot. Definitely the sort of person you would want to go for a beer with, or at least share a bit of fried, cheesy Ecuadorian street-food with.
Buy this book! You won't regret it."

– George Mahood,
author of *Free Country*

I bought it on the spot just for the title. It is truly the most hilarious book I have ever read, and I've read some good ones. It was a "In-Starbucks-laughing-so-hard-the-tears-came-and-I was concerned I was going to pee myself" kind of reading experience."

– TravelingCrone.com

Praise for *'That Bear Ate My Pants!'*
by Tony James Slater
(cont.)

"I can completely imagine Tony standing and enthusiastically delivering each chapter to a wide-eyed audience whilst they think inside their heads *This guy is a little bit mental*."

– BookC*nt

"[The] writing captures your imagination immediately and paints a picture of a world I'm unlikely to see that is so vivid, that I feel I have been there with him, every step of the way. I sweated up and down the mountains, I avoided being eaten by the Jaguar, I too chased an unruly teenage bear around an enclosure; I loved every minute of it."

– WomanOnTheEdgeOfReality.com

Fun. Fun fun fun. Did I say fun? It's been so long since I've been able to read a story that I could describe that way. You can pick this up and set it down at will. Read a chapter or two, have a laugh or a gape at the page, then go back to it in a couple of days. An easy read, and an enjoyable one at that.

Intranuovo.com

…it's pee-your-pants funny. It's like a travelogue gone horribly amuck. Brilliant.

– Shéa MacLeod,
author of *Kissed by Darkness*

KAMIKAZE KANGAROOS!

By
Tony James Slater

Various THINGS
@t **Different** *Times*

ISBN-13: 978-1514131039
ISBN-10: 151413103X

Although this is a work of non-fiction, some names have been changed by the author.

An e-book edition of this title is also available.

This first paperback edition printed by CreateSpace.

Cover Design by **Various Things At Different Times**
Formatted for paperback by **Heather Adkins**

Please visit the author's website for a selection of photographs that accompany this book:

www.TonyJamesSlater.com

Other books by
Tony James Slater:

That Bear Ate My Pants!
Don't Need The Whole Dog!
Can I Kiss Her Yet?

Yeah, I know! I'm working on it.
This is book 3. Book 4 is in the shops. As for Book 5…
Watch this space!

KAMIKAZE KANGAROOS!

Contents

(Here we go again…)

For Frieda

Concerning Rusty

When I first came to Australia, it was for pretty much the same reason that everyone comes to Australia; I was flat broke, and I had no choice.

Okay, so maybe that's not the *most* common reason...

Can I get away with just saying 'it's a long story', and leaving it at that?

No?

Okay then; here's the short-short version.

My name is Tony, and I like to travel.

I've been doing it for years...

I'm just not very good at it.

I left England in search of adventure – and on a tiny island in the Gulf of Thailand, I found it.

I'd been volunteering in an animal clinic, which is a notoriously poor way of making money. On the one hand it had allowed me to work with kittens and puppies and the occasional monkey; on the other hand I'd been bitten and shot at, had run-ins with the police and the mafia, visited hospital several times, and on one memorable occasion had been dangled from a tree by an enraged water buffalo.

Around the time I was sitting on a ferry with the decapitated head of a dog in a polystyrene box, I started to wonder – just what was going on with my life? Where was I headed? Apart from, you know, to have a dog's brain autopsied?

My love life had stalled.

Possibly because I spent most days covered in blood and poo.

As for my career... well. Did I mention that I was sitting on a ferry with a dog's head in a box?

To any normal person, these would be considered warning signs; a not-so-subtle hint along the lines of: 'Get out NOW, while you still can!'.

But personally...

I was rather enjoying myself.

At least until my money ran out.

I'd had to sell my body to medical science to get this far (told you it was a long story!), and as anyone who's seen my body can attest, it's not worth much.

Owing to a slight, ah, administrative error, I'd missed my flight home to England – by about six months – and I couldn't afford to buy another ticket.

And I didn't really want to go home anyway, because I didn't want my grand adventure to end. And also because I was still *technically* AWOL from the British Army. I felt sure this would all blow over, but it seemed like a good idea to stay out of the country for a while – you know, just in case.

So I emailed my sister, who was visiting a friend in Perth, Western Australia. They offered me a space on their couch, and a seat in the van they were fixing up – for an epic, year-long trip around the entire country! That sounded pretty good, so I told them I'd be there straight away – and then spent the next three months diving instead. Thailand is a very difficult country to leave, you see, and diving there is a whole load of fun. Still, it's not renown as a quick path to riches – and anyway, I was rubbish at it.

Hence: Australia.

When I stepped off the plane, this is what I had with me:

One pair of jeans, ripped badly (and not in an 'artistic' way); worryingly, they were also starting to fray somewhat around the groin area. I had three pairs of loose, cotton 'fisherman's trousers' – mostly blood-stained. A couple of t-shirts with the sleeves cut off, and several others branded 'LidStone', with dubious comedy slogans printed on the front. Two pairs of shorts, impregnated with sea-salt to the point where they could no longer be folded in half – and a tiny Sony Vaio laptop, on which the embryonic story of a bear was taking shape.

At least I have shoes, I reminded myself (which is a surprisingly common first reaction to landing in Australia).

I could tell the other passengers were thinking the same.

"*Thank God that bloke has shoes,*" they were saying to themselves, "*judging by the state of what's hanging out of his jeans! Now if only he could afford some underwear…*"

And that is what I was here to do: afford some underwear. And, ideally, one or two other niceties, like food, shelter, and onward travel.

At the baggage carousel I picked up an enormous holdall, crammed with every piece of diving gear imaginable – most of which I had inadvertently defrauded Lloyds bank out of.

My gaze lingered on an Italian-style espresso bar, but there was no way my bank balance would stretch to the price of a cup of coffee. That's hardly surprising though, since airport coffee costs two, or even three times as much as underwear.

Financial misfortune was preying heavily on my mind – at least until I saw the delighted faces of my sister Gillian, and her best friend Roo, waiting for me just beyond the sliding glass doors. They looked like a comedy double act, capering about in excitement; Gill, having inherited her genetic legacy from our mum, is rather gnomic in stature, whereas Roo's (apparently Dutch) ancestry meant she was so tall and slender that she daren't go outside in a stiff breeze. Gill still sported a healthy tan from visiting me in paradise three months previously, whereas Roo, despite being born Australian, was so pale she could warn ships away from the coast. After joyful hugs all round, the girls practically dragged me out of the airport, and frog-marched me over to the far corner of the car park. There, Gill introduced me to the van that would be carrying the three of us all around Australia.

"This is Rusty!" she announced, proudly.

"No shit," I said.

The door, when I opened it, came off in my hand, which was perhaps not the most auspicious start to our relationship.

"Don't worry," Gill said, "sometimes that happens." She shoved her glasses back up her nose and reached out to steady the door. "But Rusty's a good boy. I think he likes you!"

Little did I realize then, but over the next few months Rusty was to be both my salvation and my nemesis, in roughly equal measures. One thing was bothering me already, though; "*He*? Aren't we supposed to refer to vehicles as 'she'? You know, like they do with boats?"

"Don't be stupid Tony, *look at him!* Of course he's a boy."

I had looked at him. In fact I hadn't been able to look away, since first clapping eyes on him from halfway across the car park. It was kind of like watching a horror movie, when you know for sure somebody is mere seconds away from being eviscerated in a particularly savage manner, but for some reason your eyes won't leave the screen – won't even blink. And so I'd stared at Rusty as I approached, and part of me wanted to do my best Princess Leia impression and say "*You came in that?*"

Because... Hm. How to put this politely?

The girls had painted 'him'. They had cleaned him thoroughly, and very carefully masked off his windows, and then covered him from brake shoes to sunroof in bursts of yellow, green, purple and red spray

3

paint. It was very pretty. He looked like a unicorn had thrown up all over him. Inside each spray-painted circle was a white hand print; the girls had worn gloves, and had used them as stencils to create a van that was striving to give you a high-five with every square centimetre of its being.

Credit where credit's due though – the girls had done a very professional job.

Rusty looked *fabulous*.

And as I climbed into the back (and Gill replaced the sliding door behind me), I couldn't help but notice – they'd tailor-made curtains for all the windows. With psychedelic, multi-coloured dolphins on them.

I had to say something.

"You know, if Rusty is a boy, I think he might be batting for the other team."

Roo looked at me in the rear-view mirror, her eyes wide in mock horror. "Are you saying our van is *gay?*"

"Almost definitely. But don't worry – lots of my friends' vans are gay."

"Don't listen to him, Rusty," she said, patting his dashboard.

Then she changed gears, and Rusty groaned in pain.

"Also, I think he's dying," I added, "possibly of extreme old age."

"Nonsense," said Gill, "he's fine! I think of him like a young lad, really – he's trying to give us his best, only his best isn't quite good enough."

Riiight. So Rusty had not only a gender, but an appropriate character defect.

I had a horrible feeling he was being modelled on me.

But Rusty's life had been very different from my own, for which I was profoundly grateful. Roo and Gill took turns in relating this sorry tale to me, as we clunked and clonked down the highway towards Roo's home, in the hills south of Perth.

Rusty had started life as a young, brilliant-white work-van, but his innocence had only lasted until a gang of burly builders started putting their tools in him. Since then, every gruff, hairy-backed council labourer in the shire had taken a ride; he'd been used, and used hard. For more than two decades he'd been passed around the motor pool, and every tradesman they have a name for had been inside him. And most of them weren't too careful about it either.

His days as a working boy were over. And so was his healthy

prime, those middle years of taking a constant pounding with no outward signs of strain. Now, Rusty was entering his golden years – that time of life when, if he'd been an animal, he'd either get adopted by an appropriate sanctuary, or get taken out to the field and shot for dog food.

After spotting him sitting forlorn and broken by the side of the road, Gill and Roo had wanted to rescue him immediately.

In a fit of compassion they'd paid well over the odds to liberate the old van, and then they'd lavished their attention on him. Their attention, and their cash, as it turned out – Rusty had needed a fair bit more than a good clean and a few pairs of curtains. Dragging him unwillingly out of retirement had required replacing almost everything that could be replaced – from the gear box to the window latches. For anyone who is interested, here are the cold, hard facts: Rusty was bought for $2,000 – and he cost a whopping $2,500 to be made driveable!

If the girls had known this at the time, he'd have been dog food for sure.

And this eccentric, decrepit, borderline road-worthy vehicle was the trusty steed that was supposed to be carrying the three of us all around Australia. Or at least (as I became fond of saying) until it exploded in a rather garish fireball, killing the lot of us.

But that wasn't terribly likely, now was it?

Meeting The Locals

The late-afternoon drive through Perth's suburbs was an eye-opener.

Everything looked so clean and modern; so *new*, as though it had all been built yesterday, and to a plan made by someone who actually knew how roads should work. There were wide, tree-lined boulevards, uncluttered by parked cars. Junctions were spacious, and the traffic seemed suspiciously light, given how close we were to the city centre.

The only time we ever queued was at traffic lights.

Most of the other cars on the road were either huge four-wheel-drives, or something that looked like a saloon car cut in half, with a pick-up truck's tray glued on where the back seats ought to be.

"It's called a Ute," Roo explained, "short for Utility Vehicle."

"How odd. Can you sit in the back?"

"No, of course not!"

"Then... what's the point?"

"Tradies — sorry, tradespeople — use them for work. So they can carry their tools around."

As she said this, the ute sitting next to us roared, its driver flooring the gas and screeching the tyres, then it blasted off from the lights at terminal velocity.

Rusty was left trembling in its turbo-charged wake.

"That happens quite a lot," Roo noted, as our van puttered up to speed. "Maybe there's a certain kind of person that feels, I don't know, *threatened* by being close to Rusty? And they always seem to be young guys in shiny new utes..."

"Well, you're right about one thing," I said, "they seem like the perfect car for tools."

All the houses we passed were detached, on their own little plots of land. Most were single-storey affairs, the only exceptions being miniature mansions complete with Grecian columns and electronic security gates. There were enough of these, scattered around the various districts we drove through, to suggest a certain affluence;

obviously *someone* was doing quite well here.

And then the van laboured up a series of increasingly steep hills, through scrubland and forest, right to the very edge of the famous Australian Outback. This is where Roo lived with her family, in a sprawling, split-level bungalow that clung precariously to the top of its hillside plot.

"Welcome home!" the girls chorused, as Roo guided Rusty down a driveway that was more than half precipice.

My first contacts in Australia were to be Roo's immediate family – and there were millions of them! Okay, not literally, but Roo did have two parents, Gerrit and Frieda (both Dutch), and three sisters – one of whom was her identical twin, Sonja. The two of them looked… well, identical. To the untrained observer. The same wavy, mousey brown hair, the same pale, slender frame. Even my sister had trouble telling them apart, and she'd been living with them for three months already…

Which was partially my fault.

Unless you ask Gill; she would tell you it's *entirely* my fault.

Personally, I blame Thailand.

The two younger girls could have been twins too; both tall, pale and incredibly slim, Wendy and Vicky differed from Roo and Sonja only in their hair colour (they were both proudly ginger).

Roo's family gave me a very encouraging welcome, considering I was the second member of the Slater Clan to wash up on their doorstep.

After warm hugs and handshakes all round, Gill went straight to the kitchen to put the kettle on, and straight away I felt relaxed and at home. I'd been introduced as 'Gill's brother' – so I had to wonder how much further into our family their enthusiasm would extend. Next week: 'And these are all Gill's cousins…'

Eventually they were bound to run out of sofas. Even in a house this size.

And it was *huge*, at least by English standards. The living room was as long as a tennis court, and lined completely on one side with glass; from there, and from the open-plan kitchen next to it, I looked out across a wide, raised decking, and down into a sloping, garden teeming with life. All of which was alien to me, apart from the butterflies, of which there were hundreds. The myriad snuffling, scurrying and hopping creatures were harder to glimpse as they darted between the trees, but Roo, a volunteer at several local wildlife centres, could identify all of them.

But it was getting late. I'd come a long way, from the penniless vagrant that left Thailand, to… well, the penniless vagrant that turned up in Oz. It was the emotional miles, I reminded myself, that made me feel so suddenly old.

I'd left all my friends in Thailand, along with a way of life I'd been enjoying for almost a year. From here on, it was the great unknown. Which was exciting and terrifying in equal measure – and, consequently, quite draining.

Roo loaned me a sleeping bag and led me back up to the landing.

"I hope you don't mind, Tony, you're sleeping in the Games Room."

Wow.

I'd never been in a house with a dedicated Games Room before.

Most people I know are lucky if they've got space for a Games Cupboard.

I followed Gill, as she was also sleeping in there, and I was seriously impressed.

Roo's games room was of a size that, had it been in an English house, would have been called the Grand Banqueting Hall. It was massive, with chunky wooden beams supporting a pitched ceiling, and the same wall-of-glass effect that characterised the lounge. Cousins? Hell, my entire family tree would fit in there!

Probably best not to mention that, I thought, *in case they get scared.*

And so I passed my first night in Australia, surrounded and comforted by all the sounds of nocturnal life. Rustling leaves and humming insects, the constant drone of cicadas; and every so often, a clatter on the roof that sounded like a hippo had fallen off his unicycle onto it.

"SHIT!" I sat bolt upright, the first time I heard it. "Gill, was that you?"

Gill was sleeping on the sofa opposite me, dead to the world as usual.

So I lay back down, and listened to the drumming of feet on the roof. After a while I was pretty sure that something way too heavy to tap dance, was tap dancing up there.

But the big things in Oz aren't dangerous, I remembered as I drifted off to sleep. *It's the little things you've got to watch out for…*

Changing countries so abruptly can be very disorientating.

I woke up in a sleeping bag on a strange sofa, looking up at white-painted roof beams, and thought *where the hell am I?*

I've had this experience quite a few times, and normally a quick glance around the room reveals enough clues to jog my memory.

So I turned my head to the side, and there was a big lizard looking at me.

Oh, that's right! Australia.

The lizard was about two-feet long, about three feet away, and covered in sleek black scales. It looked slightly disappointed, as though it had been intending to suck my brains out through my nose while I slept, and its dinner plans had just been cancelled.

"Hey, don't be sad," I said to it, by way of an apology.

The lizard froze for a second, then skittered off under a bookcase, moving faster than something that size has any right to.

I blinked for a few seconds, and thought maybe I'd been hallucinating. But I decided to mention it to Roo, because sometimes people like to know if the cast of Jurassic Park takes up residence in their guest bedroom.

I broached the topic over breakfast, as we stood in the kitchen drinking tea and eating toast.

I couldn't really think of a polite way to bring it up, so I just waited for a natural break in the conversation and blurted, "Is there a giant lizard living in your games room?"

"I dunno," Roo replied. "Maybe."

"Oh, alright then. Because I thought my mind was playing tricks on me."

Apparently the weirdness of my mind was no match for the weirdness of reality in Australia.

Roo was quite nonchalant on the matter. "I was wondering about him. I think I've spotted him a couple of times, but he's too quick to get a good look at."

"Well I saw him pretty good. He's about this big," I held up my hands, shoulder-width apart, "and he's black all over. Looks kind of evil, actually."

"Ah! It might be a blue-tongued skink."

"A what? Blue-tongued? That doesn't sound real!"

"It's real."

"So, is that him making all those noises on the roof then?"

"No, that'll be the possum."

"Possums, eh? Those little hopping guys from the garden?"

"No, those are bandicoots."

"Okay, you are SO making this up now."

"No! Not at all. If I was making it up, I'd tell you about the drop bears."

"What bears?"

"Drop bears. It's a story we invented to tell foreigners who are freaking out about the wildlife here. Basically, drop bears are like the evil, carnivorous twin of koalas – they hang around in trees looking innocent, but when a person walks underneath they drop down onto them and bite their faces off!"

"Woah. But you *do* have koala bears…"

"Koalas," she said flatly. "They are *not* bears."

"Riiight. But drop bears are…?"

"Fictional."

"Okay. I think I've got it. Possums and skinks and bandicoots. Man, the animals in this country are bizarre! But you have kangaroos, at least?"

"Not personally! But yes, we have kangaroos."

"And you have all the world's deadliest spiders here, don't you?"

"Oh yes, spiders! That reminds me… hang on." Roo led me back into the games room, which was a little disconcerting.

She took me over to the farthest corner and pointed into it. "There! See that one?"

"OH FUCK ME!" The spider was as big as the palm of my hand. I could see every hair on its long, spindly legs. "This is just inside?"

"Yeah, this one's fine. These aren't dangerous. This is a huntsman. It's harmless."

"What, so it doesn't bite?"

"Of course it bites, but it doesn't *hurt*. Not much. It's not poisonous. And it eats all the mosquitoes and flies."

"But, it *bites*?"

"Yes, but you don't need to worry about it. *That* one, down there – that's the one you have to be careful of."

"What? Where… Oh."

Tucked further back into the same corner was a tiny little cobweb, with a tiny little black spider clinging to it.

"See the red stripe on its back?"

I shoved my head in for a closer look. "Yup, I think so."

"That means it's a 'red-back'. They're pretty bad."

"Like, poisonous?"

"Like, deadly. But no-one really dies from them these days, because there's anti-venom in all the hospitals."

"Well, that is comforting. I feel much better about having one in my bedroom now."

"Don't worry, I'm going to kill that one. They shouldn't be inside, really, but when you live out here…" she trailed off with the kind of shrug that says 'what can you do, really?' Which was considerably less comforting.

"How do you kill them?"

"Oh, I'll just squish it. With my thong."

This seemed like an embarrassingly intimate revelation, so I decided to be all manly and offer my services instead. "No need to stain your knickers! I'll do it with this shoe."

She looked slightly puzzled*, but was happy enough to relinquish spider-bashing duties to me.

"Don't get too close though!" she warned.

I froze. "Why? They don't spit at you, do they?"

"No, but you're getting close to the huntsman. And they jump."

"Oh Jesus! So, jumping, biting spiders the size of my hand?"

"Yup! Welcome to Australia! Bet you're glad you've got a lizard in your bedroom now, eh?"

*Roo was destined to remain confused on this occasion, because there is no good way to apologise for telling a girl not to stain her panties. It's notoriously difficult to pass that shit off as a cultural misunderstanding.

The Curve

All right you lot, it's time to admit it: ninety-five percent of everything you know about Australia comes from watching old episodes of *Neighbours*.

No?

Really?

Okay, then. *Home and Away.*

Don't worry – same here! Only it was more embarrassing for me, because I was actually *in* Australia.

So on my first morning in the country, I was forced to re-evaluate my knowledge.

For example, as far as I knew, it was always summer in Australia. I knew that all the blokes loved beer, and all the women were called Sheila. And I knew that Bondi Beach was the spiritual home of the nation, and that as a direct result of this, the whole population spend their entire lives in swimwear.

Right?

Wrong.

I'd arrived in mid-winter. In the hills around Perth it was freezing; shivering, ball-achingly cold, particularly at night and in the mornings. Wearing a bikini outdoors was inviting death by hypothermia – as well as earning me quite a few strange looks.

It didn't matter how good the beer was, as I couldn't afford to drink it – alcohol turns out to be eye-wateringly expensive in Australia.

I was 2,498 miles from Bondi Beach.

And if you call enough women 'Sheila', sooner or later one of them will punch you in the face.

I was now living with six women of different age groups, and not a single one of them was called Sheila. I didn't have a clue what they were called – something I only realised when the phone rang halfway through that first morning. I picked it up without thinking.

"Hello!" I said, "This is… the house of… some Australians?"

One distinct downside of open-plan living is that when you make a gaffe like this, everyone can hear it, no matter where they are in the house. All of them shrieked with laughter, and by the time I'd handed the phone off to one of the girls, the caller must have thought they'd dialled an insane asylum by mistake.

I later learned that Roo's family name was Reynen – adapted by her parents from the Dutch 'Reijnen'.

That day involved a fairly steep learning curve. I imagine that most tourists visiting Australia come and go without ever having to learn certain things, but living where Roo did, on the edge of the Western Australian outback, survival lessons were disturbingly important. I think they get taught at pre-school.

First up, I learnt that a 'thong' is not actually a skimpy piece of underwear. It is in fact a multi-purpose item of footwear, which most sane individuals would refer to as a flip-flop. I say multi-purpose, because the primary use of a pair of thongs, in Roo's house at least, was to kill things. They can also be used to fix certain parts of a car's engine, are often thrown at people to get their attention, form a miniature floating table for something light, like a bag of crisps, in the swimming pool, and – in an emergency – can even be used to paddle a canoe (though I only found this out much later). Because all Australians wear them all the time (unless they're working in heavy construction – and sometimes even then) – I was offered the use of a spare pair of thongs. They were to be worn generally outside, but I had to "be careful wearing them in the back yard, because of snakes."

I had to love this aspect of Australian culture. Rather than chaining the back door shut, and nailing thick wooden planks across it topped off with a sign saying, "KEEP OUT, THERE'S FUCKING SNAKES IN THE GARDEN!", instead they say things like "if you do go out there barefoot, try to be a bit careful."

But at least the snakes weren't on the inside. Often.

"So I don't use a thong to try and kill snakes, then?" I joked.

"No," said Roo, looking vaguely disgusted, "why would you want to kill snakes?"

Which was a fair point.

I just had to hope the feeling was mutual.

Because I'd arrived in the coldest part of the year, with no money and almost no clothing, I had to borrow a fleece from one of Roo's slender sisters.

It had 'Bush Ranger' emblazoned across the front.

I was the only one who seemed to find this funny. It was hard to tell whether this was a language-barrier thing, or whether it was because my sense of humour stopped developing at age twelve.

Regardless, now that I was suitably equipped to handle the cold, I had a busy day ahead of me. The girls had planned an epic road trip around the whole of Western Australia, and had been waiting for me to arrive so that I could accompany them.

But not only had I arrived three months late, I'd also arrived penniless.

It's okay though – we're blaming Thailand, remember?

So before we could set out on our grand Australian adventure, there were a few little details I had to take care of.

Like earning enough money to pay for it.

Luckily, both the girls had been in this situation before…

About three months ago, as it happened.

They fired up Rusty and drove me to the nearest bank, where I braced myself for an orgy of form-filling, coupled with the high probability of being laughed out of the place.

I always feel self-conscious in banks, as though the staff can see right through me and know instantly that I'm a man of very dubious financial security.

The fact that I was wearing ripped, stained jeans and a girl's jumper was also fairly poor indicator. I half expected alarms to blare, and a giant illuminated arrow to swing down from the roof with a warning sign on it blinking 'CREDIT RISK! CREDIT RISK!'

But I was pleasantly surprised to find that most of the bank's customers were covered in concrete.

"Rich tradies," Roo pointed out. "That's who owns all those mansions! Builders and plumbers, and especially the miners. The guys on the *big* money."

That was unexpected. Plumbers are expensive at home, but I didn't know many miners that had earned their fortune. I distinctly remember being threatened with mining as a job, if I didn't work hard at school and pass my exams. *The cartoons were right*, I thought, *everything is upside-down here.*

A very efficient lady typed in the details off my passport, and accepted Roo's family address as mine.

"What funds would you like to open the account with?" she asked me.

"Funds?"

"Yes, you need to deposit some money into the account to open it."

"Ah. How much do I need to put in?"

"Anything you like! A dollar will do."

"Um… guys? Anyone have a dollar they can lend me?"

Roo dug into the pocket of her jeans. "Here – have two."

She handed me a small gold coin. Travellers are often confused by this (as are the natives) – but for some reason, their two-dollar coin is half the size of their one-dollar coin.

And just like that, I had a bank account.

Next, the girls took me to an employment agency called 'Select'. They'd both got temp jobs through this agency, and they reckoned there was plenty of work going.

Now this did involve a lot of paperwork; I spent about two hours filling it all out, taking maths tests and English tests, and then I sat through the inevitable video about Health and Safety in the Workplace. It was delightfully lurid, with graphic re-enactments of accidents so improbable I had to applaud the scriptwriter. I mean, what are the odds of being decapitated by a step ladder? I was tempted to try it just to find out.

Finally, the lady marking my answer sheet came over to me.

"Okay, so, we have some labouring work for you. I'm afraid it's minimum wage stuff though."

"Ah well, that's okay! What is the minimum wage by the way?"

"How old are you?"

"Twenty-eight."

"Okay, so it's eighteen dollars thirty cents an hour."

I had to sit and think about this for a few seconds. It was tough to calculate, because I don't have eighteen fingers, and the exchange rate was a little better than one-and-a-half dollars to the pound, and I don't have one-and-a-half of anything on my body (unless you count my nose). And when I'd done the sums, I still thought I'd made a mistake.

"Is that… it can't be? Eighteen dollars is more than ten English pounds an hour? That's double the minimum wage in the UK! That's more than what my Mum earns, as a qualified nurse!"

"I know," she said, "it's not great, but we do get better stuff in. Only, you wanted to start straight away."

"Hell, I'll start right now! Where's the job?"

She looked impressed by my enthusiasm. Probably because she hadn't seen my bank account.

"You can start tomorrow, if you'd like."

Tomorrow would be my second full day in the country.

To celebrate the breath-taking swiftness of my transition from unemployed bum to valued employee, we first headed to Woolies (supermarket) to buy a chook (chicken) and some snags (sausages) for the barbie (iconic doll from the 1970s).

I also grabbed some bread to make a sanga (sandwich), and nearly bought a kanga-banga (kangaroo sausage).

It was a like free lesson in Aussie slang.

Next we went to buy some *goon*.

"It's wine in a box," Roo explained, "or wine in a bag inside a box. It's what all the kids drink, because it's the cheapest thing they can get."

But we couldn't buy it there, because the supermarkets aren't allowed to sell booze. For that we had to go to a separate liquor store, which Aussies, with their typical subtlety, call a 'bottle shop'.

Three things about the bottle shop blew me away.

First up, it was massive; not far off the size of the supermarket we'd just come out of.

Secondly, it was unfeasibly expensive. The cheapest bottle of vodka on offer was $45 – that's £30! Now I knew why the minimum wage was so high.

Oh, and the third thing that blew me away?

It was a drive-thru bottle shop!

Seriously!

I couldn't help but think this sounded like a really, *really* bad idea. Almost like an accident waiting to happen. I mean, isn't there some sort of thing about drinking and driving not going terribly well together? I was kind of surprised there wasn't a police station next-door.

I'd love to have been at the meeting where they came up with the idea.

"How bad is it, having to park up and get out of the car every single time you need to buy a beer?"

"It's a bloody disaster! If only there was something we could do about it…"

Talk about first-world problems.

Anyway, fully half of the cavernous building was devoted to wine. They had Dry, Medium, and… Lexia. It sounded more like a car than a beverage, but absolutely nothing in the whole shop was labelled 'sweet'. After reading the labels on half an aisle's worth of wine bottles, we discovered that Fruity Lexia is what everyone else in the world would call a sweet, white wine. Clearly some kind of award was in order for the most confusing labelling system in the world. But we couldn't complain too much – once we'd identified Fruity Lexia as our poison of choice, we discovered why kids loved the stuff so much; a four-litre cardboard cask of it was only ten dollars.

We were the only people in the queue not buying at least two giant crates of beer. Supermarket trolleys were provided, presumably for those industrial-size purchases that wouldn't fit through a car window. Alcohol buying in this country was obviously taken very seriously.

I felt rather inadequate, with my little box of goon, *walking* out of the bottle shop.

And the next morning, I started work – unloading container trucks of bog roll!

Alright, you can laugh now.

But it could have been worse.

Roo was working in a textile factory, categorizing towels.

And Gill was cleaning public toilets.

Oh, yes – we were living the Australian Dream all right…

Ready For The Off

And so, for the next two weeks, that was our life.

We got up early (painfully early in Gill's case), we worked hard, and we enjoyed several delicious barbecues, cooked and eaten out on the Reynen family veranda.

We even went to the park for one – because *there were free gas barbecues in the park!* And not just a couple, but loads of them, dotted around a stretch of riverbank, complete with large, shaded picnic tables.

In England, they'd have been covered in graffiti and vandalised beyond recognition within half an hour of being put there. But here, only minutes from the city centre, overlooking a wide curve of the Swan river and the million-dollar residences on the far side of it, the great steel hotplates were spotless.

"I can't believe it, they're so clean," I said to Gill.

"I know," she replied. "I cleaned them. It's not just toilets we do, y'know."

"So that's where my tax-dollars are going! Paying you to keep the barbies clean."

"Nothing wrong with that, is there?"

"Nope. I think it's the best system in the world."

It might not be a tourist's idea of the Australian Dream, but it's far closer to the average Australian's version of it; hard yakka (work), honestly done, a good laugh, and a cold beer at the end of the day.

We never went to the beach once.

We did go ice skating, though – in fact Roo's entire family squeezed into Rusty for the trip, to an ice rink amusingly named 'Cockburn'.

"Probably because that's the most common injury men get when ice skating," Gill quipped.

"No," Roo explained, "it's pronounced 'Co-ben'."

"I wouldn't know," I told her, "I've never suffered from it."

We also made a couple of return trips to the bottle shop, hereafter to be referred to as the 'bottle-o' – because Australians suffer from a pathological inability to use complete naming-words, and must shorten everything and add an 'o' on the end. Don't ask – it's the law. Even if it ends up harder to say than the original word. I found it hilarious, listening to my new co-workers call to each other around the yard. Every one of them was a 'Johno' or a 'Steve-o'. It confused the hell out of them for a while, when I introduced myself as Tony. I could see them racking their brains, trying to figure out where to put the 'o'. They had to call me 'mate' for the first couple of hours, but it didn't take them too long – halfway through my first morning I was rechristened 'Tone-o'.

Sitting with Roo's family on their deck, watching the sun set through the trees, I took a swig from my stubby (small beer bottle), and breathed a sigh of relief. "That's what you need – a nice cold beer, after a hard day's work."

Gill was quick to respond to that; "Awww, you poor man! Is it heavy, lifting all that toilet paper?"

"Hell yeah it is! I can steal you some, if you want."

"Dude, I work as a toilet cleaner. One of the few perks is a endless supply of free bog roll. And unlimited bathroom breaks."

After ten days of work, I had amassed a little more than eight-hundred dollars.

After tax.

It was a stunning revelation. To achieve the same level of income back home, I'd need a qualification considerably more impressive than my degree in Acting. Admittedly, every qualification is better than a degree in Acting, with the possible exception of a degree in Philosophy.

But there was no doubt about it; my earning potential, at least in Perth, was incredible. In my last temp job in England, it would have taken me a month to accrue this much money. Now, after just two weeks, I was good to go.

The long-awaited road trip was about to commence.

It was time to head north.

Step One: pack the car.

This can be a bit of a chore, especially when you're travelling with two young women.

Neither Gill nor Roo were particularly ladylike at this point, so at least I wasn't loading suitcases full of cocktail dresses and Jimmy Choos. They didn't even pack a hairdryer! But still, they conjured up an impressive amount of gear, from pots and pans to folding canvas chairs. My sole contribution came in the form of one large holdall crammed with diving equipment. I managed to wedge it under the last row of back seats, well out of the way – and there it stayed, completely untouched, for the entire time we travelled in Rusty.

It was a bit of a mistake, that. But how was I to know? Australia – at least the bit we were planning on visiting – is defined by its distinct lack of water. Damn it.

And speaking of water, we put a twenty-five litre plastic tank full of the stuff in the boot, because getting stranded in the outback kills dozens of people every year. Most die in less than two days – of thirst. You've got to respect that kind of environment.

For the same reason, we added a jerry can with 15 litres of petrol in it. Not to drink of course; north of Perth, fuel could be hard to come by. Gas stations were generally spaced a full tank apart, so too much detouring could leave us unable to reach the next one. 'Avoid becoming stranded in the bush at all costs,' is the advice routinely dispensed by the AA and the RAC. We had membership of the latter, but would be well beyond their call-out range for much of the trip. Beyond the range of mobile phones, even.

"What happens if you get lost?" Roo's sister Sonja asked. "Do you want to take my GPS?"

"Nah, we'll be fine," said Roo. "We've got a map."

"That map is ten years out of date," Sonja pointed out.

Roo wasn't fazed. "Don't worry! I'm pretty sure there's only one main road, once you get out of Perth."

I admired her confidence. Even if I didn't share it.

"What if we do get lost?" I whispered to Gill.

"That's alright, we've thought of that."

She led me around the back of Rusty, and pointed to a sign stencilled across the tailgate.

It read, 'Don't Follow me – I'm Lost!'

"See?" she said.

"Fair enough."

It took us a day and a half to get Rusty fully packed.

Because I had so little equipment, I had to borrow various things from all three of Roo's sisters. A sleeping bag, a pillow, cutlery and a plate – and most importantly, a towel with a purple octopus embroidered on it. Any fan of Douglas Adams can tell you, when setting off on an adventure such as this, you must always know where your towel is.

Rusty's boot was stuffed to the gills. A tent and blankets, cooking gear and clothes, a huge plastic crate full of all the food we could scrounge from Roo's parents' kitchen – and another, not substantially smaller, plastic crate of books. Books? Well, we had a van instead of a bunch of rucksacks – might as well fill it!

Poor Rusty. With the three of us sat inside, it was a miracle he could get out of the driveway – which, like all the driveways in Roo's home town, angled downwards at about forty-degrees.

We said an emotional farewell, particularly to Frieda and Gerrit, who had fed and sheltered us without a second thought. Roo was particularly upset, leaving her entire family all at once, for an unknown length of time. We'd all had to do it at some point; my family farewell was now almost a year behind me, and yet not a day went by when I didn't miss my parents. I worried about them constantly, because… well, if you'd met my parents, you'd know.

And so, we pointed Rusty north, and set off into the wilderness…

Heading Up

As we drove through Perth's charming outer suburbs, Gill and Roo explained their carefully crafted plan for this trip. They'd had three months to prepare, to research alternative routes, to pick desirable stopping places and to choose which of the attractions along our path were 'must see'.

This is how they laid it out for me:

"We're going north," Gill explained.

"Okay! Why north?" I asked.

"I dunno. Just 'coz."

"Ah."

"We can't go west," Roo pointed out, "because Rusty can't swim, and west goes into the sea. To the east, there's nothing between here and Sydney but the desert, and I'm not sure Rusty would survive that trip."

"And south?"

"Ah, well... we already went south," Gill admitted. "A bit..."

So they took turns in describing to me the trip they'd undertaken as a maiden voyage for Rusty, weeks before I was due to land in the country.

To say it was a rip-roaring success would be a lie.

Roo's mum Frieda had accompanied the girls to see a massive rock formation, which was known as Wave Rock because... What? Oh, you've got there before me? Well I can't help it if the Aussie style of naming things lacks creativity. Then again, what else do you call a fourteen-metre high chunk of rock that looks like a wave?

Answers on a postcard...

Anyway, about halfway there Rusty had started to overheat, so they pulled off the highway onto the amusingly-named 'Strange Road'. They'd waited till he cooled off, put loads of water in him, then went to start the engine – and nothing.

Just a click. The battery was dead.

Noticing they'd parked Rusty on a slight incline, the girls decided to try jumpstarting him. Backwards, because that was the direction the slope was in…

They'd had no problem picking up speed, but it was around that point that Roo, in the driver's seat, had realised that Rusty's brakes were hydraulic, and only worked when the engine was switched on. As did the power steering.

Careening backwards at quite a clip, Rusty had left the road, ploughed down a steep bank, and crashed arse-first into a stout wooden fence. The fence snagged the bumper, and luckily so; otherwise, it would have been all downhill from there.

After several hours waving at the handful of cars that passed, they'd managed to enlist the help of a group of local farmers. The guys drove off and came back with a beat-up old tractor. Together with chains, elbow-grease and a goodly amount of swearing, they extricated Rusty from the fence, hauled him back up the hill, and got him running in an epic eight-man push-starting marathon.

Before they drove away, the helpful farmers had given them two pieces of advice; one, to drive without stopping until they found a place to buy a new battery, and two, join the RAC.

Which is why we now had a membership.

Because it always pays to be prepared.

After hearing how scary and remote the outback seemed, the reality was somewhat softer and less threatening. As the buildings became more sporadic, the urban areas gave way to farmland. Before long we were enveloped by it; thousands upon thousands of acres of wheat crops, wilting in the afternoon sun. Stands of tall, white-barked trees broke up the monotony, adding to the foreignness of the landscape, but what set it apart most of all was the scale. I was used to seeing fields neatly divided up by hedgerows and roads, littered with electricity pylons and never far from a village or six. Here, the fields stretched to the horizon in all directions, with only log fences and the occasional barn to prove that humans laid claim them.

The further we got from the city, the less tamed the land became. Red dirt showed through a covering of spikey-looking grass and shrubs. We'd gone from arable, wheat-belt farming to a much harsher wilderness frontier; probably whilst I was asleep. I know, this was my first taste of rural Australian countryside; but it was lovely and warm inside Rusty, with the throb of the labouring engine and the rumble of the road beneath our wheels…

Sleep was impossible to avoid.

But don't worry! I wasn't driving.

I was cabbaged full-length across the middle row of seats, with my head on a pile of blankets. I defy anyone not to doze off under such conditions!

Almost at sunset, we arrived at our destination; an area of desert full of strange protruding rock formations called The Pinnacles. They were like the stalagmites that form on the floor of caves, only here there was no limestone dripping from the ceiling – just the rocks themselves, thrusting up through the earth like talons. Or termite mounds.

We parked right amongst the rocks, having arrived late enough to avoid both the crowds and the admission fees, and Rusty was dwarfed by the stony spires. The girls ran around, taking far more photos than was strictly necessary. I had to point out that when they looked at them later on, all they'd really have were dozens of pictures of pointy rocks. "It's gonna make for a fairly boring slideshow," I warned.

But there was a raised wooden viewing deck, which we duly climbed up to investigate. The added height meant we could see *even more* rocks – and could confirm for ourselves that they were, in fact, *all* pointy, for as far as our new vantage point allowed us to see. Oh yes! None of this fobbing-you-off-with-a-few pointy-rocks-when-the-rest-of-them-are-completely-normal shit. You get so much of that these days.

As a tourist attraction… well, it's never going to rival Disneyland.

"We should probably go," Gill said, "because there's only so long you can run around a bunch of big pointy rocks and go 'oooh!'"

We stayed for the all-important sunset photo opportunity, and the girls were suitably impressed. The flaming orange sky cast a dramatic silhouette, which looked remarkably like the shadows of lots of big pointy rocks.

"Shall we rock on?" said Roo, climbing back into the driver's seat.

My response was a stony silence.

It wasn't hard to locate the campsite, because there was only one; it was on the road, of which there was also only one. Roo had been dead right – since leaving Perth's northern suburbs, we'd seen exactly one junction. We were only a few hours north of the city, and already the land felt… desolate. Empty. Wild.

We set up the tent, for the first time, in complete darkness. Which is easy enough, if you know the tent, and each other, and can work as a team. But there were three of us, all with our own opinions, and one rather small tent which seemed to be missing most of its vital components. By the time we thought of using Rusty's headlights it was fully night-time, and we still hadn't had anything to eat.

"Right!" said Roo. "To the kitchen!"

"Woah? There's a kitchen here?"

"Of course! All campsites have kitchens. How else would we cook dinner?"

"I thought that was what the little gas stove was for."

"Only in emergencies. If we're free camping by the side of the road! But no, this is a proper campsite." She held up the paper map we'd been given on arrival. "There's the kitchen, and there's a games room, a TV lounge – ooh, and a pool!"

"Wow... that's just... wow."

"Don't they have this stuff in campsites in England?"

"Um... no. They're more like, a place to pitch your tent. Some grass, you know. And that's about it."

"Oh, we have those too. We call them fields."

All Creatures Great And Small

The next morning, after a leisurely breakfast of leftovers, we carefully packed all our gear and ourselves back into Rusty.

Our first stop-off, just down the road, was Lake Thetis, an inland salt-water lake that was home to The Stromatolites. No, not a cheesy rock tribute band – they are unique, microscopic creatures, known from the fossil record as the earliest form of life on earth.

It's Gill's fault for raising my expectations, by telling me we were going to see the oldest living organisms in the world. When I hear something like that, my mind goes instantly to T-rex. Sadly, the stromatalites were small lumps of rock at the edge of the lake.

"You can see the bubbles, where the bacteria is doing… whatever it does." Even Gill sounded disappointed. How excited can you get over bacteria?

"Maybe we should come back in a few million years," she added. "By then they may have evolved into even bigger creatures that blow even more bubbles…"

"The possibilities are endless," I agreed.

So we decided not to sully their three-and-a-half billion year legacy with our continued presence.

"And no," I told Gill, "before you suggest it – we do *not* need a pet stromatalite."

"Aw! But they hardly eat anything…"

Since leaving Perth, the temperature had been rising dramatically. Now, only three-hundred kilometres further north, it was already becoming uncomfortable. Sitting still for ten minutes had turned the inside of Rusty into a sauna. We opened all the doors to vent the baking hot air, replacing it with marginally less hot air from the surrounding desert.

And then we drove, and drove, and drove.

If we'd been back home in the UK, we'd have fallen off the edge.

Not so in Australia; one of the few things I had known before coming here was that it's a fairly big place. Size, I feel, is a relative concept, and my idea of 'big' was limited to things I already knew that fell into that bracket. Like my credit card bill. Well, I was about to gain a new understanding of 'big'.

Starting with kangaroos, which are commonly represented in the western world by cartoon characters and cute, fluffy toys, giving the impression that they are small, friendly, somewhat comedic creatures.

They are not.

The few we saw in the distance, as late afternoon tinged towards evening, were the size of Gill – which, I'll grant you, isn't huge. But I'd been expecting something the size of a dog stood on its hind legs, so to see animals weighing in at close to what a person does, was a bit of an eye-opener.

As was the fact that Roo kept referring to her namesakes as 'cute little greys'.

"They come bigger than that?" I asked her, when she pointed out another *little* group.

"Oh yes! Wait till we get a bit further north. The reds are everywhere out in the bush."

"How big? Like, my height?"

"Yeah, I'd say the girls would be about your height."

On up the western edge of Australia we journeyed, the road now hugging the Indian Ocean to spectacular effect. After the previous day's drive through over two-hundred miles of flat red dirt, the change of scenery was a welcome relief.

The beauty of that coast is in its raw elements; the rust-coloured rock giving way to a narrow fringe of golden sand, and then to the sea – the water mirroring the sky, both of them as blue as any postcard of paradise. The wind blasts and buffets, carrying a hint of Antarctic chill as it surges inland; there's nothing to stop it, no obstacles either man-made or natural. And above it all, the sun rains down its fire, more potent here than almost anywhere else on Earth. That hole we tore in the ozone layer back in the 1980s might have dropped out of the spotlight of the world's media, but it's still around – and Australia is where it likes to hang out. So while the rest of the planet views Aussies as a nation of sun-worshippers, the vast majority of them avoid going out in it as much as possible. Skin cancer is rife, owing to dangerously high UV levels, and TV ads regularly drive home the message: *Slip, Slop, Slap*. As in, *slip* on a shirt, *slop* on the sunscreen, and *slap* on a hat. 'Because you don't want to end up wearing your bum on your face!' (A reference to skin cancer surgery, where they replace the cut away bits – commonly on the nose and cheeks – with a graft from your nice, soft buttocks!)

It's an environment that bites back alright.

And that's even before we consider the wildlife.

But it is beautiful.

It was dark by the time we reached Geraldton, but we were delighted to discover that this particular dot on the map belonged to a *real town* – and the first supermarket since Perth. To celebrate, we bought an entire tub of ice cream, a bottle of caramel sauce, and some 'Tim Tams' – delicious, chocolate-coated biscuits that were set to become my newest addiction. The girls had a tradition, established on their trips around America and Europe, called 'Ice Cream Wednesday'. They used it both as a reward, and as a way to mark the passing of the weeks. Weekends can cease to have meaning when you aren't working, and endless days of long-term travel have a way of blending into one another. I've lost count of the number of times someone's asked me what day it is, only to watch me glance around for any clues, and come up with nothing. So Wednesday became the new Sunday, with the consumption of ice cream as our chosen mechanism for marking it. I tell you what, it beats the snot out of going to church!

Perhaps in response to this blasphemy, the heavens opened, and as we sat in Rusty eating huge bowls of ice cream we decided not to bother pitching the tent. We found a campsite, drove right up to the kitchen, and de-boxed just enough stuff to cook a nice chicken korma.

By which I mean, three bowls, three spoons, and an industrial-sized tin of microwavable chicken korma.

Then we settled down to spend our first night in the van.

I don't know if you've ever slept in the back of a car or not.

I have, for several reasons, ranging from poorly-anticipated poverty, to extreme stupidity, to accidents involving me having a mouth the size of the Rift Valley. What I will say about it, is this: cars are not designed for sleeping in.

Well, except the ones that are designed for sleeping in. And even those ones are bloody uncomfortable.

Sleeping in Rusty was like some kind of Chinese torture. At first, it seemed quite inviting; with the seats all flattened out and Gill's psychedelic dolphin curtains at every window. With the low-drain strip light (helpfully fitted by Roo's Dad) glowing, and our sleeping bags disguising the contours of the back-seat-cum-bed, Rusty looked quite cosy.

But Rusty, as we were already starting to realise, had a spiteful streak.

For starters, he was too narrow. The middle row of seats, where three pairs of legs wriggled and writhed, were full width; not so the back row of seats, which coincided with our shoulders. At the broadest part of us, Rusty was only two seats wide – and those seats were tilted steeply upwards, because all our worldly possessions were crammed underneath them.

Seatbelt holders, reclining levers, arm rests – all these things, so convenient whilst driving, dug into the soft, fleshy parts of us. The seats undulated in exactly the opposite way to my spine – so that, no matter which side I lay on, it felt like I was being folded in half. It was hot and it was cramped, and we couldn't open the windows for fear of a full-scale mosquito invasion. Sweat ran down my legs. Condensation dripped on me from the seal above the side window. And every time I tried to squirm into a more comfortable position, something hard and unyielding jabbed me somewhere delicate and tender.

If there's a less pleasant place in the world to sleep, I have yet to discover it.

All three of us lay awake for hours.

At about 4am the rain stopped, and I realised I'd been listening intently to something else that was going on outside. It had grown, from background noise to a deafening shriek; magnified by my mind, perhaps, but drowning out any further chance of rest.

"What the hell is that noise?" I moaned. "I can hear the cicadas, but that other sound? It's high-pitched, like a police whistle?"

"Oh, that's the frogs," Roo said.

"But why are they whistling?"

"Because they're frogs," she explained, "that's the sound they make."

"Eh? No, that can't be right. We have plenty of frogs in England. Frogs croak."

"Frogs don't croak! How stupid is that? Birds croak."

"No, no! It's frogs! Everyone knows that. Like in that cartoon with the frog and the chicken in a library. And the chicken goes 'Book, book, book,' and the frog goes 'Readit, readit, readit.' You know?"

Apparently she didn't know, which resulted in me spending the next ten minutes gurgling in my throat, trying to create an adequate frog noise.

You should try it, next time it's 4am and you can't sleep because you're lying in a padded oven with two other people. It gives everyone a good laugh, especially when you choke on your own spit and segue into a coughing fit.

There passed another of those mutually-agreed sleep attempts, where everyone tries really hard to get to sleep, only to have the bugger next to them turn over and knee them in the back just when they were drifting off.

It was no use. With the door open briefly to exchange the air, another peculiar noise was coming to my attention.

"Roo, what the hell is that, then?"

"Is what?" she yawned.

"That… pinging noise. It's all around us. It goes like: Boing! BAUung. Bong! It sounds like a midnight ukulele convention. Are there red-necks in the bush? We're not going to get raped, are we?"

"I keep telling you, that's the frogs!"

"You said the whistling was the frogs."

She sighed, and started speaking more slowly. I think my intelligence had just dropped a notch in her estimation. "The *whistling* frogs are whistling. That's why they're called *whistling frogs.*"

"Right."

"And the ones that sound like a banjo string being plucked – those ones are the *banjo frogs.*"

"You are absolutely shitting me right now."

"No, not at all! I can't believe you haven't heard them before. Do you know about motorbike frogs then?"

"Motorbike frogs? No! What do they sound like?"

"Well, like a…" she paused. "You're taking the piss out of me, aren't you?"

"A little."

"Then you can bugger off, with your stupid croaking frogs!"

"Go on, do an impression! Please?"

"No. You'll hear them, soon enough."

Around us, the banjo chorus continued.

Roo rolled onto her side, squirming in a futile bid to find a comfortable position.

"So frogs don't whistle at all in England," she muttered to herself. "How weird is that?"

Happy Returns

The next morning there was cause for celebration – for me, at least.

It was my birthday! Somehow, more by luck than by design, I had achieved the ripe old age of twenty-eight.

That's a good age. A *responsible* age. People I knew back home had started families already, had good jobs with potential for career-progression, and mortgages to match.

Whereas I had... what exactly? Freedom? Happiness, certainly. Hell, I had a rucksack full of that.

And not a whole lot else.

And as for responsibility...

Making sure the ice packs were frozen before we left the campsite was mine.

And that was about it. But, you know, ice packs can be important.

Buried in Rusty's boot, we had what Australians call an 'Esky'. It's a brand name which is used to refer to any type of portable cold-storage unit.

In Oz, they have perfected this technology – either because their environment is so unforgiving that access to cold water can mean the difference between life and death – or because they place a similar importance on keeping their beers cold. I'll leave you to decide which is more likely.

So any decent camping store stocks a whole range of options, from lowly insulated picnic bags to diesel-powered, climate-controlled mobile fridge/freezers. The Esky Roo's dad had lent us fell somewhere between these extremes, and was the kind of hamper-sized plastic cool box that most Brits would be familiar with. They don't work too badly either – in England.

Out here, after spending the morning baking in Rusty, it was no match for the searing daytime heat.

"The ice cream is a bit, um..." Roo said, stirring it with her finger.

"It'll still taste the same," said Gill.

"Maybe it will. Only it's *warm*."

We'd spent the morning raiding the two-dollar shops, which were oddly abundant in Geraldton. Now we were sitting down for a celebratory birthday lunch in the park, under the shade of a single stunted tree.

On the menu, we had left-over curry – on sandwiches. We washed this down with a bowl each of warm liquid ice cream – with caramel sauce, of course! And then, the pièce de résistance: a donut.

This one was all for me.

At some point one of the girls must have scurried off to a different two-dollar store, and bought a packet of birthday candles. We couldn't get enough candles on top because of the extremely limited surface area of donuts (and because, in my extreme old age, I had crossed a certain threshold and was now nearly *two* packets old). And when three people try simultaneously to light birthday candles on the ground in strong wind, all you tend to achieve is the loss of a few eyebrows. We stood considerably more chance of lighting the donut to be honest, so eventually I waved the girls off and claimed my prize. It was gooey and jam-filled and partially blackened from some over-enthusiastic lighter-action. Mmm! Singed donut. Just how I like 'em.

Then Gill held out her hand to me and opened it. "Happy birthday, Tony!"

"Gill, I don't know what to say! It's… it's a plastic… fish."

"It is! And you can't actually have him, because he's mine. But I wanted to have something to give you. So – say hello to our newest travelling companion!"

"Is he an air freshener? From the two-dollar shop?"

"He is! And he's spradoingey!" For proof Gill flicked the fish, making it bobble around on its spring.

I thought about the kinds of presents other people my age would be receiving. A couple of X-Box games perhaps. Or an actual X-Box. A new helmet to wear when riding their motorbike. A new set of speakers for the home cinema…

But they do say you should be grateful for the little things in life.

I bet whoever coined that phrase had never been given a spradoingey plastic fish for their birthday.

It redefines the boundaries of little things.

But I loved him all the same. Even if he wasn't mine.

The girls also bought me a t-shirt, possibly because I'd been wearing the same two t-shirts since we started the trip, and alternating them rather than washing them on the grounds that they were 'okay again' after a certain length of time away from my body.

Both girls strongly disagreed with this philosophy.

In fairness, Rusty was a mobile oven, and within minutes of climbing inside him we were all dripping with sweat. Even on the coolest days, the sheer amount of glass turned the inside of the car into a hot box, and apparently opening the windows only helped to circulate any smells developing in the back.

Sigh.

There were advantages to traveling with two attractive women. The street cred, mostly. Being constantly reminded to wash more often wasn't one of them.

I promised them that I would shower and put on the clean t-shirt as soon as we got to the next campsite.

My last birthday present came from Frieda, Roo's Mum – she'd sent it along with us for me to open on the right day. It was a black baseball cap with 'Australia' proudly emblazoned across it. I loved it, and wore it almost constantly. In fact I only took the thing off for sleeping – and whenever I was wearing my new t-shirt, which coincidentally also had 'Australia' written across it.

Don't want to look too much like a tourist, I thought, as I climbed back into our multi-coloured, hand-print-covered van.

That evening, a hundred miles further north, we sat around a camp fire, eating fish and chips, drinking *goon*, and discussing our plans. We'd been lucky enough to arrive just as the supermarket was closing, and we'd bought all the sandwiches they were about to throw away for next to nothing. That sealed it – our intention for tomorrow was to drive into the nearby national park, take our packed lunches, and do a spot of hiking.

I sat up late that night, watching the stars twinkle brightly in the absence of other light. I was in a philosophical mood, either due to the significance of the day, or more likely the significant amount of cheap wine I'd consumed.

A year ago I'd been in England, desperate to be anywhere else; now here I was, on the other side of the world. Just achieving that much felt like a victory; the fact that I was fulfilling a long-held dream of traveling Australia – and doing it in such *style* – that was an unexpected bonus.

The icing on the cake, you might say.

Or the donut.

I decided that, no matter what happened from here on in, on future birthdays I would remember this moment. How happy I could be living so simply, and how grateful I felt to be so completely and utterly responsibility-free.

I owned almost nothing. I owed nothing to anyone – well, unless you counted the credit card company – and I wanted nothing more than what I already had.

Although, a hot naked woman waiting for me in my sleeping bag wouldn't have gone amiss. *Perhaps I'll ask for one of those next year.*

It didn't seem terribly likely, given my current living situation, but then that was the exciting part; literally anything could happen in the next three-hundred and sixty-five days. I was looking forward to every single one of them.

I'll remind myself, wherever I am next year, that life is for living, I thought. *If I'm not in the middle of some crazy adventure, that will be my wake-up call – to get out there and have some fun, to live a little. Before I get to the point where I lose the option.*

For now though, the closest I would get to adventure was a stumble through the darkness to the toilet block, followed by bed.

Tomorrow was a new day, and it glistened with promise.

It was going to be one hell of an interesting year.

Parklife

I haven't mentioned it yet, but the roads had dwindled since Perth. Not only in number, but in size. In the UK our major cities are connected by huge, six-lane motorways – it's only when we reach those cities that we sit in gridlock, amidst networks of tiny medieval streets governed by countless traffic lights and archaic one-way systems.

And punctuated by those hell-spawned mini-roundabouts.

In Perth, the biggest, widest roads ran right through the city. Freeways led to every different area, and even the streets of the central business district were several lanes deep. Conversely, once we got out into the open, the solitary road between Perth and the cities further north was a narrow ribbon of tarmac; a single carriageway in each direction with no crash barriers, no hard-shoulder – not even fences to keep livestock off it. The crumbling edges of the road blended seamlessly into the rocky red dirt, and the vast majority of the junctions – the few that we saw – were wide swathes of dust and gravel, where unsealed tracks branched off into the wilderness.

It was down one of these dubious tracks that we turned Rusty, heading into Kalbarri National Park on a route which can only be described as off-road.

We regretted it almost instantly.

The action of the wind, and an endless succession of four-wheel-drives ploughing up and down, had sculpted the surface of the road into millions of ridges, like miniature speed-bumps less than two-inches apart. It was like driving on a corrugated tin roof.

For fifteen miles.

Noisy doesn't even come close.

Rusty started shaking the second we left the tarmac. Really shaking I mean, like a knackered washing machine on the spin cycle.

It made my teeth chatter so hard I was worried about chipping them.

It made Rusty's bodywork and innards vibrate so hard they

became a blur.

And every knife, fork, spoon, pot, pan, plate, tent pole, tent peg, food can, drink can and gas can, chattered and clattered like an earthquake in a tambourine factory.

A succession of big four-wheel-drives cruised past, each effortlessly chewing up the road and engulfing us in their dust trail.

'Tryy speeedingg uup?" I suggested. "Mayybe itss eeeasierrr att speeeed…"

Roo pushed a quivering foot onto the accelerator and Rusty leapt forward as though he'd been stung.

The rattling grew to a deafening roar. I was sure there were pieces falling off the car. Rusty drifted as he shook, the loose dirt under his tyres behaving more like ice than gravel.

"ARRRRRRR!" I cried.

"ARRRRRRRRRRRR!" cried Gill.

"ARRRRRRRRRRRRRRRRRRR!" cried Roo (which was more worrying, as she was driving).

"SSShHIT! SSSSssssLlllowwW DdDooOWwn!"

Dust billowed around us, blocking the road from view as we skipped and skidded along it. When Roo brought Rusty under control again, we agreed that the speed theory had been adequately tested. We renamed it the Certain Death theory, and decided to take full advantage of having lived through it by never, ever repeating it.

Eight miles an hour was the most we could manage. Even at that speed, Rusty was shaking himself apart. It felt like we'd replaced his wheels with square ones.

"W-w-we sh-should t-t-turn b-back," I stammered, managing to bite the tip of my tongue twice in one sentence.

"We c-can't," replied Roo. "N-n-nearly there!"

She was lying.

It took us two hours to reach the car park.

By the time we got to the end of the corrugated road, we'd discovered our first casualty. The spradoingey fish had been shaken up so much that scented gel was leaking out of his gills, making a sticky pile of smelly pink fish-innards on the dashboard. Gill declared the little fella dead on arrival, and I soothed her grief by pointing out that he was the lucky one; he'd escaped.

We had to make the same trip back.

If you've ever tried to walk after being on a boat for a long time, you might have experienced land-sickness – the feeling that you're still moving, and that the ground under you is heaving and swelling.

We suffered from vibration-sickness; the feeling that someone nearby was using a jackhammer with such ferocity that the vibrations were travelling right through the ground and up our legs. We staggered around the car park like a bunch of drunks, while our central nervous systems tried to adjust to the sudden stillness. It was probably hilarious to watch; like an old episode of Star Trek, when the cast really try to sell the effect of the Enterprise taking a direct hit.

Finally, I felt I'd recovered enough to use the toilet without pissing all over the place. It was a long-drop; the kind of 'outback dunnie' that consists of a garden shed containing a box with a toilet seat over a very deep, very smelly hole.

Not the ideal facility to use when one's ability to stand upright has been compromised.

I bounced off several walls, and emerged feeling worse than when I'd gone in.

"Why did we come here again?" I asked.

Ah, yes. Hiking.

The main selling point of Kalbarri National Park was Nature's Window – a natural archway formed right on the edge of a precipice. It framed a panoramic view of the vast, empty landscape, and the narrow gorge that cut through it. The view was even better from the top of the arch, which was easily reached by climbing on an ironically placed sign warning 'Climbing Danger!'

Far below us, the river winding through the gorge was emerald green, reflecting the scrubby vegetation that clung to every nook and hollow. The cliffs were a dark, dusty red, and in the bends of the river yellow sand had accumulated, forming a series of miniature beaches. It was a stunning essay in the colours of nature – here, even the barren rock put on a pretty show, as though to make up for the complete lack of anything else to look at.

"Gorgeous," I commented. And not for the first time.

The next warning sign we encountered was where the trail petered out – about ten paces from the car park. Evidently this chunk of unspoilt wilderness was particularly unspoilt.

'GORGE RISK AREA', the sign read. 'TURN BACK UNLESS YOU ARE: CAUTIOUS, FIT AND AGILE, PREPARED TO SCRAMBLE, COMFORTABLE WITH HEIGHTS, CARRYING WATER'.

"Well, you're screwed straight away," Gill said to me.

"Why? I'm great with heights! I'm fit. And I love to scramble."
"Yeah, but you're the least cautious person I've ever known."
"Oh, screw caution. Who needs that?"
"Exactly."

We descended into the gorge, picking our way down tracks that probably weren't tracks at all. The strata in the rock ran horizontally, giving it a stripy appearance. The eroded layers formed flat planes and step-like edges, inspiring those of us who love to climb (me) to venture further and higher than was probably wise.

It was so easy, and so much fun, that before long both the girls were scaling the cliffs in all directions. Nature had provided us with a wonderful playground, and after making a supreme effort to get here, we figured we might as well make the most of it.

The river was so still in places, so unaffected by the wind racing across the flat desert above, that it became a mirror. The doubled view of rock and sky, reflected in the tranquil water, was made even more impressive by the complete lack of anything man-made to spoil it. There was nobody there but us – and looking around the place, I could easily imagine that there never had been. No litter, no graffiti; no sign of human passage at all.

It's possible we were a bit lost.

But never mind! With a bit of narrow-ledge work we followed the river on its serpentine path, sometimes walking three abreast, sometimes single file, crabbing sideways on our tip toes, hugging the rock.

In one of the narrower sections, where the walls closed in above us, Gill paused. "Woah, listen," she said.

We stopped dead, and listened. "Listen, listen, listen," echoed faintly back down the rock towards us.

"Ha ha! Echo!" I called, listening to the reverberations as 'echo, echo,' was repeated up and down the length of the canyon.

Just then, a deafening shriek rent the air:

"AAAAAAOOOOOOOOOOOOOOOOUUUUUUUWWWWEE!"

The sound wave billowed out all around us, crashing into the walls of the gorge and bouncing back to wash over us again. It sounded like those monsters from *Pitch Black* were coming from every direction to tear us to shreds.

Rocks fell in the distance.

I think I pooed a little.

When the sound abated and the echoes subsided, Gill and I dropped our hands from our ears and turned to look at Roo, from whose throat the unearthly noise had come.

"What?" she asked. "You don't do that in England?"

"Um, no. We mostly just say 'Echo'."

"Where's the fun in that?"

As the afternoon wore on, we started looking for a route back.

Every curve we rounded offered another rugged vista.

It was absolutely… *gorgeous*.

"If you don't stop saying that, you'll be swimming in it," Gill informed me.

We came across a wooden signpost with what looked like a line drawing of a colon on it. We assumed this was a route marker, but there were no notes to accompany the bowel diagram; no 'You Are Here', with an arrow pointing to the sphincter, and no clue as to which direction the stomach was in. I was assuming the car park was at the stomach end – otherwise we were *incredibly* lost, and would be exiting via the rectum – neither of which appealed to me.

We were, unsurprisingly, rather late getting back to the car park. Rusty was the only vehicle left, and we still had the agonising two-hour trip out of the park to look forward to.

Only this time we would have to go slower, because it was getting dark, and there would be kangaroos on the road.

"But it's so barren," I said, "it's hard to imagine anything surviving here."

"Oh, there were loads of signs of life back there," Roo informed me. "There was wallaby poo all over the place."

"Really? And it was *definitely* wallaby poo?"

"Yep," Roo said, thereby admitting that she could tell the difference.

I decided to take her word for it.

Because when you're traveling with someone for the first time, it's always good to find they know their shit.

Getting High

I have been told, on occasion, that there is something wrong in my brain. Not by doctors, you understand – just by… well, pretty much everyone else. So as I stood at the base of a hundred-foot cliff, looking up, some mis-wired chip in my head fired up. Where most sane people would have said, "Fuck me, that's a big bugger!" and carried on walking, I turned to the others and said, "We've *got* to do this one!"

It had been another long day of hiking and climbing – same gorge, different day. Okay, technically speaking it was a different gorge as well, but it looked identical to the last one. We were several days and over six-hundred kilometres north of Kalbarri, in yet another national park with the equally ambiguous name of Cape Range.

The girls looked at each other, then back at me. I could tell they were hesitant, but this didn't sound any kind of alarm in my head. Okay, it did – but the alarm was saying 'Quick! Get started before they have chance to think up excuses!'.

We'd done some great climbs already, and both girls had grown in confidence since this morning. I knew they had it in them to manage this one – as long as I could get them started before nervousness set in. This one would be our crowning glory.

Our ultimate challenge.

Plus, I *really* wanted to climb it.

I've always loved climbing stuff. Some would say, I've always loved to climb stuff that I really shouldn't climb. Not too long ago this habit had come to a head, in a tricky situation in Thailand which had very nearly cost me my life.

Afterwards, I'd promised myself that in the future, I would *think* before I climbed. That I would analyse the situation and weigh up the dangers – even do something previously unheard of, and actually consider *not* climbing something!

I think it's a testament to my strength of character that today was the first time in almost six months that I broke that promise.

Up I went, an easy scramble for the first few body-lengths. I looked back over my shoulder at the sky, realising that Roo and Gill were already quite a way below me. But, in fairness to the pair of them, they were both trying it.

"You're doing great," I called down to them. "See, this bit's not too bad!"

Roo was having an easier time of it than Gill, purely because she was built for it. Climbing is all about strength-to-weight ratio, and Gill, for her size, is fiendishly strong. But Roo was strong too, and she had less body-weight than some insects. Her long, lean limbs splayed out in all directions to find holds even I hadn't been able to reach. She wasn't relying on strength, at least not yet. Honestly, if we'd have filled her lungs with helium, I think she'd have floated to the top.

First Roo, then Gill, reached me. I'd decided to wait for them because the next section looked quite steep. Well, steep for a cliff…

I think the appropriate term is *sheer*.

But I was confident, and I sought to give them confidence by pointing out the hand and foot holds as we went.

It was an arduous climb, but not impossible. Slowly but surely, we inched our collective way upwards. Gill called up to suggest a brief rest, and I agreed wholeheartedly. The next ledge above me was an obvious choice, so I hauled myself over its lip and thrust my hand down to help Roo. Gill powered over the edge herself, huffing and puffing a bit, but exhilarated with the accomplishment.

She stood and looked out at the view, empty air stretching all the way across to the opposite side of the canyon.

"Beautiful," she said.

"MotherFUCKER!" I replied, which startled both of them.

They looked confused until they saw me slapping at my legs. Giant red ants had climbed me in a fraction of the time it had taken me to climb their cliff, and unlike our little group they weren't stopping for a rest.

"Shit!" said Roo, "Those things bite really bad!"

Then both girls started swearing as they swatted at dozens of insects that had already ventured onto their shoes and up their trouser legs. Cries of "ARR!" and "OWW!" mingled with the profanity, as the creatures began to take their revenge.

"We can't stay here!" I said. "Climb!"

And climb we did, with a purpose.

Thankfully, we left most of the freakish ants behind, though every few seconds another one would emerge from the neckline of my t-shirt and take a bite out of whatever it could reach.

"Argh! You little bastards!"

The ants paid me no heed.

Still we climbed, slowing now, as the route became more and more difficult. I thought I could see the top, but it looked like the final push would be the biggest challenge so far. Behind and below me, the two girls battled on, though there was rising panic in their voices when they asked me where to put their feet next…

"A ledge!" I cried. "Let's get up there, and we can have a breather!"

"Thank God," said Roo.

"How?" said Gill. "I can't see where to go!"

"Just a little further," I told her. I grabbed hold of a twisted tree trunk that seemed to grow right out of the rock, and dragged myself up onto the ledge above it.

Roo followed, taking my hand, clearly straining to lift herself over the edge. It had been a long climb, and she immediately set about pulling ants from her clothes and squashing them.

Gill reached the last section below the ledge and baulked at the height of it. "I'm not tall enough," she said, her voice shaking with exertion and fear.

"It's okay," I told her, "just grab onto this tree. You can haul yourself right up on it, and I'll grab your other hand."

"I don't know, it's very high…"

I could tell she was about to panic.

"Don't worry, it's easy," I told her. "Roo just did it, and I helped her up too. Come on, you'll make it!"

She didn't sound very confident, but she gave me a shaky, "Okay."

Then she stretched out for the tree trunk, grabbed a hold of it, and pulled.

And the tree trunk came straight out of the cliff face as though it had never been attached in the first place.

Gill fell.

I know it sounds hopelessly cheesy, but time really does slow down in moments like this; or at least, it does for me. I had thoughts that would have taken me minutes to speak aloud. Chief amongst them was my voice repeating over and over, "I just killed her. I just killed my sister. Gill's dead. I've killed her."

I saw it all in a flash; her body, smashed and bloody, in a pile of rocks at the foot of the cliff; the horror in Mum's face as she looked at me.

And, according to Roo, I screamed.

Gill did not scream.

She also did not die.

Scrabbling at the rock like a cartoon character, she fell about ten feet in the blink of an eye. Knees, elbows and fingertips bounced off the cliff, scuffing and scraping, and then her feet found a narrow lip and stuck there.

By terrified reflex she wrapped her whole body around the cliff face, hugging it for all she was worth, and her trip downwards was over.

For now, anyway.

"GILL???" I shrieked down at her.

She didn't reply for what seemed like eternity. Then a croaky, "I'm okay," floated up.

And Gill lay against the rock, breathing heavily, and quite possibly crying a little bit. But I could hardly blame her for that. I was crying too.

I think we'll call that 'shock', and say no more about it.

After a few minutes, Gill regained control over her body. She was weak and trembling – but she was alive!

And she was about to face the ordeal of climbing back up again. Because there really was no other way but down. And it was a long, long way down.

Roo and I stared at her, and Gill stared back up at us. "I'm going to take a picture," she called.

"Eh? Oh, okay."

I could see what she was up to. Faced with continuing the climb, and well aware of her failing strength and shaking limbs, she'd found an excuse to extend her breather. Her camera was dangling from the back of her belt, and with one hand she reached around and unzipped its case. Laying there, sprawled across the rock like it was the living room carpet at home – only with about seventy-five degrees of difference – she pointed the camera up at us and killed a couple of minutes trying to get a clear shot. Roo even took one back at her.

Which was nice.

But it still didn't solve the problem, so eventually, with much cajoling, we coaxed Gill back up the cliff. With no tree to haul on, the last section was a toughie, so I climbed down again to help her up. And then, rather than rest and risk losing heart, I mercilessly bullied the others on up the last stage of the climb.

It was the hardest part yet, even without considering our mental state, but somehow we pushed on through and made it.

I consider it one of the most difficult free climbs I've done – not the hardest, or the longest, but certainly the one where I came closest to shitting myself.

For the girls to have managed it was nothing short of miraculous.

I told them so, too, as we lay there on the flat top of the gorge.

"That was amazing," I said, "the best climb I've ever seen either of you do! It's something to be proud of. A real achievement. You guys were incredible!"

To her credit, Gill agreed. "Yeah, that was amazing," she said. The elation of pulling off such a feat was flooding through her, overwhelming the despair she must have been feeling only minutes earlier.

Roo's face was flushed with excitement too. "I've never done anything like that before!"

"I knew you could do it," I said. "Both of you did so well… Next time it'll be loads easier, because you've got this experience now. Next time you'll *know* you can do it."

Gill pushed herself to her feet. "I don't think there should be a next time *just* yet."

"Well okay, that's a fair point. We've definitely done enough for today! And anyway, it'll be getting dark soon."

Roo was standing now now too, admiring the view from what felt like the top of the world. I stood up to join them, and studied the path we'd been following along the bottom of the gorge. It looked like a dark red pen line, drawn all squiggly across the lighter dirt.

"That is a long way," she said.

"It is," I agreed.

"So, I was wondering. How do we get down?"

Why Not To Drive At Night

It took us hours to find the car.

Forced to walk back along the top of the gorge, we headed in what we hoped was the right direction, but couldn't quite be sure. And it wasn't like we had much choice – whereas before we'd been following a mapped out (if terribly sign-posted) route, now we were wandering fairly randomly along the flat, dry landscape. We stuck close to the edge of the canyon, but the route below soon vanished in a direction we couldn't match without growing wings. And from there on, it was all guesswork.

We walked for miles that evening, finally discovering the car park as the last of the light ebbed over the horizon. Thanks to the featureless flat plain, we'd used every last ray of sunlight, arriving back long after night had fallen down below.

When Roo's sharp eyes picked out the squat silhouette of Rusty, sitting alone in a cleared area, she gave a whoop of joy.

She and I jogged over to our beloved vehicle – sprinting in mind, if not quite capable of doing so in body – and wrapped ourselves around him.

Gill, even less inclined to run, hung back to take a photo.

It's a strange picture, with the two of us hugging the van; it's caused a few raised eyebrows over the years. But we didn't care. We were sweaty, aching, exhausted – and in Gill's case, still bleeding quite substantially.

We were very glad to see Rusty indeed.

All we had to do now was drive back down one of those delightfully corrugated roads – for about an hour – and then we could start looking for a place to spend the night.

It was Gill's turn to drive.

She insisted, saying that it was only fair she do her share, and that the bleeding had mostly stopped anyway.

"Be extra careful," Roo warned her, "there'll be kangaroos about. They mostly come out at dawn and dusk, and this place will be full of them."

"Don't worry, I won't be going fast enough to kill anything!" Gill replied.

And she didn't. But that didn't stop the kangaroos from trying.

"They must have a death wish," I commented, as we crawled past dozens of the critters, lining both sides of the road as though they were expecting a parade to come down it.

"The plants they eat grow better along the edges of the road, because of the moisture and carbon dioxide from car exhausts," Roo explained.

"That doesn't explain why they keep leaping out in front of us!"

Gill swerved to avoid another apparently suicidal kangaroo.

"Sometimes they use roads," Roo continued, "because it's easier than going through the bush. But they're jumping at us because they're scared. You've got to remember, kangaroos evolved without any natural predators, so they don't have a fight-or-flight instinct like most animals. So when something scares them – like the noise of a car passing – their brain short-circuits, and they jump randomly. Quite often, straight into the car that spooked them."

"So what you're telling us is that kangaroos are mind-boggling stupid?"

"Yep. They have the tiniest brains, like walnuts. And they have two penises."

"What? That's… also very stupid."

Suddenly Gill swerved, and there was a loud thump on the front wing.

"SHIT!" she bawled.

All eyes swung to that corner, where a smallish grey shape was bounding off into the darkness.

"He bounced right into me," Gill said. "No warning! I was already past him when he jumped."

"Looks like he was okay though," Roo said.

"Yeah, he picked himself up and bounced right on. But I hope Rusty's okay!"

It was a tense drive after that, as we all sat in silence, scanning the road in front and to either side. Gill crawled Rusty forwards at a snail's pace, and finally the headlights picked out the junction with the tarmac road.

I breathed a sigh of relief. "Let's not do this again, okay?"

Both girls turned to glare at me, at which point I remembered why we were out driving so late. "Oh, yeah. Sorry about that folks…"

Night had fallen long before we located a campsite entrance.

As Gill pulled up in a car park across from the office, Roo slid off her seat in the back, and lay down in the footwell.

"Are you okay?" Gill asked.

"Yeah," came the stage-whispered response, "I'm hiding! It's dark, so they'll never notice. Go in and pay for the site, and if they ask if it's just the two of you, say yes."

Gill gave me a nervous glance, then reached back and pulled a towel over Roo's head. "In case someone looks in," she explained.

It seemed to take the receptionist forever to arrange a pitch for us. I was starting to get paranoid, picturing us walking out of the office to find the van surrounded by site wardens or police.

How embarrassing would it be, to be busted for this? Roo squatting on the floor of the van, covered in towels, just to avoid paying an extra twelve dollars for camping. But even my basic maths skills could calculate how quickly money was running out. Sneaky, underhanded tactics like this were all that stood between me and bankruptcy – which in any case was inevitable in less than a fortnight.

The woman behind the desk clucked her tongue as Gill handed back the form she'd been filling out. One night. *Two persons*.

"Did it work?" Roo whispered, when we climbed back into Rusty.

"Shhh! Yes and no."

"What?"

"Yes, they just charged us the price for a Wicked van."

"Did you tell her this is *not* a Wicked van?"

"No, I was too worried about her asking if we knew there was a Roo hiding under our towels!"

"Bloody Wicked vans," she grumbled.

"But the bad news is, you've got to stay down! The woman from the office is coming out to show us to our pitch."

"Oh… shit!"

"I know!"

There followed a tense few minutes, as Gill guided Rusty along at walking pace, following the woman who was pointing out the way with a torch.

Finally we stopped. Gill jumped out to talk to her, and came back a few minutes later with the news that the woman was leaving. "But stay down for a bit," she advised Roo. "She might come back, if she's forgotten to tell us something."

So Gill and I put the tent up that night, and when it was ready Roo scurried inside, still wearing a towel over her head.

"That's not going to help much," I pointed out, when she was safely inside.

"Hey, it worked, didn't it?"

"But was it worth it?" Gill asked.

Roo thought about that for a few seconds. "It was," she decided.

And by the end of the trip, taking it in turns to hide under a pile of towels during check-ins, between us we saved over $300.

So yeah, she was right. It *was* worth it.

We stayed up late that night in the luxurious camp kitchen, laughing about the crazy day we'd had, and about the craziness of Australia in general.

Like most former British colonies, Australia is littered with place names 'inspired' by the UK. Gill had been amused to find 'York' on the map, as she'd been born there (in England, obviously). This York, a farming town only an hour's drive from Perth, had a population of less than 4,000 – not quite a match for the magnificent medieval city it was named after, but then I'd rather live an hour's drive from Perth, Australia, than Perth, Scotland. Only because of the weather, I assure you.

But now we were camping in…

"Exmouth? Come on! There isn't even a River Exe here to need a mouth!"

There wasn't a river at all, which offended my sensibilities a little. "If we're going to ignore naming conventions wholesale, I might as well pick a random patch of desert and call it The Isle Of Wight!"

This silliness put me in the mood to do some writing. I'd been spending most evenings squinting at the screen of my miniature Sony Vaio, trying to add a few chapters to the book I was working on. Often I'd sit up quite late after the girls had gone to bed, nursing a last glass of wine and reading through my notes.

It was still too early to make claims of greatness, but I was pretty happy with the way it was turning out. The memories of my time in Ecuador, volunteering in an exotic animal refuge, would eventually be lost if I didn't record them – but I had high hopes of finding a publisher for this little memoir.

After all, it had a cracking title.

So I picked up the bag with my laptop in, to move it from table to chair – and as I did so, it slipped from my fingers, falling the remaining distance to the concrete floor.

It struck with a sickening thud. At the same time as I heard the impact, I felt it somewhere in my stomach. A lurch, and a sudden queasiness. A dread.

I pulled the laptop from the bag, swearing frantically, and pressed the power button.

The tiny machine clicked and whirred for a few seconds, the battery light blinked – and 'OPERATING SYSTEM NOT FOUND' appeared on the display.

And that, for now, was the end of 'That Bear Ate My Pants!'.

I went to bed early that night.

Rest and Repair

Exmouth was a tiny place compared to its English compatriot; in fact there was so little there that driving through town in Rusty caused quite a stir. The sea-front road – also the only road – was lined with onlookers as we cruised down it in search of a campsite. People smiled and waved – some even held up their phones to take photos of us. Perhaps they thought the circus had come to town. It was always weird when we met this kind of reaction, as we'd become so used to Rusty that we only paid attention to him when smoke was coming out of him.

Gill or Roo would be first to notice, as I'm fairly oblivious to the world around me. "Those people are staring at us," one of them would comment. "So are the guys over there! Wait – that woman and her daughter are waving at us... do we know them?"

This would be followed almost immediately by the realisation; "Oh, we're in Rusty! That's why everyone's looking!"

So we'd smile and wave back, feeling rather like we were making an official visit.

It was like the best parts of being a celebrity, without the crowds of paparazzi hassling us when we got out. And without the millions of dollars and the rock-star lifestyle, but we were working on that.

Starting with saving my book.

Amazingly, for a 'town' the size of Exmouth (population 1,998!), there was a laptop repair specialist listed in the phone directory. He worked from home, so we paid him a visit in Rusty. I left the computer with him, and spent the next couple of days feeling sorry for myself. We'd planned on being much further up the coast in Broome by now, but there was nothing else we could do; so we waited. The girls weren't gutted, to be honest; they needed a break from the tedious days of driving, and by pure chance they discovered a late-night trampolining emporium right outside our campsite. What are the odds? Exmouth didn't even have a public swimming pool. As we were the only customers, we got chatting to the owners, and I had to admire their vision. Some things are worth sticking your neck out for; late-night trampolining and homemade ice cream – despite being a fairly volatile combination – was one of them.

So we stayed for a week.

And Roo continued to hide under a pile of towels every time we drove past the site office, which averaged around six times a day.

Every single time we pulled up outside our tent, guaranteed someone nearby would say, "Oh look, that Wicked van is back!"

It set our collective teeth on edge.

But what is a Wicked van, you ask?

Wicked Vans, or 'Wicked Campers', to give them their slightly misleading title, had been a constant thorn in our side. They weren't campers – they were regular vans, like Rusty only in an even shittier state of repair. Their back seats had been ripped out, and a bed made from a sheet of plywood. Then they were spray-painted all over with rebellious graphics and slogans, and hired out at obscene prices to backpackers who had no other way of exploring. Their main selling point, aside from their graffitied bad-assery, was that *you were allowed to crash them*. Seriously – there was no charge for 'minor damage', which might give you a clue as to the general condition of the vans on offer. At one point the entire Sydney Wicked fleet was suspended from driving, pending a state-wide series of road-worthiness tests.

So understandably, Rusty being mistaken for a Wicked van bothered us.

Rusty's colourful paint job was what we'd come to call 'Granny-friendly'. Utterly inoffensive. We loved it when whole families would smile and wave as we went past.

Wicked vans had a similar effect – well, the ones that didn't have naked tits or crude sex scenes daubed all over them. On approach, the first thing you'd spot is some indecipherable nonsense scrawled across the front. Next, the big cartoon on the side would slide past, featuring the boys from *Southpark*, or maybe flaming devils, or cats chasing a ball of wool. Kids would shriek in delight, and adults would turn to look, just as the back of the van slid into view – emblazoned with an appropriately witty counterpoint, like: "Every time you masturbate, a kitten dies!"

Cue much awkwardness.

There was usually a big space around Wicked vans in car parks, for this reason – and presumably so that any bricks thrown at the van wouldn't bounce off and hit more respectable vehicles.

Amongst the slogans we spotted on our travels were some vaguely amusing ones, like 'If Quizzes Are Quizzical, Then What Are Tests?' – some slightly controversial ones, like 'Save a Whale – Harpoon a Jap!' – and some that seemed likely to get their drivers lynched – like 'It's better to be black than gay, coz U don't have to tell your parents.'

Argh.

So whenever people made the assumption that Rusty was a Wicked van, we were quick to correct them. In Exmouth, Gill came up with a better way of making our point. It was July, so she tore the first couple of months off a calendar we'd picked up in one of Geraldton's two-dollar stores. She taped them together, and made a sign for Rusty's back windscreen.

"We'd Rather Push Rusty Than Hire A Wicked Van!" it read.

"That'll tell 'em," she said.

Finally, I got a call from Mr Fixit. I walked into his house with a long face, and walked out with the empty shell of my laptop and a plastic carrier bag full of its guts. The prognosis: terminal.

(Bit of computer-based humour there, to lighten the mood!)

On the upside I also had a CD-ROM, which – so he told me – contained all the data he'd been able recover from the shattered hard drive.

Now I had the world's most agonising wait to find out how much, if any, of my book had been saved; the first place we'd be able to check would be Broome.

So we buggered off Broome-wards at top speed.

Road Trip

Broome, from Exmouth, is quite a drive.

It's a little over a thousand miles away – not the kind of place you nip over to because they've got cheese on special offer.

It was going to be an epic journey, spanning several days, so we had a last bounce at the trampoline place to prepare ourselves.

What? That *totally* helps.

We were heading straight towards the Northern Territory, but the landscape was nothing like the swamps and jungles from *Crocodile Dundee*.

Something seemed to be missing here. It was… everything! The plants. The animals. The bush! All I could see, for miles and miles in every direction, was flat, red dust, with patches of low, scrubby grasses dotted here and there. It was about as desolate as you could imagine… and it went on *forever*. This was the real Australia – the hundreds of thousands of square miles of empty, red desert. From here, on the eastern-most edge of Western Australia, it stretched most of the way across the country, a vast swathe of barren no-man's land known as The Red Centre.

The wildness of this landscape was at once its rugged beauty and its deadly teeth; there was no help out here for anyone in need of it, no easy way to return to civilization – just the long, straight road you drove in on, and the possibility of the occasional car heading back your way. If you went off-road, there wasn't even that. No tracks, no landmarks – no water. To go out there you had to know exactly what you were doing. If you didn't, chances were you wouldn't be coming back.

On those long, lonely stretches of road, other vehicles of any description were a welcome break from the monotony. The first clue would be a tiny cloud of dust on the horizon; then, undoubtedly, one of us would cry "Look! A car's coming!" with the same trill of excitement normally reserved for pointing out a roadside burger bar.

The conversation would pick up as the other vehicle approached;
"I wonder if it's a farmer?"

"Who else would be out this far?"

"Hope it's not a road train…"

By this point the car had grown from a speck to an identifiable shape, with predictable results;

"I told you it'd be a farmer!"

"Well, who else would be out this far?"

"Thank God it's not a road train…."

And then the vehicle – which was *always* a substantial four-wheel drive, like a Land Cruiser, and was always covered in a thick layer of dirt and dead insects – would hurtle past, rattling the van and showering us in freshly churned-up dust.

We'd feel an instant kinship with the occupants, as they became visible through the windscreen; more often than not a single, weather-beaten Aussie battler, bush-hardened and confident, driving with his window down and his *Akubra* (cowboy hat) on.

Inevitably our eyes would meet, and some signal of recognition would be exchanged between the two drivers, each according the other a measure of respect just for being here.

Sometimes a single grubby finger would lift from the steering wheel to acknowledge our passing; sometimes we'd receive a cheerful thumbs-up, or a mock salute – or, on the few occasions when the car was fully occupied, enthusiastic double-handed waving from everyone inside. There were as many different road-greetings as there were vehicles on the road.

In other words, about ten.

And then, as the car receded into the distance, the chatter would resurface;

"He didn't *look* like a farmer."

"Well, why else would he be out here?"

And speculation would keep us occupied for the next ten or fifteen kilometres.

Unless it *was* a road train.

Gigantic trucks pulling four, or even five, extra-long, extra-wide semi-trailers; seeing one of those monstrosities bearing down on you is like staring down the barrel of a loaded gun. No, scratch that – I've only ever done that twice, and both times I had no idea what was going on, so I can't really claim to understand it. Let's say it's like… preparing to catch a small crocodile bare-handed. You know that you're about to put yourself in the worst kind of harm's way – but you have absolutely no choice. All you can do is tighten the muscles around your bladder – because you can't know if you're going to pee yourself until you've tried it – then grab.

Or in this case, grit your teeth, brace yourself against as many fixed surfaces as possible, and start reciting the *Our Father*.

Road trains don't just bring dust; they often brought substantial pieces of road with them, torn from the sealed surface by the violence of their passing. The slip-stream they produce is gale-force, buffeting the car and pushing it off the road, then dragging it back on in the monster's wake. Some careful steering is required, combined with a grip like iron on the wheel, nerves of steel all round – and a pair of those adult incontinence knickers wouldn't go amiss. Road trains really are the kings of the road, and the general rule of thumb which applies in these encounters is this: get out of the fucking way!

We'd been out of mobile phone signal pretty much the whole time since we'd left Perth. Some of the tiny towns we'd passed through could boast reception on one mobile network or the other, but rarely both – and once beyond those tin-pot places, there was simply… nothing.

It was liberating and terrifying at the same time.

I made this point to Gill, as we pulled up in the middle of nowhere to take a bathroom break. I mean, it was literally the middle of nowhere. The road stretched arrow straight to the horizon, both in front of us and behind. The same low, scrubby bushes spread from either side of the tarmac, blending into a seamless blanket of brown-green ripples. The landscape was flat in every direction, as far as the eye could see, and there was absolutely nothing else in it.

Well, apart from us.

It made for a dull game of 'I Spy'.

Roo and Gill scurried off into the bushes, straying far enough from the road that they felt safe from prying eyes. I had to wonder at their caution.

"We haven't seen another car for over an hour," I shouted over the van. "Are you trying to hide from low flying aircraft? Because we haven't seen any of those, either…"

Gill was first back. "It's Sod's Law and you know it. The second I try to take a piss beside the road, we'll have three school buses and the Prime Minister's motorcade coming through here. I'm comfortable with my arse, but I don't want to see it on News At Ten."

"Honestly Gill, you worry way too much about that stuff."

And to prove my point I stood in the middle of the road, faced away from her, unzipped, and emptied my bladder right along the dotted line.

"Ahhhh! You see?" I called over my shoulder. "I bet there isn't another human being within a hundred miles of—"

And that's when I noticed that Roo had emerged from the undergrowth just in front of me. She was frozen in shock – possibly because I was standing there with my cock in my hand, or possibly because I was halfway through desecrating Highway One with my bodily fluids.

Either way, it probably wasn't something she'd expected to witness.

Poor girl.

It was only going to get worse from here on in.

A couple of hours later we were treated to a spectacular outback sunset. Shades of orange and purple hung in the sky for what seemed like an eternity, before the last sliver of sunlight slipped over the horizon. Twilight came and went; Roo slowed, and we all took up intensive kangaroo watching.

Driving at night hadn't been part of our plan, but neither was being marooned by the side of the road; the extreme temperatures in the middle of the day had forced the girls to nurse Rusty, keeping his speed down to avoid overheating. Now though, with the 'roo danger lessened by the darkness, and the air outside cooling, we made a last sprint finish towards the nearest roadhouse.

Roo was peering through the windscreen, striving in vain to see beyond the weak cones of light that passed for Rusty's headlights. She was tense, hunched over the wheel, well aware of how vulnerable we were out there at night.

Suddenly she yelled, and stamped on the brakes.

Rusty skidded and fish-tailed as he screeched to a halt – and there, not a metre in front of us, was the biggest bull I'd ever seen. Blacker than the night around him, with tiny curving horns, the bull stood motionless, dead centre in the middle of the road. He was so big he filled the carriageway, and as he stared back at us, his eyes gleamed red in our headlights.

"How the hell did you see him?" I asked Roo. I was amazed, as was Gill. Even from this distance, we could barely discern his silhouette; it was like he was absorbing the light from Rusty rather than reflecting it. Only those eyes glinted evilly…

"It was the eyes," Roo confirmed. "I could see something,

but…" She shuddered. "Holy shit. If we'd hit that…"

She didn't need to finish.

That bull had to weigh at least eight-hundred kilos; Rusty would have crumpled like tinfoil, crushing the girls and pitching me through the windscreen.

Dead, is what we'd have been. For sure.

We sat there, waiting for the giant beast to move, but none of us felt brave enough to get out and try to shoo him. There was something about those eyes… the red gleam, caused by his pupils being dilated in the low light, lent him a certain air of… *malice*.

Eventually Roo backed up, drove off the road onto the hard packed earth, and went around him. The demon-beast receded into the distance, and only the burning smell from Rusty's brake pads remained to prove we hadn't imagined the whole thing.

"I still can't believe I saw him," Roo admitted. "We must have been a hundred metres away. But I knew… I knew there was *something* there."

"No-one will believe us though," I told her. "Precognition? Near-death experience? Invisible ghost-cows on the road late at night? What a load of bullocks!"

Beachin'

Travelling up the coastline, we'd been awed by two things: the raw, elemental beauty of the land, and its incredible emptiness.

Broome distilled both of these characteristics into an ambience so poignant you could bottle it.

After hugging the coast since Exmouth, the road to Broome swerved inland, catching up with the road out of Broome. From there we swung back on ourselves, and entered a narrow nubbin of land jutting out into the Indian Ocean – and there it was. A small, sun-kissed paradise of a place, almost entirely surrounded by beaches.

The nearest town of any size was Port Hedland – a mining town with the genius catchphrase, 'It's Ore-some!' – over six-hundred kilometres to the south-west. And such time as we decided to leave Broome, we'd be going the opposite way – slightly north and slightly east – and we'd be driving until we hit the nearest real town in that direction.

Which was Kununurra, a little over a thousand kilometres away.

Between here and there were a few farms and homesteads, the occasional petrol station, a couple of one-horse hick towns – and the vast expanse of the outback.

The campsite was doing a brisk business, between backpackers with knackered vans like ours, and a collection of die-hard Aussie pensioners in shiny new motorhomes – but other than that, the town seemed devoid of tourists.

No holidaying families, no weekend-breakers; it was like every island paradise must have been, a decade before you went there on holiday.

Oh yes – Broome was my definition of unspoilt.

Probably because it was such a bastard to get to.

Only minutes from the campsite was one of the most amazing beaches in the world, which we went to check out as soon as we'd pitched the tent and eaten; fourteen miles of pristine white sand, wide, flat and level enough to play football on. The sea was warm, and the breeze kept the temperature bearable – but for all this, no-one was there.

Possibly because of the weird haze that had descended.

The sun was clearly visible in the middle of the sky, yet it looked like sunset; the stunning reds and oranges I would normally associate with the last rays of daylight were out in force, spreading to the insubstantial horizon.

We were all amazed by the colours, and the girls devoted a fair bit of time to capturing this phenomenon on camera.

"It's smoke in the atmosphere," Roo said. Which sounded ominous.

"Smoke as in, fire?" I asked.

"Yeah. They must be back-burning."

"Eh?"

"Oh, it's where the local park rangers set fire to all the undergrowth, to burn it away in a controlled manner. So that if there's a bushfire, it hasn't got as much fuel, and it can't spread so quickly."

"I see. Shit, living with fire is like a daily thing for you guys!"

"Yeah. Because the climate is so dry, fires are inevitable, so our ecosystem has adapted to include fire in its life-cycle. The burning away of the undergrowth is what allows new plants to grow, so most of the native tree-seeds, like the honky nut, can only be opened by fire. Animals can't eat them. They can lay dormant for years, and when they open they're sure of a chance to grow because there's less competition, and the ground is fertilised by ash. The trees are all fire-resistant – you'll see if we pass through a burn area – the bark blackens like charcoal, but the tree inside stays perfectly healthy."

I sometimes fell into the trap of thinking about Australia as like England, only hotter and with more kangaroos, but this kind of insight reminded me just how different it really was.

Evolved for fire.

The animals had clearly got the shitty end of the stick though, having evolved no better defence mechanism against fire than to run the fuck away. Whereas the Australian human male had lucked out – he'd evolved the ability to start the fire, ideally in the heart of a big stainless steel barbecue, and to cook the animals over it.

While drinking a beer, naturally.

Later, we discovered that the 'MCG' campsite was a Mecca for backpackers. The surf culture had drawn them here in droves, despite the remoteness – or perhaps because of it.

Over the inevitable box of *goon*, we got chatting to Richard and Kate, an English/Aussie couple who'd spent the better part of a year backpacking around Australia, focussing heavily on the beaches.

"I fly kites," Richard explained. "You wanna come to the beach tomorrow and fly my kite?"

Well! How do you refuse an offer like that?

Broome had an internet café, and the following morning I was able to discover that the text files for my book had been saved. There wasn't much I could do with them, as my laptop still looked like someone had been playing football with it, but for now 'That Bear' was safe. I hastily made a couple of copies, and posted one CD home to my parents in England. I'd learned a new mantra: Always Back Up.

After spending the rest of the morning exploring Broome on rented bicycles, we showed up at the beach expecting to find Richard holding a plastic handle with fishing line wrapped around it, and Kate carrying a diamond-shaped kite like you'd see in a kid's drawing of a trip to the park.

Instead, straining at the leash was what appeared to be a special forces parachute. The curved silken sail was bigger than our tent, and control over it was only achieved by means of two padded, foot-long steel bars, connected to the kite by heavy duty paracord.

Holding it felt like restraining a pair of bull-mastiffs hell-bent on rabbit for dinner; aiming it at the sky with both hands, it was impossible not to imagine I was firing the turret guns on the *Millennium Falcon*.

Gill had a go, and her low centre of gravity, combined with decent manual dexterity, allowed her to loop it around the sky like she'd been doing it all her life.

Then Roo had a go, and the effect was somewhat different. I'm sure there's some kind of lesson about levers in here, but Roo's long, narrow frame was no match for the raw power of the kite.

She took a firm grip on the handles – gave a brief cry of "SHIIIII…" – and was airborne, legs flailing, as the kite dragged her off down the beach.

"ROO!" I shouted.

"My kite!" Richard yelled.

"Let go!" I called to her.

"NO! Don't let go!" Richard corrected. "Hang on – I'm coming!"

And he raced off after Roo. Not because she was in danger, but because kites don't heal like people do.

"Hold on!" he called, as he ran.

But Roo wasn't making those kinds of decisions. A sudden gust of wind ripped one of the handles out of her hand, and in a flash the kite veered back on itself and arrowed towards the beach.

Richard must have seen it coming, but it was over far too quickly for him to turn away – the kite plunged towards him, angling straight for his head – and smacked into his face with the full force of... well, a kite.

It can't have been that bad.

I think he was just being dramatic – rolling around in the sand moaning, "My eye!"

Still, we decided a retreat was in order.

"Shall we, ah, go for a quick swim?" I asked the girls.

"You can't right now," Kate said. "They just closed the swimming beach, 'cause of a shark sighting. Reckon it'll be at least an hour before they re-open it."

"An hour? Why only an hour? What if the shark comes back?"

"If they see him again, they'll probably close it for another hour."

"That's crazy! Surely they should shut the whole place down, for a few days at least! Give him time to bugger off."

"You can't close the whole beach all day! Everyone wants to get in the water."

"Even with a shark out there?"

"Oh, he'll be long gone by now."

"But... *hello?* Shark! What if he's hanging around, waiting for the beach to re-open? *What if he knows it'll only be closed for an hour?*"

"They're mostly just passing through. If there's nothing to attract them, they move along pretty quick."

"I'm... not really sure I trust that."

"Honestly, most sharks never bother anyone. Giving them an hour is just being cautious." Then she gave me a cheeky grin. "But if you see one wearing a digital watch, then we're in trouble."

Horseplay

A few nights later, there was a treat in store for us; the Broome Rodeo was being held in a field on the outskirts of town, so we bought tickets (and cowboy hats) and headed out in Rusty to see what it was all about.

A rough ring of dirt had been fenced off for the competition, and was surrounded by eager spectators. Surrounding them were the food stalls and barbecues, selling drastically overpriced sausages which smelled so damn good the girls had to physically restrain me to stop me wasting five dollars on one.

The commentator sat in a garden shed that had been raised up on a platform of rusty scaffolding poles. From this rather ridiculous perch he held sway over the crowd – with possibly the worst display of commentating that has ever been heard by human ears.

Some people seem born for their jobs – many of the braver cowboys amongst them. They had the instinctive horse control, the split-second reflexes, the flawless hand-eye coordination; all essential qualities for casting ropes over enraged animals more than ten times their weight. A few seemed less confident, or else their timing was a bit off – and these were the cowboys that, whilst learning, would never be as good as the best. They were also the most likely to be going home in an ambulance.

But of everyone in that competition – nay, everyone in the stadium; hell, everyone in the damn *country* – no-one was less suited to his job than that commentator.

"This… is… John…" he said, introducing the first rider to tackle the bucking bronco in a drawl so monotone it was like a general anaesthetic. "John is… a local boy…" every word was so drawn out I had time to throw my hands up in despair before he got to the next one. I've heard more inflection from the speaking clock.

Even speaking at the same speed glaciers form, he still hit the limit of his repertoire within two sentences.

"John has won… some awards… for his… Oh!" By this point the staff had got sick of waiting and had released the thrashing horse unannounced.

John was clinging on for dear life while the horse unleashed its rage. Bucking furiously, it flung the man skyward again and again; every time he crashed back into the saddle my balls winced in sympathy. John's chance of having children looked less likely by the second.

"Oh!" the commentator repeated. "They're off. That's it, John. Stay on, John. Stay on, mate. Ride him, John. Ride him, cowboy. Ride him, mate. Ride hi… oh, he's off."

John, having been thrown violently, was now limping towards the stock fence, as two other cowboys rode in and effortlessly lassoed the rampaging animal. Their job was over in seconds; far too fast for their impressive efforts to be acknowledged in the commentary box, and the next cowboy was already springing onto the back of his bucking bronco.

"This is… Fred," came the commentary, "Fred is… another local lad… Fred is… ah… oh, they're off. That's it Fred. Ride him, cowboy. Ride him, mate. Stay on, mate. Stay on, Fred. Stay on ma— oh, he's off."

By the time Bill was announced, the three of us were in fits of laughter. "Stay on, Bill!" we called between guffaws, as the commentator found himself with enough time to elaborate. "Bill's riding a local steer, owned by… oh, they're off. That's it Bill. Ride him, cowboy. Ride him, mate. That's it Bill. Stay on. Ride him, Bi— oh, he's off."

And the crowd went wild.

In the wild-eyed chaos of the arena, Bill had been thrown so hard he couldn't stand up. A bent old bloke in a gigantic Akubra shuffled in and dragged the barely conscious cowboy to his feet. Bill looked dazed and beaten, but he managed to give his supporters a wave.

Screams, hollers and cat-calls erupted from the fence line.

"Well done, Bill," said the commentator. Flatly.

We decided it was time to go. For one thing, this could never get any better. For another, there were dozens more cowboys lined up to take their chances, including most of the ones who'd had a go already. This was shaping up to be a long event. But most importantly of all, was that there were no toilets here at all. And if I had to listen to one more bout of commentary, I was definitely going to piss myself.

In the corner by the entrance gate, a band was clearly raring to go, strumming their instruments in the gaps between riders. "We're not staying for the band, then?" Roo asked.

Gill shook her head. "I heard them warming up."

And so we traipsed back through the mud and sawdust towards Rusty, all the time with one ear tuned to the events in the ring:

"Sam's from… just up the road, here. He's… oh, there they go. Ride him, Sam. Ride him, mate. That's it, Sam. Ride him, cowboy. Ride him. Stay on mate. Ride him, Sa— oh, he's off."

And that was our first rodeo! Which has allowed me to say, whenever the occasion allows, and with complete honesty: "This ain't my first rodeo…"

I'm told I use that phrase far too often.

Sleep was a long time coming that night. Every time we were about to drift off, one of us would mutter, "Ride him, cowboy," and we'd all crack up again.

But there was something else keeping us awake, too.

In the middle of the campsite there was a small tent, not unlike ours – and inside that small tent, a new couple were… Hm. How to put this delicately?

They were shagging like deranged monkeys.

That was delicate, right?

Because tents aren't famed for their sound insulation, the entire campsite was in on the act – from first whispered suggestions to every groan and moan of pleasure.

And because the clever couple had left a light on – an iPhone, by the looks of things – a detailed silhouette of every thrust and every jiggling boobie was writ large across the skin of the tent. It was like drive-in movie, except we didn't need the radio to hear the sound track – they could probably hear it in Perth.

He had some stamina, that lad. It went on for hours.

When a last shuddering gasp announced the end of the evening's entertainment, a spontaneous round of applause erupted from the surrounding tents.

I joined in, whilst also pretending to share Gill and Roo's disgust.

Secretly, I had to admit – I'd have been quite proud of that, if it had been me in there.

That was the last thought I had, before I dozed off.

I woke up with a horrible realisation that the worst thing in the world had just happened.

I looked around me in the darkness, searching for clues to this sudden feeling of dread in the pit of my stomach. What on earth could be so wrong?

I couldn't figure out what, or why, until I'd given up trying and snuggled back into my sleeping bag, seeking the threads of my last dream. It had been something particularly delicious…

And then I knew it. Just like that – all bets were off.

Suddenly I perceived what the worst thing in the world was – and just why I'd been unable to place it before. It was because it was disguised most cunningly, as one of the best things in the world – all the better to take me unawares.

I'd had a sex-dream about Roo.

It changed everything. Because now, instead of being a carefree traveller, bunking up with his sister and her friend, at the start of a potentially endless adventure – I was Man. And in my sights was Woman.

I knew from past experience that once my mind got a grip on an idea like this, it wouldn't let me rest. I could tell myself to forget it all I wanted, but I had no control over my mind. Sometimes, I swear it does things just to piss me off.

This was a prime example. Out of all the women it could have started to fantasise about, why did it have to be Roo?

Roo had very gallantly been sleeping between Gill and I, simply because it felt a bit weird for us to be sleeping right next to each other. I mean, we'd done it before of course – whilst renovating a house in the Welsh Valleys, where we'd had no choice – but this was a different environment. People were bound to ask about our sleeping arrangements, when we rocked up at a campsite and pitched a single tent between the three of us. So Roo had slipped in between us on the first night, and although we'd never felt the need to discuss the arrangement, I'm sure we were all fairly happy with it.

Until now.

Because suddenly, I was sleeping right next to the woman I wanted most in all the world. In fact our feet were touching. I was awake, I was aroused, and all I could think of was how close she was. And how delicate. How tiny her earlobe looked, on the side of her head that wasn't currently pressed into a foam roll-matt. She breathed so peacefully, so regularly, so gently, so… seductively.

Ohhhh…. Shit.

This was going to be a problem.

A stronger man might have forced those images from his head. Might have laid back down, facing the other way, and made himself think about war movies, or poverty in the third world, or a possible link between relativity and quantum theory (perhaps my ideas of 'strong' and 'geeky' have gotten a bit mixed up over the years?) – but no. Sadly, I am not that strong.

So I did what a weak man would do: I rolled over, away from Roo… and continued fantasising about her. *This will all blow over*, I told myself, *just as soon as I get some action. It's an infantile fantasy based solely on the fact that I'm sleeping less than six inches away from the most desirable woman on the planet. Once we hit a real town, I'm bound to meet some other chicks. Then I won't even notice how biteable that earlobe is. Or how soft the line of her jaw is… that smooth patch of skin below her cheek that would just tingle if I were to stroke a fingertip along it…*

Oh, bloody hell!

There was no two ways about it: I was in trouble.

Hell's Crack

Leaving Broome was one of the more contentious decisions we made.

I loved the place; I'd have happily stayed there, if I'd been sure of a job. Sadly, we were all running out of money; traveling in Rusty was proving to be more expensive than we'd expected. Broome, though delightfully laid back, was a tourist-town – one without tourists, for the most part. Jobs for three of us in such a tiny place would be difficult to arrange.

So we hit the road, heading inland, leaving behind those crystal clear waters and that infinite expanse of white sand. In return, we got dust; and the further inland we went, the more dreamlike the lush green coast seemed.

On our second day of driving we came across a rest-area with a billabong, or swimming hole. Exerting a great effort of will, I managed to avoid peeking at Roo as she changed into her bikini, and we swam, leaving plumes of red dust in our wake.

It wasn't until we'd dried off, climbed back into Rusty, and were preparing to re-join the highway that we saw the warning sign; it was cunningly positioned on the exit slip road, at least for anyone traveling in our direction.

'DANGER – CROCODILES INHABIT THIS AREA,' it said.

'Do NOT enter the water. Attacks cause injury or death.'

"Glad they waited till now to tell us," I said, "or we'd never have got to swim!"

Our second brush with death came just a couple of hours later. We were cruising along at top speed, when there was an almighty BANG! – and the car slewed across the road. It would have been right into the path of the oncoming traffic, except we hadn't seen another car for almost an hour. Suddenly we were skidding, swerving, and someone was screaming.

"FUCKFUCKSHITFUCKAAAARRRHHH!"

Back on the right side of the road, Rusty slowed to a halt as Roo smoothly applied the brakes. And we sat there for a few seconds, in a swirling cloud of red dust, and caught our breath.

"Everyone okay?" I asked the girls.

They were both staring at me. Ahh! So *that's* who'd been doing the screaming. In my defence, I'd like to point out that I was in fact screaming for two, as Roo had remained so calm that she obviously hadn't noticed the danger we were in.

"Did we explode?" I asked her.

"Ah, a little. But don't worry, it's just a blow-out."

"A blow out of what?"

"A tyre! That's all. When you mix hot roads and old tyres, this *always* happens. No biggie."

"NO… no biggie? If that had happened… in the middle of…"

Roo had the grace to ignore me. She jumped out to check on the damage. Gill was already staring at it, a look of awe on her face. I slid the side door open, trying to be gentle in spite of the adrenaline coursing pointlessly through my body. The tyre – Rusty's front left (passenger side) – was ruined. I mean, I've seen some punctures, but this was something else. The whole tyre was torn apart, a tangled mess of steel wires and shredded rubber. For the last fifty metres we'd been driving on the wheel rim, and it had gouged a perfect pattern of swerve-arcs into the sun-softened tarmac behind us.

"See?" said Roo. "Just a blow-out. Let's get the spare."

I was still in shock. The state of the tyre suggested we'd run over a land mine, but this wasn't a good time to stand around discussing it. Rusty had a rack mounted underneath his back end to carry the spare wheel, but like everything else on him it had been broken when the girls had bought him. Unlike everything else, they hadn't bothered fixing it, which meant that the spare lived in the boot – underneath every other piece of gear we owned.

It took a good ten minutes to unload, by which point our possessions were stacked all over the highway. Crates of food wobbled unsteadily atop piles of books, folding chairs lay in a heap with rucksacks stacked next to them – and the wheel itself was finally liberated from the bowels of the vehicle. Deciding I needed to display a more manly aspect from here on in, I volunteered to change the wheel, and was again amazed at the wreckage of a tyre I removed.

"Careful," Roo pointed, "the metal bits are sharp!"

Honestly, I never even knew there were metal bits in a tyre.

Back in, repacked, and rolling once more, I asked Roo how she had remained so calm.

"That's all you can do, really," she told me. "The heat of the road makes the tyres so hot, that if they have a weak spot they're bound to blow. All you can do is try to keep the car under control, and slow down gently. If you panic and brake too hard you could spin around and flip the car. You just have to not freak out, really. And keep both hands on the wheel."

I glanced at Gill. Between my tendency to panic, and her patented one-finger driving technique, we weren't best suited to handle this sort of situation. But… realistically it would never happen again. Right? I asked Roo if it had happened to her before. Her response was less encouraging that I'd hoped.

"Oh, not for a while," she said.

We limped into a tiny town called Halls Creek, Roo taking it nice and slow, as our spare tyre had originally been the worst of the bunch. Losing one shitty tyre to the super-heated road was unlucky; losing two would be careless. Not to mention, it would have been a very long, very hot walk into town to buy a new one. So we rolled calmly up the main street and discovered a garage fairly quickly – because there was sod all else in Halls Creek, beyond a bottle shop and a library.

No prize for guessing which was doing the most business!

I hadn't encountered many aborigines so far, and this first glimpse was less than ideal.

Although the vast majority of Australia's original inhabitants have either integrated into modern society, or continue to pursue their tribal way of life in more remote areas, there are, of course, outcasts. Alcohol abuse proved to be a particularly difficult issue for indigenous communities, and the collision of Western values with their own has produced its fair share of casualties.

Hall's Creek, it seemed, was where they'd ended up.

Sitting around town, in every patch of shade they could find, were family groups large and small, all dressed in dirty, ragged clothes (except the children, who were naked). They sprawled on the grass around every tree – and in every single hand, there was a can of beer.

The garage mechanic was missing half his teeth, more than half his wits, and was far more focussed on scratching something nasty on the back of his neck than he was on our ruined tyre. He took one look at Rusty and did that drawn-out whistle thing mechanics do. It must be taught on their apprenticeship, as a way of softening up customers before the hammer-blow of the price quotation. To me, it signals that a con is about to be attempted – and in this case, I was dead right.

"Yeah, you'll be needing a light truck tyre for one of those."

"Really? A light truck? Is that… big?"

"It's expensive. Can't just use yer regular tyre, not on that thing."

"What have we got on it now then?"

"All different. I'll have to do both your front ones, or they won't match. It'll be $150 per tyre."

We exchanged shocked glances. $150 was more than we'd bargained for. Twice $150 was…

"That's ridiculous!" said Roo. "Thanks, but I think we'll try somewhere else."

"Nowhere else in town," the bloke said.

Luckily, he was lying about that too.

On the second of Halls Creek's two streets, we had much better luck. A slightly more honest mechanic sold us a $50 stock tyre for $90, and we decided to get the hell out of Halls Creek as fast as possible.

It was a run-down junkyard of a town, with weathered, ramshackle buildings and a populace of shambling, incoherent, unwashed drunks. It seemed like no-one wanted to help us, or even wanted us there at all. There was something unwholesome about the place; we had no scientific basis for this feeling, but we all shared it.

If the zombie apocalypse had happened a decade ago, Halls Creek is what the whole world would look like now.

Gill summed it up best, as we sped past a 'Welcome' sign riddled with bullet holes; "That place was an absolute shit hole."

"Yeah, glad we're out of there," I added.

"Let's never go back," said Roo.

Return To Hell's Crack

An hour out of town, Roo started swearing under her breath. This was very unlike her, from what I knew so far, and enough to be of concern. But even more concerning was the fact that I couldn't quite see her anymore. The air in Rusty was rarely what you would call wholesome, but this time it had a definite opaque quality to it.

To put it another way, Roo was engulfed in smoke.

"I'm gonna have to pull over," she said, tension in her voice. "The temperature is off the gauge. I think... I think we've got a problem."

The words had barely left her lips when there was a 'CLUNK' from somewhere beneath us, followed by a regular clicking, as of two metal things hitting against each other. I have a fairly limited experience of cars, but as I understand it, this sort of noise is rarely a good thing.

There was a rest-stop just ahead. Roo coasted into it and brought Rusty to a shuddering halt.

"Lucky there's a place to stop here," I said.

"For what it's worth..."

She waved her hand at the view from the windscreen. This 'rest-area' was little more than a flat semicircle of dirt and gravel, separated from the road itself by a narrow strip of dead brown grass. The 'little more' came in the form of a single stunted tree, which Roo had brought us to rest alongside.

We piled out into the blazing sun, and gathered around Roo's door. Rusty's engine was underneath the driver's seat, which was every bit as bad a design flaw as it sounds. Access required folding the seat back to reveal a small hatch – a hatch that, at the moment, seemed to be spewing steam...

We set up our chairs in the tree's scant shade, and dragged out the Esky. Then we sat and ate sandwiches, feeling very civilized about it, if a bit ridiculous. No cars passed in this time. When we felt Rusty's engine had cooled enough to risk a look, we crowded around the driver's door while Roo popped the seat catches. Smoke or steam or some noxious combination of both spilled out of the engine hatch as she folded the seat back out of the way. Inside… well, it looked like an engine. I craned my neck for a better view, and saw a complex assortment of interconnected parts, all covered with thick red dust. Yup – it was definitely an engine in there.

"So, Roo, what's wrong with it?" I figured she had the best chance of knowing. At least I hoped so. Because for all I knew, we could have blown the flux capacitor.

"Hmmm…" said Roo. She poked a finger in and pressed delicately on a few different components. "This fan seems a bit loose." She pressed on it to demonstrate, and it gave a couple of inches before springing back into place.

"Is that normal?"

"It's… I don't know. Maybe?"

"CAR!" yelled Gill. She'd been at the back of our little scrum, and was too short to look into the engine compartment anyway, so she'd been watching the road. Now she ran out and waved at the car – a typically monstrous four-wheel-drive truck.

The car slowed – drivers out here being more prepared to help than the average – and it pulled into the rest-stop in a cloud of dust.

"G'day fellas!" The car's occupant was a cheerful Aussie bloke, wearing the ubiquitous white vest known (to the people that don't wear them) as a 'wife beater'. "What's going on?"

"Well…" I gestured at the car.

The bloke wasted no time. In less than a minute he had his hands deep in our engine, fiddling with something or other. Now, most Aussie blokes know their cars. Kind of like English blokes and football. Anyone living this far from civilization has to have a bit of technical know-how. But sometimes they can be a bit like me – their enthusiasm outstrips their ability.

"I reckon this is your problem," he said, giving the fan a firm shake. "No way it should move like this…" there was a muted CRACK! from the engine compartment.

"Oh shit! Look!" he lifted the whole fan, plus the white plastic tank it was attached to, right out of the car. "Yeah, this *definitely* shouldn't come out."

Ah. You don't say.

"So, is there anything you can do?" I wasn't very hopeful by this point.

"Nah, mate. She's knackered! You'd better call the RAC. Get a tow back to town."

Ohhhh crap. Not *that* town.

"You're in the RAC, right?"

"Oh, yeah."

"Right-o! On me way back, I'll bring you a bag of ice, if you're still here. It's getting hot, eh! And you're stuck right out in the middle of it!"

And with that, he was gone. I couldn't be sure, but I had a feeling we were substantially worse off than before he'd arrived. If only his technical skills had matched his ability to state the obvious, we'd have been well on our way by now. But he'd been dead right – it *was* hot. And getting hotter. We had to get out of the sun, if we could.

A few hours later, the same bloke pulled up going the other direction. Good as his word, he'd brought us a bag of ice big enough to fill the Esky. "Still here, are ya?" he asked.

I considered it a rhetorical question.

"We tried to call the RAC, but we couldn't get any signal."

"Oh yeah, phones don't work out here, mate."

"Yes, we figured that out."

"But I see you've got yer tent up!"

He was right – in the paltry shade of that single stunted tree, on the verge beside the carriageway, we'd pitched our little tent. It was an act of desperation, the only thing we could think of to keep out of the sun – though it had pretty much the opposite effect on heat. Sitting inside was like being trapped in an industrial oven, and we could only manage it for short bursts. Sweating was bad, because it led to dehydration. We had plenty of water with us, but in these temperatures we should be drinking constantly. And we had no idea how long we'd be out there, next to that long, empty road, in the middle of nowhere, with sod all around us but one measly tree.

Three days, as it turned out.

The Very Helpful Bloke agreed to call in to the local RAC branch on his way back through town. Just to be on the safe side though (having already been on the receiving end of his help once), we stopped every car that passed that afternoon. All three of them. Each driver promised us faithfully that they'd have a word with the RAC rep in Halls Creek, and that he'd be back to get us in no time…

On the second day, we mostly lounged around, splitting our time between the car and the tent. Both were insanely hot, but moving between them gave us some illusion of choice – as though we were here by design, for the fun of it. In any case, we tried to stay positive.

We cooked and ate food, much as we had when camping beside the road previously. A few more cars stopped by to offer help that day, some bringing us ice, some offering to give us a lift into town – but much as this idea appealed to us (it didn't), we had some logistical issues to contend with. We couldn't leave the car. This place might look deserted, but everything we owned was inside Rusty. Guaranteed, within minutes of us leaving the whole car would be stripped bare. We'd be lucky to find the wheels still on him when we got back – and we already knew how much those puppies were worth.

I fancied going to town myself, to get a hold of the RAC dude – literally grab hold of the fucker – and ask him why the bloody hell he wasn't out there, rescuing us. But then, I didn't fancy leaving the girls here all alone. Equally, though I wouldn't mind waiting with Rusty, neither Gill or Roo liked the idea of setting off in a strange man's car – and wandering the streets of Halls Creek seemed like a nightmare.

No – he had to come. The RAC guy – it was his whole *raison d'etre*. Surely?

We spent the second night in the tent, clustered together under every blanket we owned. As hot as the day was, the night was colder. I'd read about that happening somewhere. Oh, yes! The desert. The Australian Outback was remarkably like a desert.

Only with road trains.

When one thundered by in the middle of the night, giant wheels chewing up the gravel only a few feet from our heads, we understandably shit ourselves. There wasn't much sleep to be had for the rest of that night, and we lay awake listening to the howling of wild dogs in the distance. At least, we hoped it was the distance…

Escape From Hell's Crack

Halfway through the next day, the police showed up.

"We kept getting reports that you were out here, but we didn't believe it at first," one cop said.

"We thought we'd have to have a look for ourselves," the other added.

"So, if you know, and presumably the RAC know, then why are we still here?" I asked.

"Search me! I reckon we'd better go and ask old Mick what he's playing at. Does one of you want to come along?"

Roo offered to go – but just then, the officers got a call on their radio, and they "had to check this out," so Roo had to stay with us. "But we'll speak to Mick about you," they said.

And left.

That evening the cops returned, with the news that RAC Mick was 'busy'. The bastard! They'd had a few choice words with the grumpy old bugger, presumably mentioning that it was his job – and they'd convinced him to come and get us in the morning.

"But we can't leave you out here all night," one of them said, "it's far too dangerous."

We loved hearing stuff like that.

So we piled as much gear as we could into the back of their truck, bid a nervous farewell to Rusty, and tried not to picture him being a burnt-out wreck when we returned. The cops dropped us at a campsite – sorry, *the* campsite – in Halls Creek, and, well, that's where we stayed.

For quite some time…

Amongst the delights the next morning brought us, was discovering that RAC Mick was the same asshole who'd tried to sell us light truck tyres for Rusty the last time we visited him. Top of my list of questions was, why the hell he hadn't come for us himself when the police told him to – forcing us to abandon Rusty to Fate and the wilderness. But this question was answered long before I had to get angry about it; as we approached Mick's garage, we couldn't help but notice that the tow truck sitting outside was missing the entire front section!

No headlights. No grill. No windscreen.

No wonder he couldn't drive at night!

The whole cab was stripped down, as though being repaired after an accident. This did not instil much confidence, either in the tow-truck, or in the ugly old git that owned the thing, but it did give us a moment of comedy: what was left of the vehicle was parked directly in front of a huge sign that read '24 HOUR TOWING'.

Indeed! 24 hours a day – so long as it wasn't dark.

Mick was none too pleased about being made to fetch us, so Roo and I climbed into the half-cab and endured his constant stream of complaining in silence. I started out on the journey wanting to strangle the bugger, and by the time we reached Rusty I had to sit on my hands to stop myself reaching for his neck. Only the disturbing way he kept scratching it kept me away. Nothing was right in Mick's world. Everyone was out to get him. And you know what? I was more than happy to join the queue.

He brought Rusty back and ditched him outside the campsite. Almost for a laugh, we'd asked Mick what it would cost to get him fixed. He'd had a rummage around in the engine while we were making Rusty ready to tow, and he didn't hesitate to give us his opinion.

"Busted water pump, it is. Cost yer two grand, yeah, at least that."

Laugh or cry? I chose option 3. "Bullshit! Why?"

"It's a Nissan. A Nissan Nomad van, yeah? Not many of them about."

"Seriously? We only saw eight cars yesterday. Three of them were this exact same van."

"Yeah. Imported, they are. Can't get the parts. Very hard to find."

"Riiight. Thank-you."

And so we spent most of the afternoon emptying Rusty completely – and then pushing him back through town towards the mechanic that had sold us the right tyre.

His verdict was the same; a new water pump would have to be ordered, and couriered in from Perth. But his price? $350. Which, whilst still heart-stopping, was within the bounds of possibility. Now all we had to do was wait…

For a week.

In Halls Creek.

Where waiting was no.2 on the list of fun things to do – right behind shooting yourself in the forehead.

"You could get a job in the hotel," the campsite owner suggested, when I mentioned why we were so eager to reach Kununurra.

I just smiled and nodded, as there's no polite way to say 'Honestly, I'd rather be raped by a cactus.'

The campsite in Halls Creek – or Hell's Crack, as we'd come to call it – did have two redeeming features. One was the campsite swimming pool, our only respite from the baking heat, to the point where we spent all day, every day in it; and the other was the three backpacker chicks who showed up there the day after we did. None of them were particularly attractive, but they had redeeming features of their own – and they weren't ashamed to show it. Within minutes of their arrival, all three of them were in the pool with us – and all three of them were topless!

And they stayed that way the entire week.

I tried to ignore it, of course. I mean, I didn't want to be *that* guy; the one always staring at boobs. But when they're right there in your face? And we were in Hell's Crack – a place so barren, there was literally nothing else to look at...

If I passed those girls in the street tomorrow – and they had their clothes on – I don't think I'd recognise a single one of them.

At least it helped me to conceal my growing obsession with Roo.

The balance of bad luck continued though – both Roo's shoes, and then my shoes, broke; our tent collapsed, snapping one of the poles in the process, leaving us even closer to being homeless than we were already.

And on the evening of our first night, a fight broke out just beyond the campsite fence. It sounded ugly; screams and yells from dozens of throats pierced the air, and we huddled in our tents, hiding from what sounded like a full-scale gang war.

In the morning we expected to see bodies. Blood stains, severed limbs, discarded weapons – the aftermath of a conflict so violent, the screaming had kept us awake until the early hours of the morning.

But there was nothing.

It was eerie. A brawl that protracted and brutal couldn't have been cleared away so completely, could it?

That night, at roughly the same time, it began again.

It was the aborigines; drunk to the point of psychosis and filled with hatred and despair, they apparently spent every night this way; hurling torrents of abuse at each other as part of extended family feuds, not coming to blows (presumably because they could hardly stand upright by this point) – but such passion, and such venom was in their shrieks, that we constantly expected to see corpses littering the ground outside the campsite.

When our water pump showed up from Perth and was installed a day later, we could have kissed the thing – grease and all.

Not the mechanic though, as the campsite owner had warned us he was a paedophile.

We hardly dared talk about leaving Hell's Crack for fear of jinxing it.

It seemed too fragile a dream to risk unveiling in such an awful place.

If we didn't get away this time, I would definitely consider shooting myself in the forehead.

And then, at last, we were sitting in Rusty, pointing out of the place.

"Let's get the fuck out of here," I said.

"If we can!" said Gill. "This place is like a black hole – it keeps sucking us back in! It's inescapable."

She was wrong, thank God.

Smashing Pumpkins

After the physical and spiritual desolation of Hell's Crack, we arrived to find Kununurra a thriving oasis of life.

There were *trees* here, for gawd's sake!

We checked in to a pleasant campsite on the edge of a lake, and pitched our tent amidst acres of lush green grass.

Then a day later we moved it, because all that lush green grass was maintained by a network of automatic sprinklers programmed to come on at six in the morning – and we'd pitched our tent right in the middle of them.

Rusty got a damn good soaking too, which frankly, the old boy needed; he hadn't been washed since before the girls had painted him. He'd ceased to be a multi-coloured marvel and had been completely redecorated in Insides of Insect.

The first item on our to-do list was a biggie – getting a job. We'd kept our eyes and ears open as we travelled up the coast, but every piece of advice we'd been given was the same – that Kununurra was the place to go, to work in the fruit-picking industry. And if we didn't want work in the fruit picking industry, well, there was plenty of other work – in Perth.

So we figured, perhaps fruit picking was worth a shot.

On our first trip into town we signed up with a job agency – and agreed to start the very next day.

Picking pumpkins.

"It's either that, or melons," the agency woman told us, "and you *do not* want to pick melons."

So, five o'clock the following morning found Roo prodding me insistently – with the butt-end of a torch.

"Tony, wake up! Gotta get ready for work!"

Outside our tiny tent, darkness reigned and the civilised world still slept; but we had pumpkins to pick, and one thing farm work the world over has in common, is a hideously early start. Intellectually I knew that this far north, by 7am the inside of the tent would be like a blast furnace – but I still loathed and detested 5am.

We spent half an hour stumbling around in the darkness, trying to remember the way to the toilets, and rooting around inside Rusty for hats, sunglasses, sun-screen and water bottles. Then we trekked through the campsite to the main road, where we stood waiting for the staff transport – a Land Rover so encrusted with muck and dust it was tough to tell what its original colour had been.

And from there, we were whisked away to join the other backpackers working at Ivanhoe Farm.

If there was a definition of 'back-breaking work' – picking pumpkins would be it. In no way is this an exaggeration. We'd start off quite innocently, using long-handled snips to cut the pumpkins off their stems. Now, I say long-handled, but they are only long in relation to the short-handled ones, which aren't substantially bigger than a pair of scissors. To employ these tools, we have to bend over at about forty-five degrees, make a cut, then shuffle forward two steps. It soon became too much for my lower back muscles to straighten me up after each cut, so I adopted the perma-hunchback position.

The rows were evenly spaced about half a metre apart – and each row was exactly one kilometre long. I tell you, by the time I got to the end of a row, I had a powerful need to stand upright!

So I did. For about thirty seconds. Then, before I got spotted by the boss (who was racing up and down the furrows on his mud-splattered quad bike), I turned around, assumed the position once more, and started back up the row next to me. By then my spirit was freshly crushed, as during my half-minute stretch, while shocks of pain and pleasure chased themselves up and down my spine, there was only one thing to look at: the endless expanse of field, rows upon rows, receding into a distance too far for the eye to measure. Infinity. Of pumpkins. In fact that would make a good collective noun for them; 'an infinity of pumpkins'… either that, or 'A Chiropractor's Delight'.

Anyway. Lunchtime, when it came, was a particularly torturous respite. Our mobile lunchroom, aka the battered Land Rover, was like a furnace. Rather than using it to ferry us all back to the break room, the boss simply left it there on the edge of the field. By the time we'd trudged back to it, our lunch break was half over, but this was a blessing in disguise; inside the car, the temperature was sufficient to liquefy every item of food we'd brought with us. Including the sandwiches.

We had to give the exposed bits of us some relief from the sun, so we crammed ourselves inside the vehicle and tried to rehydrate with water hot enough to make tea with. Flies and mosquitos were as thick in the car as they were outside, with the additional problem that swatting them usually resulted in smacking someone else in the face. It was insanely hot, ridiculously sweaty, and the supervisor sat in the cab and cranked up his Eminem CD to the point where the benches shook in sympathy.

"I think they do this on purpose," Gill said. "They make breaks so frigging awful that I actually want to get out and snip pumpkins again!"

As we poured out of the Land Rover for the second innings, the boss raced up to us with a request. "I need four of you to help me with the Jarradales."

All three of us volunteered so enthusiastically we nearly left the ground, but the boss was only interested in blokes for this gig.

"Sorry ladies," I said to Gill and Roo. "But this job could be even harder!"

Gill's response to that was a suggestive snip with her shears that brought a tear to my eye.

So off I went. To a different field, which was welcome, as I'd started to imagine the one we were working on stretched all the way around the world to meet itself. It was a refreshing sight, the end of it, even though it was very, very far away from where Gill and Roo were starting to bend over.

In the top corner of the new field was a tractor, with four enormous plastic crates strapped to the back of it. At least this looked more interesting…

The boss began his briefing while we were still walking.

"Easy, this," he said. "I'll drive that tractor. You take a row each and follow me, picking up the Jarradales and putting them in the back. Just remember, *place* them, don't throw. That's it."

"So, what's a Jarradale?" I asked, just as we arrived at the edge of the field full of them.

"That."

His foot rested on a gigantic pumpkin, like the ones kids carve out for Halloween. Except it was a greenish-grey-blue colour. And it was the size of Rusty's spare wheel.

"Oh… Shit."

And though I've had a strange and varied career as I've travelled around the world, I have never yet encountered any form of work as tough, and as painful, as picking Jarradales.

It went something like this:

1) Stand behind tractor. Breathe deeply to fully appreciate the aroma of its exhaust, as it crawls forwards in low gear.

2) Bend double at the waist. Wrap your hands and forearms around a monster-pumpkin – each weighing between fifteen and twenty kilos – take the strain, and haul that bugger skyward!

3) Ditch said pumpkin in the crate attached to the back of the tractor. Take one pace forwards.

4) Repeat.

It was agony. Periodically, the boss would up the speed a notch, confident that we were now 'getting used to it'. By the time we'd been at this for two hours, he was up to jogging speed. I had to plead with him on behalf of all of us – and then on behalf of the pumpkins, which were being thrown haphazardly at the back of the tractor from several metres away as we tried in vain to catch up to it. He relented, and passed on the good news: "Just another couple hours of this, lads, then it'll be back to the other job."

Fuck me! I've never wanted to clip pumpkin stems so much in my life.

Later, after I'd worked the kinks out of my back enough to stand upright again, the boss confided in me that we'd done well. "I've never had a crew stick at it that long before!" he said.

Which made sense, because he hadn't bothered to tell us there was an option.

And Then…

Sex.

Men, in my experience, are extremely weak in this area. I've seen good men seduced by evil women twice their age, with nothing more than a lingering gaze and a suggestively crooked little finger. Hell, I've *been* that man. It's not something I'm proud of. Okay, I'm a little bit proud of it. But I'm not proud of being proud of it. Well, not much.

All of which goes to illustrate – using myself as a prime example – just how pathetic guys can be around girls, when it comes to matters of sex. Or potential sex. Or the slightest remote possibility that some time in the distant future there's a chance that sex will be considered. Oh, yes! Those are the kinds of possibilities we live for.

If you're reading this, and you're a woman, then I guess you know this already.

If you're reading this and you're a man, stop denying it! It won't do you any good. *They know.*

So anyway, there I was; lying not-quite-in-bed with the woman of my dreams. Literally the woman of my dreams, not that she knew as much – something for which I am truly grateful. If she'd been able to see into my head… ye gods, that would have been awkward.

But I was getting worried.

I now officially had a problem.

And it was only going to get bigger.

And yes, I'm talking about my penis again.

So far, I'd managed to keep a lid on my penis. Sorry! My imagination.

Well, I'd tried to. But I could feel my willpower eroding.

At first, I'd thought working together would help me get over it. Our job was so hideous, so incredibly unglamorous, that I couldn't possibly spend my days thinking about sex. Surely not while I was knee-deep in mud, plastered with sweat, burning in the sun and aching in parts of me I didn't know could ache?

That's when I learned that, willpower aside, my mind is very, very strong.

It's just *not on my side*.

Turns out, I can think about sex all day long.

Heat, filth and pain be damned.

And with both my body *and* my mind arrayed against me, I was in serious danger of losing this battle.

It didn't help that Roo looked utterly adorable in the fields, her slender frame draped in a men's shirt at least five sizes too big for her. Somehow she managed to stay cleaner than all the rest of us – and even when she didn't, she made dirt look *sexy*.

Even the sweat glistening on her brow was somehow seductive…

Ohhh… Crap.

This was getting out of hand.

And never more so than when, early one morning, I woke to find I was curled around Roo. Both of us were laying on our sides in the foetal position. In fairness, it had been a very cold night. But laying like this, all snuggled up together, felt so *right*. I could have lain there quite happily all day, despite being poked and jabbed by every bump and rock in the ground. As it was, several sore spots in my hips were screaming at me to turn over. It would only be a temporary respite from the pointy lumps beneath me, and soon enough my other side would be feeling the pressure – but I couldn't make myself do it. Because no-one could expect me to control what I did in my sleep. I'd woken up this way by accident, and as far as I was concerned it counted as a completely legitimate sleeping position – at least until I turned over. There was no chance I'd get away with doing this again; accidental snugglage is inevitable when three full-size people are sleeping in a tent barely big enough for two small children. But *deliberate* snugglage? That way lay trouble. And possibly some kind of sexual harassment charge.

So I ignored the messages from my whinging body, and curled myself a tiny bit tighter around Roo. After all, I figured, that's what I'd be doing naturally in my sleep! If I was sleeping. Which I wasn't.

But you know what? As I drew my legs up fractionally, and braced myself for the disappointment of Roo turning away from me and breaking our bond – I felt something else instead.

At the place where our sleeping-bag-clad bodies were touching – where I could feel the warmth of her even through two layers of shitty microfiber – my chest was pressed up against her, leaning on her slightly with the merest fraction of my bodyweight.

And, almost imperceptibly, Roo was pushing back.

It had to be my imagination. She was asleep anyway, so surely this was the unconscious act of a body seeking greater warmth? There was only one way to test this theory. I leaned in a little heavier, and waited again to be thrust away as she rolled over onto her front.

But no. This time… she was *definitely* pushing back!

What to do? My subtle moves were all used up. I was in quite a bit of pain, and couldn't snuggle any closer without dramatically altering my position. Since we were both at least pretending to still be asleep, any such disturbance would wreck everything, and I'd be back to square one. Which, to be honest, was probably for the best.

Nothing good can come of this, I told myself. No matter how much I wanted it…

And then it came to me. A last ditch attempt, disguised as the innocent act of one fast asleep, to push this envelope far enough to be sure.

Keeping my eyes closed, I tried to relax my breathing to a regular, slow rhythm.

I sighed for emphasis.

And then I freed my arm from the sleeping bag and casually draped it across her.

Instantly her whole body tensed, for a fraction of a second. It was like an electric current ran through her. *Here we go*, I thought. *Explanation time…*

And then Roo reached out to grab my arm, and pulled it tighter across her chest.

Across her… well, anyway. The point is, she did it.

On purpose.

And that was the most fascinating, most delicious, most exciting thing that had happened to me since arriving in Australia.

And by far the most dangerous.

Gill was first up that morning.

Gill was first up every morning – something I'd never really thought about one way or another. But suddenly it created a strange situation, one that I had no idea how to deal with.

As soon as Gill stirred, I pulled my arm back into my sleeping bag. I couldn't quite bring myself to roll away from Roo, but I doubted Gill would notice anything untoward. Hell, space was so tight in that tent, the difference between sleeping next to someone and sleeping on top of them was only a matter of centimetres. So I held my position and waited, while Gill zipped herself out of her sleeping bag, cursed the tent's door zipper for being on the opposite side of the tent, found it, and freed herself from our colourful silken prison. Shivering and mumbling to herself, Gill closed the door and stomped off towards the toilet block.

Leaving Roo and me…

Alone.

Together.

And awake.

Awkward…

Oh well. He who dares, wins, I told myself silently.

Or else he ends up with a knee in his testicles.

Time to find out.

So I pulled out that arm again, that arm on which all these hopes and dreams rested – that arm of infinite possibility – and I draped it back over Roo.

"Mmm, that's nice," she murmured, pulling me close again.

And that was when I knew.

Not that I'd spend the rest of my life with her, because that's an almost impossible thing to know from two sleeping bags away – but I knew this: our cosy little world was going to change dramatically.

It might be messy and uncomfortable. It was likely to upset some people. It was likely to upset *us*, both together and separately, to cause division and animosity, to end badly, and to crash and burn right through the middle of our friendly family unit.

But for my part, I was over the moon.

And I promise, that's the last time I'll mention my part.

At least in this chapter.

Where Do We Go From Here?

The simplest thing, at least for now, was to pretend that nothing special had happened.

After all, we had to get ready for work.

It was a complex process, involving moving Rusty's seats up and down to access different areas of storage, rummaging in bags, crates and a clean laundry pile that we never seemed to get around to putting away. Only one person could get in there at a time, which is why we staggered our morning trips to the bathroom. That morning there was another reason for me to visit the bathroom. Two actually, if you want to be crude, but more than anything, I felt a powerful urge to hide. And also, to think. I dunno, does that make three things?

Work that morning was depressingly normal – and torturous – but I couldn't help it. I regularly found myself stood still, remembering, with a goofy smile on my face. Then I'd catch Roo looking at me, and we'd both look around guiltily to see if anyone else had noticed. No-one had.

And even if they had, no-one would have cared. Hell, we could have been naked mud-wrestling, and no-one would have given a shit. Well, maybe they would, but not about our relationship status; you just rarely get to see naked mud-wrestling live at work.

To us, it seemed like something forbidden and illicit had taken place – and that only we two, out of all the world, could possibly know about it.

But to everyone else... well, to be honest, they had the right of it. Nothing actually had happened.

Sweet, sweet nothing!

I was quite excited about it.

And because we were at work, and the boss could zoom up at any time to inspect our progress, we couldn't say anything about it to each other. It remained trapped in a bubble of fantasy, or nostalgia.

Thank God!

I had no idea what I was going to say to her if we ever found ourselves alone again.

And then, at lunch, Roo and I were chosen to join a group digging irrigation ditches. It's hard to believe I know, but this job sounded infinitely preferable to picking pumpkins.

And it was.

Water flowed around each field though a main channel, which we crossed and re-crossed on narrow wooden planks. All we needed to do was divert it to run into each successive furrow, by taking chunks out of the bank here and there with our bare hands (I don't think they trusted us with shovels).

Of course, when hand-digging ditches there was the omnipresent danger of falling into ditches – and due to the clumsiness which is my genetic legacy, I did so quite frequently.

Roo – being far more poised and in control of her limbs – required pushing.

By the end of the day we were both caked in mud from head to toe – so much so that the boss gave us a lift home in the back of his filthy ute, rather than letting us wreck the inside of the staff minibus.

We got home before Gill, but couldn't do anything because Rusty was still locked, and she had the keys – so we lay around on the grass outside the tent, laughing at the extended mud-fight we'd not only managed to start, but had been paid for having.

Gill, when she got back, was more than a bit pissed off that she hadn't been involved. We hadn't really broached the topic of what to tell Gill, possibly because we hadn't really broached the topic of what to tell each other. Neither of us knew what was going on – if anything even was going on – but I was pleased to find I didn't feel awkward around Roo, despite the elephant in the room.

Our ritual, regular as clockwork, was to shower immediately after getting back from work – because stopping to catch our breath often resulted in us being unable to stand up again.

As Gill marched on ahead, desperate for the loo, I hung back with Roo. An idea had just dropped into my head. Now, how to phrase it...?

"Do you want to save water?" I asked her. "You know – shower with a friend?" I said it half-jokingly, so that I'd have a get-out clause in case she was offended.

But she wasn't.

"Yes please," she said, "I'm all for saving the environment."

So, after washing myself thoroughly in the men's shower block (because no-one wants you to shower with them if you actually *need* a shower – sweat-stink, dried-on mud and navel fuzz are notoriously unromantic) – I sneaked around to the women's bathrooms, ventured inside, and tapped gently on the door to the only shower still in use.

There were definite advantages to being the only people at the campsite, and this was one of them; I was fairly certain it was Roo in there, though I poised myself to flee just in case.

Roo was in there. And she opened the door, suppressing a nervous giggle, and then I was in there too.

It was the first time I'd seen her naked, and I drank in the sight in case it was also the last. I had no idea what the future would hold for us. How Gill would cope if she ever found out, and if we'd decide to nip this in the bud before we risked going down that route.

But for now, it was breath-taking.

Roo was as pale and slender as an elf-maiden, only she was real – and she was naked – and she was within reach. Elf-maidens are almost never like that.

Roo was also very shy, so I pressed myself against her, and we held each other as the warm shower water cascaded over both of us.

It was a long time before we let go.

Back at the tent, there was no sign of Gill. We'd worried, as we dressed, dreaming up elaborate stories about looking for a lost necklace, an accidental clothing mix-up, or having to kill a horde of giant spiders (guess which one was mine?). We never actually settled on a convincing version of the truth to tell her, so it was perhaps for the best that we discovered her on a bench in the kitchen, fast asleep.

I gave her a gentle shove, and then a slightly less gentle one when she didn't stir straight away.

"Eh? Oh!" she sat upright and scrabbled around on the table for her glasses. "Sorry, I must have dozed off. What are you up to?"

"You know, the usual. Lost necklace. Roo had my jumper. Giant spiders. How are you?"

"Um, I'm okay. Um... what?"

"You want a cup of tea?" I asked her. It was a sure-fire way to distract a confused member of the Slater family.

"Oh. Yeah, thanks!" she said.

And that was that.

At least for now...

And still, neither Roo nor I were sure how to proceed.

But I knew one thing – this wasn't just going to go away.

Not this time.

Luckily for us, Gill sleeps like the dead. Well, she doesn't go stiff and decompose, at least not that I've noticed, but once asleep she was almost impossible to wake.

She also tended to pass out around 10pm, giving us the opportunity, should we so desire, to misbehave quite extensively.

The only problem was, we lived in a tent.

And Gill was already in it.

If only we had another place, some kind of alternative sleeping space – not too far away ideally, but padded and discreet…

Poor old Rusty. He'd seen a few things in his time, but I'm not sure he was ready for this. Neither were we, to be honest – even the discomfort of sleeping in Rusty hadn't prepared us for just how awkward sex in him could be. Rusty seemed to have protrusions everywhere, all made of the hardest, most unyielding plastic, and I swear they multiplied in the dark.

Every move was accompanied by yells of pain, swiftly stifled, or the muffled sound of knees and elbows smacking into inconveniently placed bits of console.

If I had a penny for every time I sat back to find the handbrake probing its way into places best not probed… well, let's just say I gave it a damn good rub with a pair of socks before I felt right about letting Gill handle it again.

It's a testament to the strength of our desire that we managed to overcome these obstacles – night after night after night.

It was a pretty good week, all things considered.

Back To Nature

As the days wore on it became more and more difficult, finding ways to sneak away from Gill.

Not because she was suspicious or anything; Gill, bless her heart, was as innocent as a person could be. Or, so I thought.

But when you're living as close as we were – literally in each other's pockets – discovering a bit of privacy becomes as challenging as it is rewarding.

And oh boy, was it ever rewarding!

So one night, weighing up our options while Gill was in the kitchen making her tenth cup of tea, we decided to take more advantage our gorgeous surroundings. We were, after all, living in a place of outstanding natural beauty, and it also happened to have a very forgiving night-time climate.

In other words, we were going to do it outside.

It came about because Roo was complaining that she was getting a permanent indentation in her lower back in the shape of a seatbelt holder.

I too had suffered at the plastic latches of these little buggers. There were six of the damn things in the back seat area, and somehow, whenever I tried to do anything, one of them got in the way – either knelt on, or leant on, or more often than not working its way uncomfortably between my bum cheeks.

It was getting to the point where if I'd inserted a seatbelt into my asshole, it would click in.

There had to be a better way than this.

And I had just come up with it.

"Outside?" Roo sounded nervous.

"Yeah! We're pretty much the only people here. There'll be no-one around that late. We could lay by the pool. We could use the picnic blanket!"

I consider it a measure of how strong our lust was for each other, that none of this seemed even marginally questionable at the time.

And so, our chance came. Gill went to bed early, and Roo and I stayed up reading by torch-light. Then, when we guessed enough time had passed, we rummaged through the junk in Rusty in slow motion (for the sake of quietness), discovered the picnic blanket, and set off across the campsite.

Now, the pool area itself was dimly lit by solar-powered globes scattered around the enclosure. It's quite possible that, in the reflection of this light, the soft glow of Roo's body could be seen from outer space. We were in serious danger of attracting helicopters on bushfire patrol, and I was forced to consider going back to Rusty to look for my sunglasses.

This being the case, we decided to take the party a bit further out, finally settling in the shadow of a big shrub by the fence. Perfect!

And now…

This was the moment I'd looked forward to all day at work, and all evening whilst sitting around in the kitchen drinking endless cups of tea. It was my time, alone in the dark with Roo, and it had become my refuge; a part of my life that was, in spite of all the odds, actually going *well*.

And better than well.

I made a pillow for Roo from our discarded clothes, and fumbled for a little cardboard box I'd managed to buy earlier on…

Let me just point out that it was quite difficult to buy anything in secret when all three of us did all our shopping – and paid for it all – together. There seemed to be no need for one person to sneak off on their own to, let's say, a pharmacy. Not without arousing suspicion. I needed a reason, and it had to be good. If I suddenly remembered I wanted a different brand of shampoo, the girls would naturally expect to accompany me, to browse the bins of discounted nail polish. So I took my chance when it presented itself. At the moment of maximum distraction, when the girls were busy bagging up our food as it was beeped through the supermarket check-out, I blurted out the first thing that came to mind: "I've got to run to the pharmacy and get some cream, 'cause my balls are really itchy."

Ha! That'd keep them away.

It also earned me a concerned look from the lady behind the cash register – and from three or four of the customers queuing up behind us – but no matter. I'd done it! I was free. I raced out of the supermarket, all the way down the road, and sprinted up to the pharmacy counter with the biggest box of condoms I could find. Sweating and panting, I pushed them forwards and wheezed "Just these please!"

A ripple of disgust ran through the girl serving me, but luckily sheer breathlessness saved me from telling her, "don't worry, they're not for me!"

That would have been even more awkward.

But never mind that; I'd got what I came for. And according to the box, I'd even scored some free lube. Result!

So. Back to the present. Roo lay back on our picnic blanket, looking… magical. I was breathless all over again. I groped around in the shadows, finding the box and pulling out a condom, giving Roo my best 'bedroom eyes' the whole time.

(I have since been asked not to do my 'bedroom eyes', after Roo caught me making bedroom eyes at a bacon sandwich I was about to eat, and decided it makes me look like Gollum from Lord of the Rings.)

But anyway, I digress.

I moved closer to Roo, and bit open the packet.

And then gagged, as my mouth was flooded with an entire sachet of complimentary lube.

"EUURRGHH!"

I coughed and spluttered, hacking and spitting into the grass, as Roo shrank back out of range. God, that stuff tasted vile. I was choking on it, and swearing viciously between heaves, which kind of ended the stealth part of the operation right there.

As if to prove this point, I heard a voice from the other side of the bush.

"Tony? Is that you?"

I froze. Roo froze. I could almost hear her heart beat over mine.

"Tony?"

Ohhhh… Shit.

It was Gill.

For reasons unknown, she must have decided to visit the farthest toilet block instead of the near one – and now she was standing, somewhat confused, by the entrance – directly on the other side of the fence.

"Is there someone there?"

She sounded nervous now. Poor girl! But DAMN IT! But also…

poor girl.

"Yes, it's me," I said, trying to keep the soul-crushing disappointment out of my voice.

"Oh! I thought I heard you. Where are you?"

"I'm in the pool area."

"Oh. What are you doing?"

"Just, um…" I glanced around me for inspiration. Roo had curled herself into a ball, as though that would make her any less naked. She had one hand ineffectually covering her bare ass. "Just… looking at the moon."

There was a few seconds of silence.

"Are you… okay?" Gill asked.

"Yeah. I just ate something unpleasant. A bug."

"Oh. Okay. Are you… coming back to the tent?"

"Yeah, I might just have a walk first. That's what I'm doing, you know, having a walk. At night. A night walk."

Roo gave me a kick, which I took as a sign to shut up.

"Do you know where Roo is?"

"Ah… yeah, she's here too. She wanted to have a walk. To look at the stars! We left you asleep."

"I woke up to go the loo. They've closed the toilets near us."

"Oh? Really."

"Yeah. I had to walk all the way over here."

"Ah, I see."

Gill said nothing, and I could practically feel her confusion through the shrub.

(Not a sentence I get to use very often, that one.)

"The stars are so beautiful tonight…" I offered.

"Uh, yeah," said Gill. "So anyway, I'm going to go to the loo."

"Alright. Enjoy yourself!"

"Thanks. I will."

And she shuffled off. I heard the creak of the bathroom door as it opened and closed.

"I think we got away with it," I told Roo. She was dressing with a speed and ferocity that said she disagreed.

"Come on, quick," she hissed.

"Wait! Wait a minute. We can't go back *now*. Not before she does! We have to wait, like we're walking around for a bit. That'll be less suspicious."

"*Less* suspicious? Less suspicious than what? Than huddling in the nude behind a bush while she shouts at us from the other side?"

"Well, I just think we should wait a while… Maybe she'll go back to sleep?"

Roo stared at me.

"Think about it! She's not expecting us to be here, doing this. She doesn't know anything. Plus, she's still half asleep. I bet she believes we're out here to look at the stars. You guys used to do that, right?"

"I guess so. In America, in the desert."

"See! We'll be fine."

"So, what, you want us to wait for her to go back to sleep? Just sit here and do nothing?"

"Well, I didn't mean we should do *nothing*. We are here, after all…"

"Bloody hell! You're– I don't know if there's a word for it! Impossible, and irresponsible, and, and… too bloody horny, all rolled into one."

"But in a good way, right?"

She wisely left that one unanswered.

This event has gone down in history as the greatest failure of stealth since Moses tried to sneak a bunch of Israelites out of Egypt by parting the Red Sea. On the upside, no-one drowned – though I came close to it, thanks to the free packet of 'Play' Gel. On the downside, there was a lot of wandering through the metaphorical desert, parched, so to speak, before we dared try it again.

I thought about sending a sternly-worded email to the Durex company, complaining about the damage they'd inadvertently done to my sex life.

I mean, they should *warn us* about shit like this!

But then I noticed that someone had beaten me to it.

Maybe this was a more common problem that I'd realised.

Because Durex had already been compelled to add a warning to the packaging of their complimentary lube.

'DO NOT EAT' it said.

"That's the trouble with you men," Roo said, when I told her, "you never follow the instructions."

Field Day

When we heard on the grapevine about a chance to switch jobs, we dropped those pumpkins like hot potatoes. Our new job was on a sandalwood plantation, further away on the outskirts of town. We treated ourselves to a couple of days off, celebrating the end of two full weeks in the pumpkin fields. How we'd lasted that long, I do not know. My back still hasn't forgiven me.

On the first morning of our new job, we were presented with a worryingly familiar scenario.

Dawn found us sitting in a rapidly disintegrating minibus, bouncing along a knackered dirt track towards the plantation. The vehicle was in roughly the same state of repair as the road; there were holes in the roof; there were holes in the floor. It needed to be push-started every time, and was stopped by 'natural breaking' – ie, coasting until it either ran out of speed, or hit something. Or both.

Seven other workers were crammed into the torn vinyl-covered seats alongside Roo, Gill and myself, and every one of us was braced in position with arms legs and in a few cases, heads pressed against what was left of the dented metal roof.

"She'll be right!" the boss had said, in true Aussie fashion, when I'd commented to him that only the paint was holding his van together.

After which he'd introduced himself as 'Johno'.

Johno loved to drive that wreck of a van. He loved to drive it at speed. He prided himself on knowing exactly how to coax what he wanted from the ancient engine. He deftly slotted it between openings in the fence and shot across makeshift bridges over a network of irrigation ditches. He was grinning at me in the rear-view mirror, as if to say 'See?'

When suddenly the world turned upside down and the seat in front of me took a swipe at my ribs. I twisted as I fell, and ended up lying on my face across the mud-encrusted windows.

Roo was lying on top of me. And at least three people were lying on top of her. The van was on its side, nose down in a ditch, and I was slowly being suffocated.

This must be what it's like to play the Aussies at rugby, I thought.

"I can get out the window!" someone called from the front.

"Yeah, me too!"

And one by one we squeezed out of whatever opening presented itself. After all, there were plenty of them.

Johno stood on the bank, counting heads as we crawled up to him.

"Sorry lads!" he said cheerily, ignoring the presence of several women. "It gets a bit narrow there."

Apparently this satisfied him that the situation was back under control. He pulled out his cell phone and took a deep breath before punching a number in.

"Hey there Big Man! Yeah, we've, um, had a bit of a crash…"

He held the phone away from his ear for a few seconds while the swearing on the other end subsided. His mood deteriorated as the noise continued.

"Yeah… that narrow part, by the ditch… yeah, in the ditch. Upside down."

There was a final blast of abuse from the speaker.

"Yes," he agreed glumly. "Again."

The voice did not sound impressed.

Luckily for us, the crash-site wasn't far from the job-site.

Johno, eager to get back in the good books, led us straight into the field and got us started. 'Weeding' would be an accurate description of the job that ensued. Not that I was sure exactly what we were weeding and why, but the contrast with our last job picking pumpkins was unbelievable. It was just so… easy! After two weeks of straining, back-breaking toil hefting gigantic pumpkins into the back of a tractor moving at jogging pace, this wasn't even work at all.

I strolled over to Roo, who was busily pulling a small leafy plant from the soil.

"This is incredible," I commented.

"I know! Shh!" She was obviously thinking the same thing – don't rock the boat. We had to keep this job at all costs.

Another lazy hour drifted by. I wandered up another furrow, pulling up whatever came closest to hand. There was a certain dark green, very persistent weed that seemed to be everywhere. "Check this out!" I dropped a handful of the plants in front of Roo. These damn things are in every row!"

"That's because they're the support plants," she hissed. "Don't pull them out. okay? We'll get in trouble."

"Oh, really? Shit. Sorry!"

She herself was leaving a trail of remarkably similar looking plants uprooted.

"What's the difference?"

She sighed. She always had to help me with stuff like this. I was never a particularly observant person.

"These are weeds."

I took the proffered plant and studied it.

"This is the support tree." The fingers of her free hand gently lifted the leaves atop the stalk nearest to her.

To me, they looked identical.

"See?"

"Of course," I lied.

"Good."

"And what about this one?" I held up another of my recent victims. "We pull these out too, right?"

"That's the sandalwood tree!"

"Oh! Now I get it!"

In spite of herself, Roo was starting to giggle. "How many... how many of those have you... ripped up?"

"Um, well... all of them. I think."

She burst out laughing, but caught herself – with effort – after one guffaw. "Shit!" she coughed out between suppressed giggles. "Don't... pick... any more!"

It was all I could do not to crack up myself. We were halfway through the day and I must have divested about a quarter of the field of its primary *raison d'etre*.

We picked on in silence for the next half-hour.

"Woah! Careful there!" It was Johno, stomping up the furrow behind me. "Don't be pulling that one out, mate!"

I froze mid-motion.

"That there's a sandalwood – just looks a bit different 'cause it ain't grown as much," he explained.

I released my grip on the immature specimen.

"Phew! Glad I stopped you there!" And he strode past me towards the next keen plucker.

I stopped for a few seconds and mopped sweat from my

forehead with a bandanna. "So those ones too eh? This job is harder than I thought!"

As Johno drove us home in the recently de-ditched minibus, I couldn't resist asking; "Is this job real? There has to be a catch? Like, deep underground you've got some super-secret weapons lab, and we're just here to make it look innocent on the satellite photos? And you pay us eighteen bucks an hour to pick weeds so no-one rocks the boat, right?"

"Ha ha! Not quite that exciting," he replied. "See, these sandalwood trees will be producing oil in a couple of years and that oil is expensive stuff. Some trees will make loads, some not as much, but when they're mature they'll be worth between three and fifteen thousand dollars each."

There was a stunned silence. I couldn't have spoken even if I'd wanted to. My throat had suddenly gone dry.

"F-fifteen? Thousand?" I finally croaked.

"Jeez," one of the other workers exclaimed, "that's crazy man! What if someone steals one!"

"Security. Whole place is fenced all around. Got cctv cameras on all the fence posts. And our own fire station on site, in case a bush fire gets too close. Yeah, that field you were working in today is worth something like eighty-five million dollars. They go all out to protect these babies."

I felt vaguely sick. Whilst at the same time I had the hideous feeling that deep inside me was welling up a great big belly laugh. I'd worked here for one day. By my rough estimate I'd done at least a million dollars' worth of damage…

Roo was nudging me with her foot. I glanced over at her. Her expression was unmistakable; 'Say. Nothing.'

I was inclined to agree.

Back at the campsite that evening we discussed our options. Well more accurately, Gill and Roo discussed them, while I fell around the place laughing. "It'll take them a long time to get it out of my salary!"

"Come on, seriously!" Roo chastised me. "What are we going to do?"

I took a few deep breaths to calm myself and sat on the grass next to her.

"If we don't go back it'll look really suspicious," I pointed out. "On the other hand, if we do go back and they spot my little mistake, it's quite possible they'll drown us in a ditch."

"Or they could just put us in a car with Johno driving…" Roo added.

"So what do you reckon? Shall we look for new jobs? Again?"

With a theatrical sigh, Roo reached for our mobile phone. "I put Johno's number in here, I'll send him a text."

I watched over her shoulder as she typed.

'From Tony, Gill and Roo. Thanks for an amazing experience.'

Which I thought was quite generous. She paused for a moment, then shrugged. "Not much else to put," she said.

And added 'We Quit.'

Revelation

Luckily, that text message never got sent.

Gill vetoed it, on the grounds that she'd only just rediscovered the ability to walk upright again; she would far rather risk the wrath of the sandalwood owners than risk ending up back on the pumpkins.

So instead of leaving our dream job, we showed up for work the next morning all innocence and smiles – hoping against hope that no-one would link us to the wholesale destruction that had recently beset their precious plantation.

(I say us; technically it was me that was most directly responsible, but I find that in situations like this, it's good for friends to stick together. And share things. Like blame.)

There was one other pressing concern on my mind that morning.

Roo and I had made a decision. After carefully considering all the pros and cons, we'd decided that:

a) we were starting a relationship, and

b) telling Gill about it was the right idea.

What we hadn't decided, was who was going to tell her. Or how; or when.

We'd talked about it of course; the discussion had gone something like this:

"You tell her."

"Hell no! You tell her."

"You're her brother. You should tell her."

"You're her best friend! It should come from you."

"You know her better. You should tell her."

"No way! You guys are much closer. You tell her."

"Look, she can't hate you completely. You're her brother – she can't get rid of you. If she's pissed off with me, it could ruin our friendship. You tell her."

"You've seen the way we fight! If I tell her, it could be the biggest self-destruct of all. She won't go mad at you, because she values your friendship. You tell her."

"I'm sleeping with her brother. I can't possibly tell her that!"

"Well I've stolen her best friend! And… despoiled her. I am *so* not telling her that."

We thought about playing scissors, paper, rock for it – but secretly, we were both too afraid to lose. Even me, and I'm awesome at that game.

With little resolved before work, we counted ourselves lucky just to still be there. Whatever personal issues we were having could be ignored for now, while we concentrated on being the best employees it was possible to be. Or so I thought.

"You've got to tell her today," Roo whispered as we climbed out of the Land Rover.

And then, I was being singled out – and I was more than a little worried, until one of the supervisors explained that they wanted me to join the weed-spraying team for the day.

"Fair enough," I said.

So as I was led away, I gave Roo the 'looks like you'll have to tell her after all' shrug.

(In case you're wondering, this was a particularly expressive shrug, involving extensive mobility of both hands and eyebrows. I felt sure it would do the job.)

As far as I was concerned, it was now out of my hands.

But I trusted Roo. She could always get the job done.

Unlike someone I could mention, who was currently struggling with the concept that weeds are plants too. And that they look remarkably similar to the plants that aren't weeds…

Well, they're green. Mostly.

It was a long, hot, and for me very confusing, day.

I didn't see the girls again until after the minibus dropped me off outside the campsite. I walked in and found Roo and Gill taking it in turns to dig through Rusty in search of clean clothes.

Roo spotted me on approach. "Hey! How was it?" she asked.

"Oh God, it was bloody awful! Well, the job itself was fine, but right at the start they showed us which plants to spray and which ones not to. And I still couldn't tell the damn things apart!"

"Oh hell! So what did you do?"

"I just sort of sprayed shit at random. I mean, it's weed-killer, right? So surely it only kills weeds, not proper plants."

"I don't think it works exactly like that," she said.

"I'm awful at this job."

"Yes darling, I'm afraid you are."

It took a few seconds for the implications of that to sink in.

Not the confirmation that I was failing miserably at the easiest job in the world – that much was painfully obvious.

It was that first part.

Darling.

I looked from Roo to Gill and back.

"So… you know?"

Gill rolled her eyes skyward by way of an answer.

"You told her?" I asked Roo.

"I did."

"And…?"

"She knew."

"She knew?"

"She knew."

"Gill, you knew?"

"I knew."

"What? How did you know?"

"Oh, I could tell this was going to happen. I probably knew about it before you did."

"But… when did you find out?"

She gave me a disgusted look. "Duh! I knew from the beginning! From the time you guys went for a shower, and didn't come back for, like two hours!"

"Ah."

"Yes! Did you really think I'd been asleep all that time? I figured it out about ten minutes after I came back and both of you didn't. I tried really hard not to need the toilet, but you were in there for *two frigging hours!* So I had to sneak in – being really quiet – and of course, there were two sets of feet in the shower cubicle."

"Ah! So you knew, all this time…"

"I knew."

"And we were working ourselves up so much about telling you!"

She chuckled. "I knew that, too."

"You could have said something!"

"Ha! I wasn't going to make it that easy for you. And now that you know I know, there will begin a period of me teasing you mercilessly. Because you stole my best friend," she turned to Roo, "and you stole my brother! So you both deserve to suffer. For example, I know you've been sneaking out here at night, to do it in the back of Rusty!"

"No," I denied, "not at all! As if we'd do that!"

"Dude, I've driven thousands of miles in Rusty. You think I don't know the sound of his suspension creaking?"

"That could be the wind, or the trees… other camper vans… a thousand things."

Gill made a show of looking all around us, at the otherwise-empty camping ground.

"It could be the wind," I repeated, weakly.

"I can hear it when you open the sliding door. I'm never *that* asleep."

It was true that Rusty's sliding door had a very distinctive noise to it. An oil-deprived shriek, not unlike the death-squeal of a medium-sized pig.

"Why else would you keep suggesting that we leave the seats flat?" Gill continued.

"Um… it's good to hide our stuff? So it's not all in plain site…"

"Pah. Gonna have to try harder than that."

I had nothing more to add in my defence, as Gill rummaged around in the footwell in search of clean socks.

Most of our clothes lived in the furthest-back footwells, so she soon gave up and pulled the seat-reclining lever, causing one of the middle seats to spring violently upright. It also caused another, less expected phenomenon, which we shall call 'the flight of the previously concealed condom'.

The rubber, which I'd used last night and then been unable to find in the dark, was catapulted forwards, dripping with menace.

It flew past Gill's face, missing her left ear by inches, and impacted on the windscreen with a splat. All eyes watched as it slowly peeled itself free of the glass and plopped into a pile of dust on the dashboard.

Gill looked back at me and raised one eyebrow.

"We might have done it once in Rusty…" I admitted.

Departure

Legitimizing my relationship with Roo was the missing piece of the puzzle.

It made everything better – and apart from the gruelling necessity of work in the fields, our life in Kununurra was pretty damn good already.

In fact, everything was going about as well as I could possibly imagine.

Which is usually when life decides to stab you in the face with a fork.

It was a deliciously mild evening, and we were relaxing after work with a well-earned glass of wine. We were just discussing whether or not the shiny new laptop we'd bought from eBay would arrive this week, when Roo got the phone call.

It's the call that no-one wants to get.

And it changed everything for all of us, but most especially for Roo, because it was her Mum that was dying.

Now, this wasn't completely unexpected. I don't want to give the impression that a sudden accident had befallen her. Frieda had been battling cancer for several years, and there had been a time when she was winning. Then, only days before I'd arrived in Australia, the family had gathered together to hear the news. It was back. It had spread. It was out of their hands. It was now just a matter of keeping her comfortable... for as long as she had left.

It was a testament to their strength and amazing generosity as a family that they'd welcomed me into their household at such a time. For most of my stay there I had no idea just how recent, and how devastating, the news was. I didn't feel close enough to ask, and they didn't feel the need to have nosey Englishmen speculating on their private pain.

Staying with the family had never felt awkward; they'd all made supreme efforts to maintain a happy home environment, even while privately, all their worlds were collapsing. Frieda herself had insisted that Roo go travelling with us, as originally planned; she was a lifelong traveller herself, and recognised the same growing wanderlust in Roo. She knew how life-changing that could be, and was so keen to encourage it that she did so in spite of her own ticking clock.

She also didn't want her situation to inconvenience anyone else more than was strictly necessary, something which in itself shows incredible selflessness and generosity of soul.

So we'd set off on our adventures, always seeking out the most fun and excitement, even while Roo kept a weather-eye on events back home. Of all of us, only she knew just how serious the situation was.

That it was only a matter of time...

And that time had just run out.

Roo's Dad booked her a flight home to Perth the next day.

Gill and I sat in Rusty, after dropping Roo off at Kununurra's tiny airport. We held each other and sobbed; me, for Roo, and for the loneliness and pain I could only imagine that she was feeling right now; and Gill cried for Frieda, because in the three months she'd spent waiting for me, she'd come to know her very well indeed. Sharing an endless capacity for chatting, a love of traveling, walking, reading and sewing, they'd spent every morning deep in conversation about their projects and adventures, past and present.

I'd hardly known her, so brief was my time in her company. But Gill was going to miss Frieda deeply.

It was hard to get a handle on just how quickly things had changed.

Only a couple of days ago, we'd been sitting around on the grass outside our tent, eating melted ice cream, laughing at the ridiculousness of our lives.

Now we were sitting in the van, crying into each other's clothing.

I couldn't stop thinking about a similar day, just a couple of months earlier; we'd been sitting tearfully in Rusty when Frieda joined the rest of the family to wave us off.

Saying goodbye to loved ones before a long trip is always bittersweet; for Roo, never more so. She must have been terrified by the possibility that something could happen while she was hundreds, or even thousands of miles away – but she'd borne that fear alone. She'd never asked us for help, never given any indication of her own battle, going on inside her, hope against despair.

How she must have felt that day, pulling out of her driveway, leaving her mum, I can't begin to imagine. But I think Frieda was very proud of Roo, as she stood there, waving us off on our voyage of discovery.

She'd wished us all a safe journey.

And we had no idea, back then, but that was the last time we'd see her alive.

When Gill and I pulled ourselves together, and drove back to the campsite, there was only one issue left for us to discuss.

What to do next.

It was impossible to think about work. That normality seemed so remote from where we were now, so tied to a previous life, where the worst things in the world were back-ache and sunburn. But we had to go in and explain the situation at least.

And there were other mundane concerns.

Problems we'd faced as a trio, but now had to face on our own.

As always, finance was the ugliest of them.

We'd worked for a few weeks now, and had finally broken even on our traveling expenses to date. We'd even saved a bit of cash, and in a fit of excitement at our new-found affluence, we'd spent a thousand dollars buying a laptop on eBay.

The damn thing still hadn't arrived.

All of which put us in a fairly awkward position.

We were currently parked at the furthest possible point from Perth.

The only way to get further away would be to drive Rusty into the ocean. It had taken us weeks of shared driving, and weeks of shared petrol-buying, to get this far. Now we were faced with a stark reality; of the two of us, only Gill could legally drive Rusty.

We were three-thousand, two-hundred and five kilometres away from home.

And with only two of us to contribute, we couldn't afford the petrol to get there.

Not to mention the food and accommodation costs we'd face en route.

So.

We had exactly two choices.

One; stay here. Carry on working. Ignore what was going on back in Perth. Save money, plan the route home, and, when we were ready, drive it. Estimated time: a month at least.

Or two; fly home immediately. And when I say home, I mean Perth, of course. At this point we didn't know how long Frieda still had; if there was to be any chance of Gill seeing her again, before the end, this was it.

Of course, we would also have to keep our distance; the last thing a family in grief needs, is a pair of houseguests.

Gill and I chased these possibilities around and around. Neither of us were keen to go back to work in Kununurra's blazing heat, but we couldn't base a decision such as this on pure laziness.

"But what if we break down on the way back?" Gill asked. Rusty had been temperamental, to put it mildly, on our trip up here. One big bill would wipe us out, even if we worked and saved before we left, potentially leaving us stranded, penniless, in the middle of some Hall's Creek-style shit-hole.

Just the thought of that made me feel queasy.

And then, as often happens in these kinds of situations, Fate gave us a helping hand. Disguised, inevitably, as a kick in the bollocks.

We went to pay our campsite fees, and we couldn't find the wallet.

The shared wallet was how we'd been managing our funds — using it to pay for all our joint expenses, like camping and petrol, and each drawing equal amounts of cash to put into it when it became empty.

The last known sighting of the shared wallet had been on Rusty's dashboard — presumably by the person who took it. We'd been a bit lax with security in Kununurra, due to the emptiness of the campsite, but leaving the wallet out in plain sight was a rookie mistake.

Which means it was most likely mine.

But I'm a big believer in not bothering to assign blame in these cases... What possible good can come of that kind of arguing? Regardless, it made our tricky decision all too easy. We'd lost all our cash — well over a hundred dollars. We'd lost the ability to access any of my money, as my bank card had been in the wallet too. There was no way Gill's finances would get us home on their own, and my bank didn't even have a branch in Kununurra. Any replacement card would go to Perth...

So I dug deep down into the bottom of my rucksack, and there I discovered a folded, sealed envelope. 'DO NOT USE – EVER' was written on the front in felt-tip pen. Inside was the English credit card I'd maxed out to fly to Australia in the first place — and there was just enough room left on its balance for two one-way domestic flights to Perth.

Sold.

The laptop arrived the day before our flight. We got to sample the long-anticipated delights of the local DVD rental shop. Then, we packed everything we could carry into our backpacks, parked Rusty in the campsite's storage field – so close to the one shady tree that he was nearly part of it. We left our bright orange high-viz jackets draped around the front seats, and made the back look as flat and empty as possible – difficult, given that it was still rammed with almost everything the three of us owned.

We caught a lift to the airport with the campsite owner, and promised her faithfully that we'd be back to collect our bedraggled van – one day. Hopefully before Grandfather Time turned Rusty into plain old rust.

Roo picked us up from Perth airport, and filled us in on what was happening.

She'd arrived back in time to spend a last few days at her Mum's bedside, and for now, Frieda was holding on. Just about.

So Gill and I moved into a youth hostel while we figured out our next move.

One morning, at 4am, the beep of my phone woke us both up.

I knew then, without even reaching for it, that this was the message.

I checked it anyway, because what else can you do, really?

It was from Roo, and simply said, "It's over. She's at peace."

I felt hollow, that spreading numbness of disbelief that comes with an event so massive, and so dreadful, that I couldn't even begin to figure out my reaction to it.

I've no idea what I replied to that message with. Some carefully phrased platitude, no doubt, that struggled to convey in a few short words something which couldn't adequately be explained by all the flowery language in creation.

Love. Sympathy.

Support. Belief.

Peace.

All of which, to Roo and her family, were completely and utterly useless.

There was nothing Gill and I could do for them; nothing except keep our distance, and still be available, and try to understand how this delicate balance worked.

And comfort each other, because, well, that was all we had.

Each other.

And once again, time, great destroyer and greatest of healers, was our master.

Only this time, we had way too much of it.

Under Pressure

Waiting, in a city like Perth, isn't cheap.

Both Gill and I knew that sooner or later we'd be flying back to Kununurra to rescue Rusty, because nothing else made sense.

Time would pass.

Eventually, Roo would feel strong enough to venture out again – and the adventure would continue.

But until then, we needed jobs.

So following an advert on our hostel noticeboard, we scored jobs as labourers, working for a brick-paving firm called Buildcraft.

On our first day we caught the train to Joondalup station, where our new boss Lindsey had been having some difficulties.

Lindsey arrived in the biggest pick-up truck I have ever seen. It was unfeasibly large. As I stood next to it, gaping in awe, I noticed that the grill came up to my nipples. There was a small ladder to climb in and out of the cab. Most of the cars I've ever ridden in would have fitted in the tray on the back of this behemoth, but that still wasn't enough storage for Lindsey; he also towed a three-metre long trailer, which looked like it had been built to carry a train.

And Lindsey himself, when he emerged from the cab, was scaled perfectly to fit.

Actually, it looked a little cramped for him.

I've read books where someone is described as a 'bear of a man'. I always picture an excessively hairy, thick-bearded fella dressed in a full-length pelt like a Viking.

Lindsey actually was the size of a bear.

He had the beard too, but he didn't go in for fancy dress – he just wore a pair of navy-blue work shorts the size of two sleeping bags stapled together.

If I'd have been a bear, I'd have run like fuck from him.

Well, either that, or tried to shag him.

Counter to expectations, Lindsey was a gentle giant – he was friendly to a fault, and almost genteel at times – for a builder. A typical, bluff Aussie bloke – we liked him straight away.

Outside Joondalup train station, there was a vast expanse of brick-paving that one of his previous employees had painted bright yellow. Unfortunately, he'd painted it the wrong bright yellow – which was why he was no longer an employee. The paint was bubbling and flaking, clearly not suited to being outside, on the floor in a high-traffic area. Lindsey's first job for us was to try and rectify this situation… except, he still hadn't figured out how.

To start with he offered us a stiff brush and a pressure-washer. His theory was that we'd start at opposite edges and work towards the middle – by which point he'd hopefully have thought of a better plan.

Now, power tools scare the crap out of me.

I'm one of the clumsiest individuals on the planet. Even picking up a drill is enough to make Gill want to film me, in case I do anything worthy of putting on YouTube.

So I happily ceded control of the pressure-washer to her, took up the humble broom, and began sweeping piles of yellow granules off the surface of the bricks.

Gill's first experiment with the pressure-washer flung her back a couple of metres, blasting water in all directions and soaking a few inadvertent bystanders.

"Sorry!" she called, in response to the curses coming her way.

The thing was a monster – similar to the kind of pressure-washer you might buy to clean your car with, only much, much more powerful. It was able to strip the yellow paint right off the bricks, and would start to eat through the bricks themselves if trained on one spot for too long.

Watching her get to grips with it was like watching her grapple with an anaconda; she was being flung around all over the place, both hands in a death-grip on the nozzle, while the tail of the beast lashed the pavement behind her.

"Don't let it fight you," Lindsey explained, taking it off her with one hand and directing it as calmly as one might aim a garden hose.

Probably the same way he'd hold an anaconda.

I carried on sweeping, but was interrupted by a shriek from Gill. I looked up to see her soaked from head to toe, dripping muddy water from every edge of her.

"I've just found out what happens when you spray the gaps between the bricks," she said.

We spent a week trying to get the paint off those bricks.

And we still didn't manage it.

One morning, as Lindsey stood gazing in despair at the mess, Gill said to him, "Such a pity they're stuck down."

Lindsey looked up at her and grunted, "Uh?"

"The bricks," she explained. "It's a shame they're all stuck down."

"They're not."

"Oh. Well, what colour are they on the other side…?"

Lindsey looked at her like she'd just confessed to peeing standing up – then he roared, and slapped her on the back so hard she nearly face-planted into the pavement.

And we spent the rest of our time in Joondalup painstakingly lifting every single brick in that concourse, one by one – and turning them over.

That took us most of the next week.

Then we painted the other sides in the *right* kind of yellow.

At least, I hope it was…

The work was quite varied after that. We cut down bus stops, re-paved platforms, made ramps out of concrete – it was tough, physically demanding work, which left us pleasantly exhausted at the end of every day. Gill soldiered on throughout, gleefully wielding everything from concrete saws to angle grinders; on these occasions, we agreed it would be safest if I watched. After two months of hard graft, things started to shape up. Gill and I had funds again, and we had a marketable skill for the first time since… well, ever. We'd had plenty of fun working for Lindsey, but that feeling of restlessness was never far away. We were both itching to get on with our exploration of this country, with our adventures – and that's when Roo called.

"It's time to go get Rusty," she said, and Gill and I gave each other a spontaneous high-five. (We're old-school like that.)

But Roo wasn't done yet. "Oh, and you don't mind if my sister Sonja tags along, do you?"

Of course we didn't. People deal with grief in whatever way they can, and Sonja had decided that getting away from it all might help. An adventure, to take her mind off things back home. And Frieda had been a lifelong traveller; it seemed like something she would have wanted the girls to do.

So Gill and I checked out of the hostel and headed to Roleystone to help them pack. I hadn't seen Roo for a couple of weeks at this point, and was very much looking forward to our reunion.

I snuck in through the front door and tip-toed into the living room, hoping to surprise her.

Roo was wearing short-shorts and was bent over, fiddling with the zips on her suitcase. Her delectable bottom, thus presented, proved an irresistible target – so I dove right in for a double-handed squeeze.

At which point she shrieked, and straightened up – and that's when I realized it wasn't Roo.

I sprang back in guilt as Sonja gave me what can only be described as a 'who the fuck are you and why are your hands on my arse?' look.

I'd been on the receiving end of this look several times in my chequered career, but never from my girlfriend's identical twin sister.

This was going to be a confusing trip for me.

And so it was that four intrepid explorers, not three, boarded the tiny plane for Kununurra. I think we made up half the passengers.

Western Australia from the air looked like an unruly child had left their entire toy collection out, and someone had thrown a dark green sheet over the lot. A folded, crumpled landscape, totally at odds with the flat, featureless red plains we'd driven through. But then, for the most part, the road followed the coast – whereas planes could take the direct route, ignoring the lack of trails, water and landmarks, giving us a view over land where quite possibly no cars had ever been.

The owner of the campsite picked us up, and I made good my promise by settling the bill we'd been unable to pay when we left.

And then it was time to see Rusty.

I half expected to find a pile of spare parts slowly rotting into the undergrowth – but no, he was right where we'd left him. Still faithfully guarding everything we owned, Rusty was slowly being reclaimed by the forest. Tendrils of strangler vines curled around his wing mirrors, wrapped around his wheels and draped across the roof. His paintwork was fading slightly, but the sliding door still opened with its trademark squeal.

The question on everyone's lips was: would he start?

"We love you, Rusty!" Gill said for encouragement, as she turned the key.

And his engine roared to life on the first try.

We'd had occasion to say bad things about the van in the past, but now all was forgiven – and after two months without moving an inch, Rusty tore free of the grasping vines and made triumphant laps of the campsite with ease. He was eager to get back on the road too.

So, stage one was complete; we'd reached Rusty and resuscitated him.

Which meant that stage two was bound to be a doddle; all we had to do was drive him 5,838 kilometres home to Perth – through some of the driest, most inhospitable territory known to man.

The Red Centre.

Dressed To Kill

Our first major stop was Alice Springs.

This is because, at 1,052 miles from Kununurra, Alice Springs *is* the first major stop. Actually, it's the first stop bigger than a petrol station.

We had a couple of plans while we were in town. The first was to eat as much junk food as possible, because we'd been cooking for four on our tiny gas stove for the last few nights, and instant noodles were starting to lose their appeal.

The second – which was far more exciting – was to buy ball gowns.

Now, there is a reason for this. Honest.

I'm just not going to tell you yet.

So after we'd finished eating our McDonalds, I had my first experience with the Aussie phenomenon of 'op shops'.

Op shops are rather like charity shops in the UK (or Goodwill stores in the US) – but unlike most countries I've visited, here people actually donate things you'd consider wearing.

I know! Hard to believe, but there it is. I must have traipsed in and out of hundreds of charity shops in the UK, and the most exciting thing I've bought was a dog-eared copy of *Nineteen Eighty Four*. Which was crap.

But instead of a cramped little shop with racks of ankle-length pleated skirts and size 18 maternity dresses, here the op shops were big, popular, cheap, and well-stocked with genuinely interesting items.

So it was with considerable excitement that I headed for the 'size 18 Maternity Dresses' rack. The trouble with being a bloke, and a well-built one at that, is they just don't make skimpy outfits to fit me. In the end I settled on a delightful pink number with a scooped neckline – originally knee-length, it ended halfway down my thighs. Not many women reach six-feet tall, and those that do probably have the same trouble finding a nice dress as I do.

Sonja, Roo and Gill had a much easier time, taking their pick of the fancy things on offer and settling for a trio of bridesmaid dresses in assorted colours. They were delighted to discover that their dresses were less than ten dollars apiece – but not nearly as happy as I was, when I found out that I am, in fact, only a size 16.

"Does my bum look big in this?" I asked Roo.

"It looks fucking gigantic," Gill chipped in.

"And yet, weirdly appealing…" Roo said.

"Oi! Stop that!" Sonja was adamant. "We'll have no fondling in the dresses. This picture is messed up enough as it is."

And you know what? She was right.

The lady at the till offered me a matching pink handbag, and I discovered a delicate straw hat that set off my eyes. I figured I needed the extra bits and pieces if I was going to be convincing. The others dissuaded me from wearing my outfit back to the car, though. For some reason.

And then we were off, heading into Kings Canyon – where, amongst other things, the movie *'Priscilla, Queen of the Desert'* was filmed.

Now, I hadn't seen this film. Apparently it featured a bunch of transvestites driving a bus through the Australian outback, and according to the girls it paralleled our trip in some way I couldn't quite grasp. Because as far as I knew, none of us were transvestites – well, apart from me. Three girls hiking around a rocky canyon in ball gowns as a tribute to their favourite movie – that at least was understandable, if not exactly commonplace. Only I would be doing it in drag – and I didn't have a clue what the film was about!

But it sounded like a damn good idea, so I rolled with it.

We dressed ourselves beside Rusty, applying our make-up over copious amounts of sunscreen – which I'm told, in my case at least, added a certain Hammer-Horror quality to the finished effect. But no-one could deny, we looked *fabulous* in our colourful, flowing gowns.

Darling.

Sonja set up her video camera, filming a group of avid hikers as they started up the first incline. As each one passed us, we were treated to a series of surreptitious glances. Guaranteed, every single one of them was thinking, *what the fuck?* But no-one was actually going to say that to us. Or anything else, for that matter. After all, something as simple as 'hello' could result in them being trapped in conversation with a dangerous bunch of lunatics. I had to ask myself what I'd have done in their place; would I, in all honesty, have walked up to a bloke wearing a ball gown in the middle of a rocky no-man's land and started chatting?

Probably not. Folk get murdered that way.

To show the hikers I sympathised with their dilemma, I batted my eyelashes at them as they walked past.

They hiked faster than most people jog after that, showing commendable enthusiasm given they had a three-hour trek ahead of them.

Once the column had passed, we swaggered off up the same route, pausing only while Sonja sprinted back down to collect the camera. It was an interesting sprint, downhill at quite a steep angle, over uneven rocky terrain – and she was wearing a full-length royal blue gown that didn't allow much freedom of movement.

It was less of a sprint, more of a fast-motion waddle.

She complained when I pointed this out. "At least I'm not mincing like you."

"I resent that," I said. Pouting.

Then I minced off to sulk.

I'm sure that walking like a lady takes girls many years to master. Some – like my sister – never quite achieve it. So after half an hour's practice, I thought I was doing rather well… but the proof, as they say, would be in the pudding. Or in this case, the videotape.

We spent an enjoyable morning wandering around the canyon, stopping often to pose for ridiculous photos. Many other hikers passed us during these periods; old couples, young families, heavily bearded outdoorsmen.

None of them said a thing.

When we found ourselves underneath an overhanging ledge of rock, I couldn't resist indulging in a spot of climbing.

"Your arse looks really massive now," Gill informed me, as I clung onto the outcrop with all four limbs.

"She's right," Sonja added. "It fills the viewfinder!"

"That's gonna be a treat for the folks back home."

"I'm splitting my sides," I called down through gritted teeth.

"Us too!"

"No, literally – I mean my dress's sides are splitting. And the back!"

There was a tearing sound as the zip struggled to contain my flexing shoulder muscles.

"Get down, quick," Roo said, "or you'll spoil your dress!"

This turn of phrase also caused much hilarity amongst the girls.

I dropped to the ground and reached around to feel the rip in the fabric. "Is it bad?"

"It's left quite a hole," Roo confirmed. "I think it's safe to say, this dress wasn't built for extreme sports."

"Or else you needed a size 18," Gill said. "Look! You're bursting out like a skinny, pink version of The Hulk!"

I said nothing after that – just tried to conform. To be normal. Sonja was filming *everything*, in order to justify having hauled the video camera and tripod all the way up here – and Gill and Roo were taking photos of anything she missed. As I posed for the camera, I tried not to think how much fun my friends back home would have with the pictures, were they ever to see them. It's the kind of thing people do to each other as a joke, involving judicious use of Photoshop. I was doing it to myself, because… well, it sounded like a good idea at the time.

"Why do I have to do all the posing?" I asked Roo. She'd been caught on camera a few times, but in her rather flattering peach gown she managed to carry it off quite convincingly. Whereas my pictures looked decidedly seedy, no matter how much I worked my 'America's Next Top Model' repertoire.

It probably didn't help that I was sporting a few days' stubble, and was sweating profusely in the forty-degree heat. No matter what I did, I looked increasingly like a psychotic red-neck rapist wearing his mother's best church outfit.

"But you're important," Roo explained to me. "You're the only one who actually is what they say in the movie: a cock, in a frock, on a rock."

I had to admit, this was true. If not entirely flattering.

By the time we got back to Rusty, all four of us were dripping. The harsh Australian sun was unrelenting, and I'd managed to sunburn the outline of a truly impressive cleavage onto my chest. As the others started to peel off their sopping dresses, I reached into my voluptuous bosom and pulled out about half a mile of distinctly soggy toilet roll. "Anyone need to wipe their face?" I asked, offering the paper around. They all took it gratefully and started dabbing at themselves, before it occurred to Gill to ask where I'd gotten it as the van was still locked.

"Between mah titties," I admitted, which caused a round of gagging. "What's wrong? You chicks keep tissues in your bras all the time."

"Not for other people to use!" choked Sonja.

"Oh. Ah well then, give us it back. If you don't want it, I've got a use for it."

"Do we want to know?"

"Probably not, but I'm going to tell you anyway. You're forgetting, I'm wearing underwear *and* shorts under here – for the sake of decency," I thrust a hand down my pants to prove it. "Whatever sweat you've got between your boobs, quadruple it – and that's what my balls are sitting in right now. I've got to reach in there and mop it all up, or I'll make a puddle on Rusty's seats!"

She handed back her paper streamer. "Please, for the love of God, go around the other side of the van to do it."

"It's a deal," I told her, "as long as you don't try to film it."

Rockslide

Our next major stop contained the heart and soul of the trip. When we'd first conceived of driving Rusty up north, this had been the planned route back – for the sole reason that Ayers Rock, or Uluru, would be on our way.

And now we were there.

Well, we were approaching the ticket booth, praying that in spite of the crazy temperature, they'd let us climb it.

As Roo pulled up, she pointed out a Wicked Van parked in the lay-by.

We'd seen loads of Wicked vans on our travels, their daubed cartoons and graffiti slogans ranging from mildly amusing to downright disgusting – but it had never occurred to us before, that you might not actually get much choice when you hired one. Some vans we'd seen again and again, each time prompting the question, "Who would ever want to drive around in a van that says 'MASSIVE COCK' on the side? Even if there *is* a big picture of a chicken on the other side?"

Well, now we had an inkling of the answer.

Because the van sitting opposite us was entirely hot pink – and painted up as an exact replica of Barbie's camper. (I know it was an exact replica, because, um... because the girls told me? Yes, that's believable. Let's say it was that.)

Anyway, out of this glorious vehicle stepped a muscular bloke with a shaved head and tattoos covering both arms. He glanced around furtively, took several steps away from the van, and lit a cigarette.

I don't think I've ever seen someone look so tough and so embarrassed at the same time. The poor bloke was obviously waiting for someone in the ticket office, so we had a good chuckle at his expense, debating what kind of person would emerge to join him – a very wholesome young chap named Gerald, perhaps? Or a cowboy in leather trousers with the bum cut out? Or maybe a ten-year-old girl. Rusty rocked with our laughter, until I noticed the bloke glaring at us in the wing-mirror.

"Maybe we should get on with it," I suggested.

"Fine," said Gill, "but you stay here or you'll end up staring at him."

So I hid in the van while the girls went to buy our tickets. No-one else had emerged by the time they got back, and the bloke was back in his van, looking angry.

"Was there anyone else in the office?" I asked. "Is he dating Barbie *herself?*"

"Nope. Just a medium-sized English girl, who looks about as pissed off as he does."

"No prize for guessing who got the last van in the lot, then."

"I wonder if they had the choice between something really manly and pornographic, or the *Barbiemobile...*"

"Well he's going to have to do some careful editing of his holiday pictures before he lets any of his mates see them!"

This sparked a thought. "Hey, we should get a photo of him with the van!" I told the girls.

Gill and Roo traded horrified looks. "I know you're a bit short on common sense," Gill said, "but we've driven a long way to see Ayer's Rock. It would be a real shame to get murdered when we're this close."

I had to concede that point. But then I remembered that we had *Barbie Girl* by Aqua on Rusty's MP3 player. I'm not proud of that – in fact, let's just blame the girls again, shall we? – but it allowed us to roll down the windows and blast out the opening bars as Roo put the pedal to the metal.

'I'm a Barbie girl – in a Barbie world...'

'Life in plastic – it's fantastic...'

"He's still staring at us," Roo reported, checking the mirrors. "He's not happy!"

"No shit," I said, "he's probably reading the sign we put in the back window!"

Gill's handiwork, of course.

'WE'D RATHER PUSH RUSTY THAN HIRE A WICKED VAN'.

We chuckled all the way to Ayers Rock.

Ayers Rock was closed, of course.

We sat in the car park, looking over a fence at the massive hunk of red rock. I was reading the brochure, and the picture it painted didn't seem fair.

"So, it's closed because it's too windy? It's a gigantic, sticky-uppy rock in the middle of a completely flat landscape. Of course it's bloody windy up there! Every day, I'd imagine. It's closed if it rains – okay, so that's never going to happen – but also closed if it's too hot! Too hot? It's in the middle of the desert! In one of the hottest places in the whole damn country – probably in the world! Oh, and it's closed on certain spiritual holidays. And if it's cloudy. So, pretty much just closed then. It'd be easier to list when they open the damn thing!"

"The local Aborigines don't like people climbing it," said Roo, "because it's sacred to them. That might be part of the reason why it's closed so much."

"Well they need a sign that says 'Welcome to Ayers Rock – Australia's number one tourist attraction! We're open for three days every September, if you're lucky, and sometimes again in April."

No-one said anything for a while, as we sat contemplating the rock. It truly was a magnificent sight, even cast against the battleship-grey sky.

"At least our photos will be a bit different," Roo said.

"Yeah – they'll all be taken from the car park."

"No, I mean you always see pictures of it with perfect blue skies above. It's almost never like this."

"Great. We'll be the only people in the world with photos of Ayers Rock looking rubbish. Newspapers will be queuing up to buy them."

We sat staring at the rock for a good few minutes.

This is where our interesting mix of personality types came to bear:

Sonja was very responsible.

Roo, left to her own devices, probably would have been responsible – but she was easily overridden by more dominant personalities.

Gill was responsible when it suited her – which wasn't often – and had a strong compulsion to do crazy things.

And I'm a complete idiot.

So when I said, "Bollocks to it, let's climb it anyway!"

Gill said, "Okay!"

Roo said, "Ummm…"

And Sonja said, "We'll wait down here, actually."

So I jumped over the fence and ran towards Uluru.

Ancestor spirits be damned, I thought. They could bring forth their complaints if they felt they needed to. I was willing to listen to reason. I even gave them a few minutes, standing around at the bottom of the rock while the last group of tourists read the info board and moved on.

Not a single angry spirit appeared in protest, so I figured that put me in the clear.

And up I went.

I was slipping and sliding, because Ayers Rock is smooth, worn down by constant wind erosion, and the passage of the few humans lucky enough to show up on the three days a year it's actually open. And I was running, because at any moment I expected some irate park ranger to yell at me to come down.

I made it as far as the chain link fence used by regular climbers to haul themselves up to the summit, and paused for breath while I considered my options.

I was roughly halfway up Uluru. It wasn't as big as I'd expected.

I was exhausted, but I really wanted to haul myself hand-over-hand up the support chain. It didn't seem worth risking the wrath of… I dunno, some multi-coloured flying snake or something – just to climb *halfway* up Uluru.

So I took a double-handful of the rusted chain links, and as I did so I felt a spot of wetness hit the top of my head.

It was almost like rain.

Nah! Couldn't be. It never rains on Ayers Rock.

Maybe once or twice a year – in particularly rainy years. In winter.

But it was December – midsummer – and one of the hottest days on record, at 46°C (that's 126°F). It couldn't possibly be rain.

It bloody well was though.

There was a blinding flash of lightening and an ear-splitting rumble of thunder.

Suddenly the heavens opened, and more water than this part of Australia had seen in a decade poured from the sky.

I was soaked to the skin in seconds.

As was the rock.

Time to go, I thought.

But the rain had done more than make me cold and soggy.

It had turned the rock to glass.

My feet went from under me straight away. I landed on my arse, and managed to scrabble to some form of stability. I set off, scooting along on my bum, sliding more than walking, losing more and more control with each passing moment.

Then came the time that gravity took over.

One second I was crabbing my way down the rock using my balls as brakes – the next I was sliding in free-fall, bouncing off every little ridge and flailing frantically at the rain-slicked surface.

It wasn't the first time in my life I wished I was an octopus.

But it was very nearly the last.

I don't know how I regained control – perhaps those psychedelic ancestor spirits just wanted to teach me a lesson for being such a wise-ass. Maybe the lack of skin on my palms had something to do with it. But my trusty Vans found purchase on a rougher surface, my buttocks clenched the rock, and I slowed to a stop on the very edge of Uluru.

Laying flat out like a starfish, I caught my breath. Then, feeling the cold, slick surface through the tears in my shirt, I wriggled over to the boulders lining the edge of the climbing route, and slowly climbed down them. I'd been seconds away from being launched off the end of that slide like it was… well, the end of a slide.

That would *really* have taught me a lesson.

Or at least, the hospital bill would have.

Waiting for me at the bottom was a tour guide, and the windows of his bus were lined with faces eager to watch me get a bollocking.

"You're a bloody idiot!" the guide bawled at me.

He was quite perceptive, this bloke.

"Do you know how slippery it is up there in the rain?" he demanded.

Given that he'd just watched me slide all the way down, I was tempted to ask if he thought I had wheels in my jeans.

But I settled for saying, "Yeah, it is a bit."

"Do you know that's the most dangerous thing you could have done?" he asked.

"Well yes, I do *now*," I told him.

"I could pick up the phone, and have a ranger here in ten minutes to slap you with a $2000 dollar fine!"

"You're right," I apologized. "I've been very naughty. I promise that I will never again try to climb Ayers Rock in the rain."

He seemed happy enough with that.

And it was a promise I was content to keep. Because the chances of it raining again on Uluru in my lifetime are fairly slim. The chance of me being there at the time is even slimmer. And even if that exact set of circumstances did come to pass, why on earth would I want to?

Because, you know, been there, done that. Got the holes in my t-shirt.

Mine Kamp

Smack bang in the middle of the desert, we came to Coober Pedy.

Definitely one of the most unusual towns in Australia, Coober Pedy was a hard-core opal-mining town, and as tough as you get. By way of example, the sign advising travellers that they are 'Welcome To Coober Pedy!' is made of a truck. Not a picture of a truck, or a scale model; an actual opal-mining vehicle about twice the length of Rusty, which had been hauled up five metres into the air and placed on a chunky steel frame.

Which I climbed, of course.

They didn't do things by halves here, you see, so I didn't want to either.

More than any place we'd been to this land was empty and (literally) blasted. The only shapes breaking up the table-top-flat plains of rock and sand were conical piles of excavated rock and sand; nothing grew as far as the eye could see in any direction, and the only colours in sight were the vivid yellow-orange of the stone and the impossibly pure blue of the sky.

Straying off the beaten track here was as dangerous as entering a minefield – which in one sense of the word, it was. Thousands of shafts dropped without warning, littering the area like it was riddled with giant worms. Explosions could be heard – or more often felt – from the hundreds of active mines scattered for dozens of miles in every direction, where the toughest breed of Australian prospectors sought out and ripped out over eighty percent of the entire world's opals.

To survive the extreme desert temperatures, everything underground here – homes, shops, bars, and churches – all chewed from the rock by different-sized tunnel boring machines. But outstripping all the rest for sheer cool factor (at least as far as we were concerned) was the underground campsite!

Walking into it down a sloping passageway, it felt like we were descending into an Ancient Egyptian tomb. Circular ventilation shafts in the roof cast spotlights on the ground, just begging for a variety of poses to be performed – from Charlie's Angels to kung fu and ballet, we went through the lot.

Then we pitched our tents – each one in their own cubical niche – and headed back to the surface to unpack Rusty.

Rick, a charming old bloke whose cheerful demeanour belied his decades as an opal miner, owned and ran 'Riba's Underground Camping', together with his wife Barbara.

He booked us straight in for the afternoon tour, conducted in the museum that occupied what had previously been his mine.

In the tour, which he delivered in a delightfully John Cleese-esque manner, Rick explained that only individuals were allowed to dig mines here – no big companies. Each person had to pick an area to dig in, agreed to work the dig in person, and register their claims with the Department of Mines and Energy.

This granted them four wooden posts, which they used to delineate the fifty-metre square area of their claim. From then on, it was all about the explosives – drilling holes and blasting the rock, always hunting for that tell-tale blue glint, that seam of opal which could make the lowliest prospector into a millionaire overnight.

Most of them, I think, broke even.

Next we got to try dowsing, that walking-with-metal-rods-that-cross thing, which was considered to be a science by the miners. Sure enough, the rods crossed when I held them – at just the place where a small seam of opal was known to run beneath my feet. It was like witchcraft, but these guys were prepared to bet big bucks – and years of impossibly hard graft – on the outcome of a swinging piece of metal not much bigger than a tent peg.

Rick and Barbara, like more than half the local population, lived in a 'dug-out' – literally an entire house dug out from the rock. Roo blagged us a tour by mentioning to them that I was a travel writer (slight lie), and subtly suggesting that their house might be the next thing I'd write about (bigger lie!).

It's funny, because at the time I'd been so busy working and travelling that I'd all but given up on writing 'That Bear Ate My Pants'. The chances of me getting anything on paper about Australia seemed extremely remote – even more so, given my luck with laptops.

The house was incredible; cool, airy and spacious, with two decent-sized bedrooms, a galley-kitchen, and all the comforts and conveniences of modern living.

Rather than smoothing the walls or lining them, they'd chosen to leave them rough and bare, making a design statement out of the raw rock that sheltered them. Here and there, alcoves had been chipped out to provide everything from TV cabinets to niches for candles. The effect of all that stone was anything but oppressive; it was beautiful, with the veins and striations of the rock running around the walls, and the pale yellow stone giving off a cheerful, welcoming glow.

"And if you suddenly find out your wife's pregnant, as happened to us a few years back, you just have to hire the excavator and dig out another bedroom. Too easy – although it makes quite a bit of dust."

"So all this was done with a drilling machine?" I asked.

"Nah mate. I did the main rooms mesself. Jackhammerin', pick-axein', and a good few bombs went into this place! You can tell by the roof – the diggers make 'em flat and square, but I wanted something a bit different. Took me about a year with a pick-axe, to make it domed like that, but I kind of like it."

It was surreal to see the bedrooms laid out with perfectly normal furniture; Ikea double beds, even pictures hanging from nails driven into the rock. Only the variety of the colours and textures across the walls and ceiling marked it out as different – well, that and the lack of windows.

I mentioned this to Rick, and he took me to see his pride and joy: a generous picture window that looked directly outside, drenching his living room in light.

"That winda's probably one of the most expensive winda's in Australia," he said.

"Really? Because you had to hire the tunnel-boring machine?"

"Nope – did that one mesself, all by hand. Normally when I'm mining I use little bombs, so only small bits of the rock come away. But I reckoned this would look great opened right up, so I packed a really meaty charge into it."

"Did it bring the roof down?"

"Nah, the explosion went off perfectly! I had me new winda', bang on. Only trouble was, when I came to clear out the rubble, I found opal – there'd been a big thick streak of it, right through the middle! Clear as day, and twice as valuable – and I'd pulverized the bloody lot of it. Reckon it'd have been worth half a million bucks at least, if I'd have mined it properly."

"Holy shit!"

"Yeah. Still, you win some, you lose some. And it's a really nice winda'."

Rick was a character for sure, but I doubted there were any completely normal people living in a place like Coober Pedy. It was too raw, too frontier for most people – I'd have loved it, for a couple of months. It appealed to my love of weirdness. But to live forever?

The town bred unusual characters though, and there was one living nearby that we just had to visit – Crocodile Harry, the bloke who was the real-life inspiration for Crocodile Dundee. We did a quick Google search and memorized the directions to his tin shack – he was so legendarily tough that he still dared to live above ground – and set off in Rusty.

Coober Pedy isn't big on road signs, however, probably because it isn't big on roads either. We criss-crossed a variety of gravel tracks scraped out of the desert, and soon had to admit we were hopelessly lost. We couldn't just look for town as a landmark, because most of it was underground – so in the end we headed for some of the big piles of rubble we'd noticed earlier.

At last we spotted a sign, although it was facing in the opposite direction. Roo drove Rusty past it, and we all craned our necks back to read it.

'DO NOT ENTER! BLASTING AREA!' it said.

"Shit! I think we just drove through a blasting area," Sonja said.

"I think you're right," Gill agreed.

This being the case, we gave up on the search for Crocodile Harry and managed to find the way back to the campsite. Later, we confessed our indiscretion to owner Rick.

"Ah, you won't find Crocodile Harry out there," he told us.

"Oh? Why not?"

"He's dead. Died last month. Eighty-two he was."

"Oh. Bugger."

"Yeah, it was a bit. Better for you, though. He was getting a bit crotchety in his old age. If you fellas had have rocked up at his shack unannounced, he'd probably have shot yer."

The trip back to Perth was through some of the driest, emptiest, most monotonous landscape in the country. Even thinking about it bores me half to death, so I won't bother describing it here.

We did hit the coast at one point, and drove right up to the edge of the sea-cliffs known as The Great Australian Bight. It was deliciously elemental, and amazingly cold – the wind there comes directly from Antarctica, with nothing separating the two continents but a vast expanse of rather chilly ocean.

And so, as we rolled back into Perth a few days later, the first stage of our adventure was over. Roo and Sonja went back home, and Gill and I went back to work for Lindsey. We had platforms to pave, and dollars to earn – because Christmas was right around the corner.

Two weeks away, in fact!

It would be Gill's first Christmas away from home, and I'd promised myself I'd make it memorable for her; enough so that she might manage to forget how alone we were, and that on the other side of the world, the rest of our family would be enjoying their Christmases without us.

And maybe she could help me forget, too.

Strange Bedfellows

Gill and I were determined to find a hostel where at least some of the residents spoke English. The last place we'd stayed at had been entirely Chinese students, and I didn't think there'd be much of a Christmas vibe there.

Unfortunately, accommodation anywhere at that time of year is booked up well in advance. After asking almost every hostel in town, we finally managed to score the last two beds, in two different rooms, at a grubby little place called The Planet Inn.

It was a real dump – skanky, mismatched sofas that had blatantly been found on the side of the road, and grubby, mildew-stained walls. I never got to see the room that Gill was sleeping in – mostly because she was so disgusted by it that she slept on the couch – but the room my bed was in... well. It took me about half an hour just to find the bed! Everything was buried under a knee-deep layer of clothes. Hair dryers, curlers and straighteners were strewn around with reckless abandon; a fire-safety officer would have had a heart-attack before he got through the door. Plates of half-finished food perched precariously on bags of shopping, phone chargers writhed like snakes through the miscellanea, and shoes, shoes, shoes were scattered as far as the eye could see.

Which wasn't very far, because the eight bunk bed room was less than three metres square.

The furthest bunk had a sarong draped like a curtain, hanging from beneath the top bed to provide some privacy for the one below. A neat trick, I thought, particularly now I was in here – all the other occupants of the room were female.

It wasn't until later on that night that I discovered the need for that curtain; there wasn't one person staying in that bed, there were two.

And they were fairly vigorous about proving it.

It wasn't until the second night, when I joined Gill on the sofa, that I made a startling connection. The couple had been shagging every hour for most of the night, popping out for a cigarette in between each bout. I was amazed at their stamina – and a bit jealous, to be quite honest – but Gill was less than sympathetic.

"I've got one word for you," she said; "PAYBACK!"

I guess I had that coming.

"But still," I said to her, "they must be getting sore by now! I mean, I'm fairly vigorous,"

"I KNOW," Gill interjected–

"–but really! She could just be laying their and faking it, but he must be swallowing Viagra like they're M&Ms!"

"Are you sure it's always the same bloke?" Gill asked.

And that's when the penny dropped.

The girl in the bed next to me had mentioned she was entering a competition for strippers in a local nightclub, and I'd spent half the day trying to figure out an excuse to sneak off and check it out. Not that she was pretty or anything, but *hello? Strippers!*

And somehow, it simply hadn't occurred to me – there were seedier sides to living with a stripper.

Her friend in the next bed was obviously going one better. She was a hooker – and she was using our dorm room as a brothel.

"No wonder they're all so enthusiastic," I said. "I guess you would be, if you'd paid for the privilege!"

Gill snuggled down in her sleeping bag, and stretched her legs up onto the arm of the sofa. "Maybe we should find another place to stay?" she suggested.

"What, and leave all this glamour? Shit dude, it's like living in Vegas."

"Only without the drugs and guns," she joked.

And in one of those eerie moments where someone, sometime in the distant future, has just walked over your grave – we both felt a sudden chill.

"We'll move out tomorrow," I promised.

After several days of begging for beds, we finally moved into The Underground – a massive, three-storey hostel with a courtyard swimming pool and a cinema room in the basement. It was every backpacker's dream, right in the heart of Northbridge, Perth's clubbing district.

With only two days until Christmas, Gill and I could hardly believe our luck.

It was expensive, so we'd booked the cheapest (and only) beds available – in a ten-bed dorm. This proved to be a real stroke of luck, as the room was huge, with one wall entirely made of glass doors which opened onto the pool area.

Ahhhh!

We would do well here.

Not wanting to impinge on Roo's family Christmas at such a delicate time, Gill and I spent Christmas Day in the Underground hostel – getting horribly drunk on *goon*. Oh yes – that's how classy we were! Gill had a whole Christmas dinner planned, but we got as far as making pancakes in the morning, had a glass of wine with them, exchanged presents and drank wine whilst we did so… and from there events just spiralled. By dinnertime Gill was fast asleep in the cinema room, and I'd passed out on the dorm room floor – apparently in exactly the same position as Jesus on the cross, which caused our room-mates to draw felt-pen stigmata on me and dress me in robes made from soggy pool-towels.

And then they put lipstick on me and gave me a guitar, because… well, I wasn't the only one who was hammered.

Present-wise, we got all sorts of little parcels from England. Most of them contained chocolate, so most of them arrived in a liquid state – Mum not having cottoned on to the twin facts that a) they sell chocolate in Australia, and b) it was forty degrees in the shade. Not to mention, the cost of posting chocolate to Oz has got to be at least ten times the cost of the chocolate bars themselves.

Gill managed to buy me a hilarious t-shirt which I still have, possibly because I get very few chances to wear it; it had a pink dinosaur on it, with the slogan 'Lickalottapus'.

You know that awkward moment, when you realise your sister knows you just a little too well…?

No?

Just me then.

But my stand-out present for the year (also from Gill), was a cuddly toy; there were a whole series of them to collect, all scaled-up replicas of dangerous microbes – and she'd chosen to buy me The Pox. It was a cute, pink, coiled up snake-type thing, and it was adorable. It was weeks before the joke wore off – every time anyone asked me what I'd got for Christmas, I told them, "Well, my sister gave me syphilis…"

In return, I gave her a cuddly toy of a space shuttle, which I'd named Uranus.

And I spent the rest of the week saying things like, "Gill, stop playing with Uranus," and "please move Uranus, I can't see the TV."

If anyone has any doubts about the sophistication of my sense of humour, feel free to refer them to this paragraph.

Boxing Day was spent having a second Christmas, visiting Roo and her family to exchange presents with them. It was a merry occasion, and I was careful not to tread on any toes – both metaphorically and literally, what with everyone wearing thongs. It's hard for the northern hemisphere mind to get used to, it being both Christmas *and* the hottest summer on record at the same time. Even shorts and t-shirts felt like too many clothes, as the house was scorching inside and out. But at least I got to wear my Christmas hat to the beach.

Before we left to rescue Rusty, I'd been saving up my brick-paving wages to buy Roo the dress of her dreams – a pale purple silk cocktail dress from a boutique called Intangible.

She'd lusted after it for weeks, and I'd made the difficult decision to invest $200 in it, in the hope of making her happy. Luckily, most shops in Oz still do a thing called 'lay-by', where they let you pay for things in instalments, so I'd spread the cost over several weeks of working for Lindsey.

When she opened it, her face lit up, and I knew I'd done the right thing. She was surprised and delighted, and when she tried it on for me she looked absolutely stunning.

And as far as I know, that dress has never been worn since.

We don't get invited to many cocktail parties.

For reasons, see the paragraph on humour, above.

Being back at Roo's family home allowed me to indulge in another of my favourite activities – no, not what you're thinking!

From the wide deck attached to the back of the house, all kinds of crazy critters could be observed. It was still a thing of wonder to me, that in place of the small birds we have in England, like robins and starlings, Australia has parrots – and Roo's garden was full of them. Little animals I had no names for skittered back and forth, taking advantage of the shade under the decking, or frolicking in the half-acre of native forest.

Well, not all of them were frolicking – the bandicoots in particular seemed to be having a tough time. Perhaps because of the soaring summer temperatures, they'd decided to take refuge in the pond – completely disregarding the fact that they can't swim. No wonder they're endangered.

Roo had been making a list of her bandicoot sightings to report to the Dept. of Conservation, until sighting #14 was stiff, smelly and floating.

I helped her write an email to them that evening.

'Dear DoC,

Please find enclosed a report on the bandicoot that was living under our veranda until about 2 o'clock this morning, when he decided to go for a swim. He is now living in a plastic carrier bag in my bin. Not sure what the official number of them left in the wild is, but please deduct one from the total. If you're looking to wipe out any more of the little critters just send 'em this way.

Your friends in Conservation,
Tony and Krista'

Three of the poor buggers committed suicide this way, before Roo came up with the idea of leaving bowls of drinking water for them all over the garden.

This led to the creation of our first joint New Year's Resolution:
1) Drown Fewer Bandicoots

I figured, just because an animal is stupid doesn't mean it should be allowed to die.

Otherwise I'd be in serious trouble.

Incorporating Fieldwork

Both Gillian and I were in Australia on Working Holidaymaker visas. This is an awesome scheme which the UK also offers – allowing people under the age of 30 to come and work for a year, with relatively few limitations. The biggest issue is that it only lasts a year, and while (I think) a year in England would be enough for anyone, a year in Oz is hardly enough time to scratch the surface.

Luckily, there are options.

One is to marry a local. I wasn't *quite* ready for that yet.

One is to have sufficient skill in an industry Australia really needs – like, petro-chemical engineers, or doctors, or – bizarrely – hairdressers (?!). Sadly, 'shiftless layabout' is fairly far down the Skills Shortage list. In fact it's not on it at all.

So we'd have been stuffed, if it wasn't for this:

The *Second Year Working Holiday Visa!*

I mean, really? Read that again. How sweet is that?

Designed expressly for people who can't face the harsh reality of going back to the real world, this scheme couldn't have been more perfectly timed for us. There was only one major drawback: it required us to do three months of agricultural work.

Three months!

Ouch.

And what's more, this three months' work had to be completed, and signed off by an approved person, before the first year's visa was up.

Now, I don't know if you remember, but when I originally promised Gill that I'd come to Australia with her, I was sort of… *delayed.* As in, I didn't want to leave Thailand, so I stayed there as long as I possibly could, and only came to Australia because I could no longer afford to eat in Thailand (and let me tell you, eating is pretty damn cheap in Thailand). As it happened, I'd kept the poor girl waiting *almost exactly* three months. Which, although it was utterly forgivable, and not really my fault in the first place, being as how Thailand is *awesome* – well anyway, it put us in the following position:

It was New Year's Day.

I was only halfway through my adventures around Australia, because I had six months left on my visa.

But Gill only had three.

DAMN IT, GILL!

So, all of a sudden, instead of relaxing by the pool and dreaming up ridiculous resolutions to break, we had another, rather more pressing agenda.

We had to find jobs.

In 'agriculture', whatever the hell that is. I dunno? Tractors and shit.

Like, right freaking NOW.

So. New Year's Day was spent packing the car, checking out of our beloved Underground hostel, pointing Rusty southwards, and driving through the blistering heat of the day for eight hours straight.

But Gill did the driving, so I tried not to be too hard on her.

After all, starting her working holiday visa three months before mine was an easy mistake to make.

Roo came with us of course, because she'd studied agriculture at school – she'd had her hand up a cow's arse and everything – so the prospect of farm work held little fear for her. Actually, this seems like a good time to mention an aspect of Roo's schooling that amused me no end. As part of their agricultural studies, every member of her class had hand-reared a calf, feeding it, training it, and grooming it for a whole year. Then they'd taken their cows to a show, and pranced around the ring with them, being judged for the quality of the animal 'on the hoof'. The next stage of the competition was called 'on the hook' – where all the animals were duly butchered, and judged again on the quality of their meat!

Unsurprisingly, the whole class (of fourteen-year-old girls) were distraught.

It's hard to imagine them getting away with that in England.

Afterwards Roo's cow was bought by McDonalds – but I don't think that cheered her up much.

Anyway. When we arrived in Margaret River, either the circus was in town, or else the place was just full of hippies – strolling along in crazy trousers, carrying juggling clubs, with multi-coloured hair (the people, not the juggling clubs). We even saw one guy dressed as a pirate, in such a convincing outfit that I immediately wanted to emulate him.

(But I didn't tell him that, in case he decided to rape and pillage me.) As it turned out, the circus *was* in town – but that had absolutely no bearing on the dress code of the local population, which was skewed heavily in favour of New Agers (for no immediately apparent reason), and scruffy backpackers, who had come here for the same reason we had.

All in all, there were surprisingly few suits and ties on the streets of Margaret River. I liked the place immediately.

Gill and Roo, being young, female, traveller-types, absolutely *loved* it.

Which was good, because Rusty had boiled up several times on the way here. For any of you who are fact-checking out there, Margaret River is actually only three hours, not eight hours, from Perth. The remainder of that time had been spent sitting beside the road, waiting for our van to stop making 'imminent explosion' noises. I had a horrible feeling that, unless we made enough cash to replace his... well, *everything*... we wouldn't be leaving in a hurry.

Our campsite, named with typical Aussie subtlety, was called 'Big Valley'. If you can guess why, you win a lollipop. Rather than being within said geographical feature, the camping area itself was on top of the hill looking down on it.

But what a hill! From behind the kitchen we could see for miles in every direction. There were clumps of forest, a man made 'dam' (Aussie word for reservoir), and rolling, grassy hillsides that went on forever. It was like the Garden of Eden. Only, in place of a snake it had a stocky bulldog called Muzza, who marked his territory by peeing on every tent in the site. You know what? It probably had snakes too.

The owners, a cheerful, middle-aged couple called Kevin and Shelley, charged us just fifty dollars each for a whole week's accommodation – so we picked a spot for Rusty and went to do something that would profoundly alter our lives for the better.

We pitched our tents.

See how I used the plural of the word 'tent' there?

While we'd been hanging around in Perth, Roo had discovered the tiny tent she'd taken backpacking around Europe. This had now been bestowed upon Gill, by way of creating a more harmonious living environment – and Gill was ecstatic!

Not just because she was now technically a home owner, but because she'd officially moved out – and she promptly pitched her tent as far away from mine and Roo's as the camp ground would allow.

The next morning we went out looking for a job.

And we found one!

How's that for efficiency?

It had been a bit of a gamble, coming here, as we'd made a few phone calls from Perth and been told "There might be work, it depends on when you arrive."

Not really helpful when we had exactly three months to achieve exactly three months' work. If it took us two weeks to find something, we'd have to post our forms to the pumpkin farm in Kununurra and beg them to sign for the work we'd done there… Yikes.

Fate always seems to take a helping hand in these situations though, and even though the grape-picking season wasn't due to start for several weeks, the Down To Earth job agency hooked us up immediately.

We'd be starting tomorrow – at 6am.

'Leaf plucking'.

I shit you not.

It turns out, there are all sorts of jobs under the umbrella of agriculture. There are even more if you try to push your luck – we met backpackers who had worked in pubs and hotels, and got the work signed off for their second year visas because the job was 'in a rural area'. We even met people who'd been lucky enough to befriend a farmer, and he'd simply offered to sign their forms for a few pints of beer! The buggers. But we worked for ours. Although, after what we'd experienced up north, the reality of working as a vineyard labourer was considerably less arduous than we anticipated.

By now I'm sure you're expecting a tale of incredible hardship, littered with plucking puns and accidents involving me plucking something I shouldn't be plucking.

But no! *Pluck you!*

(Okay, okay, I'll leaf it alone for now.)

In fact, this job was ridiculously easy, and even though none of us knew what we were doing, there seemed very little that could go wrong.

We walked down the rows of grape vines and, whenever we felt there were too many leaves obscuring the fruit – we plucked them.

And that's it!

As for how many was too many, this was a matter of some debate, as we also had to ensure that the grapes were 'adequately shaded by leaves'. Our supervisor, a toothless idiot known as Goldie (because no-one, including himself, could remember his real name), tried to illustrate the point by demonstrating.

He'd guide us down a row, pulling off a leaf here or there, and turning to us to say "See! Like that. Gotta be careful, get it just right."

"So, that's enough?"

"Yep."

"But what about these grapes, then? They're still a bit hidden."

"Oh yes!" And he'd pluck a load more leaves. "There!"

"But… now these others are fully exposed…"

"Oh shit. That's okay, that's okay, it doesn't look too bad. Um, let's try over here…"

Basically, he didn't have a bloody clue either.

And he'd been doing this for over twenty years.

Now, the less charitable souls amongst us may well be thinking that even a retarded Chimpanzee would get promoted after twenty years of picking grapes for a living – but then again, if you'd put Goldie up against a retarded chimpanzee in a test of mental dexterity, I'd bet on the ape every time.

I'd be surprised if Goldie's IQ made it into double digits.

He never learned my name – even though I worked for him, and with him, six days a week for three months. He never learned anyone's name, which made it all the more ludicrous that his strategy for marking which rows we'd done was to scrawl our names in chalk on the end-of-row support posts.

He'd come stomping down the grape vines demanding to know who was working there. "I'm Andy," I'd say.

"Well you're not supposed to be working here! This is someone else's row!"

"Oh, really? Who's row is it supposed to be?"

And he'd furrow his brow, replace his hat on his head a few times, and then stomp off back down the row to find out what name he'd written on the end of it.

As though it made a blind bit of difference!

Goldie had six teeth left, including one of the upper-middle ones. God knows what had caused this, but he'd learnt his lesson; he sat in his car, methodically brushing them after every single break.

The car was very nearly as decrepit as he was. It was a Ford Cortina from about 1982 – when square things were the height of fashion, and poo-brown paint was all the rage. By now the car had a two-tone colour scheme; shit and rust. Goldie wouldn't let anyone touch it – probably because if they did, the whole thing would disintegrate.

Which would have been unfortunate, because it looked suspiciously like he was sleeping in it.

As I travel around, I sometimes meet people who make me feel better about choosing the lifestyle of a shiftless wanderer. Either because they've chosen the same lifestyle – and they're rocking it – or because, like Goldie, they prove that no matter how far I may sink into debt and degradation, it could always be much, much worse.

The Kangaroo Suicides

As work progressed from leaf-dropping (clawing indiscriminately at the foliage until there seemed to be enough of it on the ground) to fruit-dropping (see above), the campsite also began to fill up with workers. Amongst the new arrivals was a short, highly amusing English lad I called Comedy Dave. Gill was instantly smitten. She's always had a thing about short guys, and Dave was also cute and smart (fulfilling her dream trifecta).

She demonstrated a Tony-esque ability to put her foot in her mouth when, after spotting Dave leaving the showers wrapped only in a towel, she walked into the kitchen singing (to the tune of 'Hey Micky!') – "Oh, David, you're so fine, you're so fine you blow my mind–"

And that's when she noticed he hadn't gone back to his tent – still wearing his towel, he was rummaging around in the fridge.

Awkward!

The 'real work' of grape picking was due to start in a few weeks' time. Until then we trained the younger vines, by curling them around a series of wires strung between wooden fence poles, pruned them, 'misted' them – basically, whatever peculiar shit Goldie seemed to think these vines needed. Not much of it made any sense to us, but we were being paid by the hour to saunter up and down the aisles of the world's finest vineyards with the sun on our faces and a pair of pruning shears in our back pockets – hardly worth complaining about now, is it?

Especially as I was working next to Roo. We always chose rows on either side of the same vine, meaning we could stroll along chatting – and whenever we came across a suitably-sized hole, we could lean through and share a kiss. Aww!

We also found ourselves ferrying half the campsite's occupants to work, as we all tended to be hired by one vineyard at a time. As the workers staggered out of their tents and groped around the kitchen for boxes of cereal, Gill would try to figure out who was coming with us.

"Roll up, roll up," she'd call, "take the magic bus to see the Incredible Kamikaze Kangaroos!"

Coaxing Rusty through the pre-dawn haze, we were glad of the extra eyeballs – the kangaroos were everywhere in the fields lining both sides of the road, and when they chose to move they were ludicrously fast.

One morning Gill slammed on the brakes as the van in front of us screeched to a stop. A medium-sized roo had pounced as they drove past, shattering the windscreen and ending up on the knee of the girl in the passenger seat!

The girl was, understandably, a little perturbed.

The roo was dead, its neck broken on impact, but it kept thrashing – and bleeding – and was so heavy, and so firmly embedded in the glass, that they had no choice but to drive on to the nearest garage with it still in there.

I don't think she was impressed with that, either.

We had a few close-calls most mornings, and a couple of weeks later we clipped another small roo as it tried to bounce alongside us. We were all on edge as we pulled into the petrol station. It was common for cars to meet there to refuel, and to travel on in convoy to that day's vineyard – but this time, not everyone would be leaving.

Halfway between here and the campsite, one old estate car had been leapt on by a giant. The big roo had completely crushed the front of the car; bonnet, grill, and the engine inside were a crumpled mess. The car was totalled; it had been towed this far by another worker with a 4x4, but it left that forecourt on the back of a wrecker's truck.

So, all joking aside, those things were damn dangerous.

I mean, every country has pest animals – but it's not often that they're bigger than we are. Or that they outnumber us – thirty-four million roos, against the twenty-three million-strong population of Australia.

That's a lot of extra penises.

As befitted a town with a population entirely composed of hippies, Margaret River had a healthy selection of op shops. It became a regular ritual of ours, visiting each of them in turn – not because we needed more clothes, but because op shops were the perfect places to acquire bits for fancy dress costumes. Week after week we went from place to place, relentlessly hunting down components for three perfect pirate costumes, to be used at some unspecified point in the future.

This idea was Roo's brainchild, but Gill agreed that it was vital we complete this task – because, as Roo said, "you never really know when you're going to need a good pirate costume."

You can't argue with logic like that.

In my time I've met hundreds of backpackers, but as far as I know we were the only ones who travelled the length and breadth of the country with a dedicated box of dressing up clothes in our van. It was bigger than our food box, and contained several varieties of wings, tutus and corsets, boots, belts, myriad garments which had been purchased purely for their material – which was either shiny, or sparkly, or leather – and before long, three complete, very convincing, pirate costumes.

I've still got mine.

But don't tell anyone.

The girls' other regular haunt was something I'd only ever come across in Margaret River: an entire shop devoted exclusively to beading. Literally thousands of different types of beads lined every wall in matching screw-top jars. It was like an Aladdin's Cave… well, to anyone who actually gave a shit about beading.

The girls would rush in, gasping with delight – as though they hadn't been in there three times that week already.

I would hang around in the middle of the shop, trying to look manly. Which, by the way, is utterly impossible in the middle of a bead shop, for two reasons; one, you're in the middle of a bead shop. Hello? It's been scientifically proven to lower testosterone levels *just by walking past* a bead shop. And two – standing there, swaying unconsciously in time to the soothing New Age music, I'd inevitably spot something really interesting – like tiny jade dragon heads, or crocodile teeth with hieroglyphs carved into them – and before thinking of the consequences I'd call to Roo, "Hey, these beads are really cool!"

And… yeah. That's one of the least manly phrases ever uttered.

So, fail on that score.

The girls bought dozens of beads, plus the string, clasps and other fittings, home in big paper bags, and set to work eagerly outside our encampment.

And despite what you may hear, I *absolutely did not* join them.

At no point did I spend several evenings crafting beaded necklaces and bracelets for me to wear. If you happen to see any photographs of me wearing these kind of items, you can rest assured that I bought them that way.

Okay?

Good.

So, late one evening, as I was sitting around doing something suitably manly (and absolutely *not* making myself a pretty necklace), Roo held up her latest masterpiece.

It jingled.

"Look!" she exclaimed, "I've done it! It's an anklet, made entirely of bells!" And she shook it in the air to prove it. It sounded like a tambourine orchestra.

I was already wary. "Uh, what are you going to do with that, exactly?"

"I'm going to wear it around my ankle, silly! So you'll be able to hear me coming!"

To which Gill replied, quick as a flash; "Roo, the whole campsite can hear you coming."

Touché, Gill, *touché*.

There was an awkward silence after that.

But the crowning achievement of Gill's time at Big Valley was the creation of Andy's Prayer.

Shortly after our first pay cheque, we made an investment that was to forever alter the course of human history. Well, it made us happier, anyway: we bought a toastie-maker. Not just any toastie-maker – one of those posh sandwich press thingummies, with two flat plates that come together to produce miracles.

Eating a simple toastie, with the cheese liberally coated in Mexican fajita spice, was a borderline religious experience.

Hence, after only a couple of days in the kitchen, our sandwich toaster had become a celebrity. There was a queue to use him at every meal time, and we quickly decided to invest in a length of chain and a miniature padlock, in case anyone leaving Big Valley tried to abduct him.

It wasn't long before we named him Andy – an in joke, because every time Goldie asked me my name I said a different one; eventually I'd got tired of the game, and settled on 'Andy'. There was no-one working in the fields called Andy, and no-one on Goldie's paperwork by that name, but the others found it amusing to play along, so everyone had taken to calling me that – both at work and at home.

If ever I had an alter-ego, it was the toaster, and thus was he christened.

That afternoon, Gill put in ten minutes at the internet café, and emerged with a sign to stick in the kitchen above Andy. It was her own take on the Lord's Prayer:

Our Toaster
Who art in Kitchen
Andy be thy name.
Thy wrap or bun
Or toast be done
With cheese, and it tastes like Heaven
Cook us this day, our Pitta Bread,
And forgive us our impatience,
As we forgive you, for taking more than 10 seconds!
Lead us into Taste Sensation,
And deliver us our meal,
For Thine is the Breakfast,
The Lunch and The Dinner,
For snacking and munching
Oh, Yum!

It caused us much hilarity, though as I write this, I feel sure this one short piece of blasphemy will earn me more hate mail than anything else in all my books put together. Ah well; such is life. At least it won't be a *Jihad*. This time…

Good Company

As people came and went with the tide, into the mix was thrown Lauren; a pretty American chick with a voice so voluble I thought she'd swallowed a loudhailer. Now, everyone has irritating habits, and living this close together tended to bring them to light fairly quickly. Lauren was one of those people who always had to have the last say about everything – and always had to go one better than anyone else in the conversation. We call that 'black-catting' – as in, 'my cat's blacker than your cat' – but Lauren was also touchy and argumentative, so if I'd dared mention black-catting to her, she'd probably have denounced me for racism.

Shane, a big brash Geordie with long, dishevelled hair, was a more amiable companion. Every morning we'd struggle out of our tents, cursing the cold, cursing our lateness, and empty a bowl of corn flakes down our necks before leaping into Rusty with anyone else who needed a ride.

Without fail, as we inhaled our breakfasts, Shane would be stood there at the barbecue, frying up a huge pile of bacon. He was late for work every single day, but he didn't care; his bacon ritual was more important.

"Why don't you just scoff some cereal and save yourself some grief?" I asked him once.

"Becaaaauuse," he slurred, "I LOVE PIG IN THE MORNING!"

Seemed like a good enough reason to me.

Every morning, our extra seats filled up with the last workers to drag themselves out of their tents. One morning Gill was incensed to see Lauren coming out of Dave's tent, obviously late because she'd spent the night getting more intimately acquainted with him. Gill's fondness for Dave was well-known throughout the campsite, and to see that her arch-enemy had moved in for the kill put Gill in an unspeakably foul mood. She sat in silence while she ate her breakfast, then climbed into the driving seat and gunned Rusty's engine so hard he roared.

The van was already moving when Lauren piled in at the last possible second, slamming the door shut behind her.

Just as Gill gave vent to her frustrations. "I'm going to KILL someone!"

"Sorry, dude…" I started.

"I'm going to fucking KILL someone! I fucking HATE Americans!"

"Um, Gill, maybe you should—"

"Bitch!"

"Gill, you should probably know—"

"Fucking BITCH!"

"Steady on," I warned. But I had no chance to elaborate further, as Gill was far from done.

"Fucking Americans! Why are they always so fucking loud, so *irritating*, and… and… BITCH!"

There was absolutely nothing I could do. Apart from boot the back of the driver's seat. Maybe that would distract her.

"OW! Stop fucking kicking me!"

I almost believed that had done the trick – but no. Gill wasn't letting go.

"When we get back I'm gonna take the fire-axe and make fucking firewood out of that bitch!"

"Gill hey, chill out a bit—"

"ARRRRH!" She pounded the steering wheel in rage. "Fucking Americans!"

Every fibre of my being wanted to scream out "SHUT UP GILL! LAUREN IS IN THE FUCKING CAR WITH US!" – but I couldn't. Not without making it even worse. Diversion was all I could try, though it was a fair bit late for that already.

"Hey, not all Americans are like that…"

"No. Just *one particular* loud-mouthed, fat, ugly, dumb-assed devious *bitch!*"

And then Lauren spoke up.

"Hey, that is pretty hurtful, you know, to me, because I'm an American, and we're perfectly nice people."

You know you've been travelling with someone for too long when you can read their "OH SHIT!" body language even though you're sitting behind them. Gill's head and neck went suddenly stiff, which can't have been healthy, given the terrain we were bouncing over.

"But…" her mental gears were spinning so frantically I could almost smell them burning. "But… Lauren… you're not *American*, are you?"

"I SURE AM!" Lauren sounded a little indignant, but that was all.

"Oh!" said Gill, "Sorry! We all thought you were *Canadian!*"

And somehow, unbelievably, she'd pulled it off.

Lauren chattered away quite contentedly for the rest of the journey, blissfully unaware that she'd been savagely insulted for the first five minutes straight.

It was a testimony not just to Gill's mental agility under pressure – which I have to say, was brilliant – but also to the incredible density of the foam Lauren's brain was carved from.

Gill's tirade may have been a little inappropriate, but she was bang on the money.

Either Lauren was so self-centred that she couldn't believe anyone would purposefully want to insult her, or else she genuinely hadn't realised what was going on.

Which meant that, as well as being annoyingly loud, irritatingly whiney, exceptionally abrasive and about as attractive as a poorly-shaved pig in a tracksuit, Lauren was also considerably dumber than that pig.

Probably dumber than the tracksuit, too.

One of the dangers inherent in fruit-dropping was that every person in the vineyard had hands full of excess fruit. Every few minutes a weighty bunch of grapes would arc through the sky, rising from one aisle and descending in the next. You could tell from snippets of conversation how far along the person next to you was, and it was utterly irresistible to try and smack them in the face with a bunch of airborne fruit from the other side of the vines. Goldie himself was target *numero uno* – not only because he was the boss, but because it made him so hilariously frantic. I'd caught him a couple of times, but when I heard him stomping down my row I had plenty of time to drop a veil of concern over my smirk.

"Not me," I told him, "try next-door!" It was what we all said, but he never cottoned on – he just stormed off to the end of my row, did a u-turn, and went back down the next one. Which was Shane, the pig-loving Geordie's row.

And Shane really loved to bait Goldie.

"Did you throw that bunch of grapes at me?" Goldie demanded.

"Which one?" Shane replied. He continued his lazy stroll up the row, forcing Goldie to chase after him.

"Just now! You threw a bunch of grapes right at my head."

"Oh, that wasn't me," Shane told him, "not *just now*."

Holding my breath so as not to draw attention, I snipped a heavy green bunch into my hand. Goldie was just explaining to Shane that throwing grapes was *not* big and it was *not* clever – when my bunch came sailing over the top of the vines, and clouted him right on the schnoz.

"HEY!" he yelled – at Shane! "What have I just been telling you?"

It was more than I could take. I chopped the nearest bunch I could find and lobbed them over on the same trajectory. They landed with a thud on Goldie's head, prompting him to yell at Shane once more; "I TOLD YOU TO STOP THAT!"

Shane was standing in front of him, empty palms held out for inspection, saying "It's not me, man! I'm right in front of you!" – when the next barrage hit. Only this was an orchestrated strike, from several rows on both sides of us, and it targeted the argument with deadly accuracy.

Goldie was foaming at the mouth as the grapes continued to pelt him, shaking his finger in front of Shane's chest and shouting, "STOP IT, STOP IT, STOP IT!"

Shane was creasing himself laughing, as was every vineyard worked for ten rows in every direction.

"I'm going to find out who that is," Goldie fumed, clearly missing the obvious – that by now, it was everyone. "You're in for it, whoever you are!"

Never had a threat seemed more impotent.

Because Goldie didn't possess the intelligence to figure out who was targeting him – even though he'd been writing our names on the end of our rows *all day*.

And even if he'd managed that, he had less power than he had teeth.

Which is to say, none.

When it came to winding Goldie up, Shane knew exactly what buttons to press.

It was Shane who came up with the idea to release the handbrake on Goldie's car and push it halfway down a random row; it was he who created the 'see how many bunches of grapes you can hang off Goldie's jacket without him noticing' competition. Not satisfied with knowing that Goldie could never remember any of our names, he went one step further by wiping the chalk names off the end of our rows, and writing gibberish there. It was quite amusing watching Goldie trying and failing to read it – he'd shake his head in confusion, clearly convinced that he'd written something he could no longer understand.

But Shane's best trick was one he'd learned from me and Gill – from the earliest days of Goldie's idiotic demonstrations, we'd discovered that if we kept looking confused, and asking inane questions, he would repeat his demonstration ad infinitum – effectively doing our job for us, for whole rows at a time, while we strolled along next to him saying thing like, "So you're clipping the *green* ones, right?"

Oh yes, we had fun with Goldie alright.

I could take the piss better than any urologist in history – but hats off to Shane.

He truly was a master baiter.

Something for Nothing

When work shifted gears into proper grape picking, we rapidly began to wish it hadn't.

Picking meant even earlier mornings; we'd get a text message before 5am, telling us if we were working and if so, where. The work itself was fast and ferocious – at least, it was for the hordes of professional pickers that descended on Margaret River like vultures on a dead bullock's bollocks.

They picked grapes with a mindless ferocity, having learned from experience that the only way to earn anything approaching a sensible wage was to attack the bunches with such savagery that they shit themselves and jumped into the bucket of their own accord. These people shredded the vines, when we'd been repeatedly admonished just for looking at them too hard. They were delicate structures, but that didn't seem to matter one whit to the hardened nomads of the fruit-picking industry.

Consequently, Roo, Gill and I trailed along in their wake, plucking what grapes we could from the devastation and praying we wouldn't get blamed for it.

Some days we hardly made enough to justify getting out of bed.

But the best days? Those were when we woke before the alarm, to the forceful drumming of rain on the tent. Wet days were non-picking days, which meant we could snuggle back into our blankets and snooze; we'd earn less – nothing at all in fact, which was marginally less than we earned on a working day – but the extra hours of sleep were worth every lost penny.

We took advantage of a run of bad weather to drive Roo back up to Perth; she was doing a sponsored bicycle ride with her sisters, in aid of a cancer charity that had helped make Frieda comfortable towards the end.

Driving through the suburbs was oddly refreshing after seeing nothing but nature for several weeks. It was also my first introduction to a fascinating phenomenon which takes place in Australia cities every few months.

"Is it an evacuation?" I asked Roo.

"Eh? Oh, that! No, that's just the verge collection."

Lining the street on both sides were piles of stuff. Almost every house had something on the lawn out front, whether it was a splintered old rocking chair or a pile of TVs. Some places had colossal stacks of what they must have considered to be rubbish – entire three-piece suites, mattresses, book cases, exercise bikes… you name it, it was there.

"What… why?" It was all I could get out.

"The council comes to collect things that are too big to put in the bins. You get a flyer to let you know when they're coming, and everyone has to pile up what they want rid of on the verge. Then the council guys come with trucks and take it all away. What, you don't have this?"

"NO!"

"Oh. Happens pretty often around here."

"But… you could just… take it all! Steal it, I mean!"

"Ha! Feel free! It's all junk, but they do say that 'scavenging is encouraged'. No need to throw it all away if someone else can use it. Loads of people go around in vans and utes, picking out the best stuff – that's how Dad got our TV."

"He got a TV?"

"Yeah, there's loads of TVs. Especially now everyone is upgrading to those massive flatscreens. Some work, some don't, but Dad can fix them, so he got the best one he could find. We've had it for years!"

The concept was still blowing my mind. "So, really, anyone can just take any of this stuff?"

"Yeah – you're supposed to. But you're not supposed to make a mess."

"Wow. Just… wow."

One disadvantage of going from student, to the world's crappest actor, to a backpacker, is I've always been broke. Free stuff – even half a jar of jam two months past its sell-by-date in a crusty hostel kitchen – is very exciting to me.

To see this – all of *this*… Well, it was very nearly too much. I was getting all emotional about it. I mean, lust is an emotion, right?

Roo could tell from the excitement in my voice, so she nipped it in the bud; "No. My Dad's house is already full of junk. You cannot fill it full of more shit."

"Awwww…?"

"No!"

"STOP!"

Roo slammed on the brakes. Never a good idea in Rusty, as they didn't always come off again. "What's wrong?"

"Look! That sofa is perfect! Pristine!"

"Oh, bloody hell! It's a crappy old sofa someone's throwing away. It's probably been there for a week."

"But it's sooo preeeety! We could… we could use it…"

"For what? We're twenty miles from my house. No way it'll fit in Rusty. And we couldn't do anything with it."

"Not true! We could do *anything* with it! If we owned a sofa like that… Gill and me can walk twenty miles. Gill? Get out and grab the end of that sofa."

"It's uphill. All the way."

Gill didn't look thrilled either, I have to say. But I knew, deep down inside, that she also wanted that sofa. I mean, it was *free*. Who wouldn't want it?

The rest of the journey was punctuated with excited cries (mostly from me – okay, entirely from me) – of things like "Look! Multi-gym! They cost thousands!"

Roo: "No."

Me: "ARMCHAIR!"

Roo: "No."

Me: Holy SHIT! Did you guys *see* that pile of computer stuff? It was taller than I am! I bet some of it still works fine…"

Roo and Gill together: "NO!"

We dropped Roo home, and Gill took the wheel for the drive back to Margaret River. By this point, I'd been forced to admit that a lot of the roadside piles did contain junk. Broken furniture, useless electronics; the occasional busted-up washing machine, or a giant CRT TV with a Post-it note on the screen that said 'still works!'. Not much we could directly *use*, as Gill pointed out, *because we live in a tent*.

I was also forced to concede that point.

But Gill is far more like me than she cares to admit, so we spent the whole morning cruising slowly up and down residential streets, carefully studying each pile as we passed, always on the look out for that one sweet item of treasure that we knew would make it all worthwhile.

And then we saw it.

"It'll never fit in," Gill said.

"Or will it?" I countered.

"It WILL," Gill decided.

"Awesome. Let's get it."

A bright blue La-Z-Boy reclining armchair, fully cushioned, it screamed comfort and luxury in a way that couldn't be denied.

"Who would throw this away? It must be knackered!"

But no. At some point we'd crossed the line into a posh suburb, and as we all know, rich people have a better class of trash. Looking up the driveway at the house responsible for our find, I could well imagine that they'd thrown it out because they'd decided to redecorate, and it no longer matched the curtains.

"Score!"

It took us over an hour to get it into the car.

By then we'd emptied Rusty completely (which by itself takes twenty minutes), tried to manhandle the La-Z-Boy in through every opening Rusty had. It wouldn't quite go in through the tailgate, even with the back seats flat, but by turning the thing on its side, it went in through the sliding door – and, tipped upside down, finally came to a rest filling the whole back section of the van.

Gill and I did our little victory dance (thankfully no-one was around to film us this time), and spent the next ten minutes congratulating ourselves on our find.

And then, we saw another one.

Not an armchair this time, but a bizarre kind of wickerwork basket-chair. It had a separate base and a giant, soft cushion the size of a duvet.

We'd thought nothing else would ever fit in Rusty (apart from a few books, and a spare hammock, and a football, and a PlayStation that I was *sure* would work again once it dried out) – but this was different. Because it was hollow, a sort of skinny round frame… and because we wanted it badly enough to *make it fit.*

And we did.

Unfortunately, Rusty punished us for stuffing him full of skanky old furniture, by boiling up just as we were leaving the hills. It had never happened without Roo there to advise us, because Roo was always there to advise us. So in her absence, I did the most sensible thing I could think of – wrapped my hand in a tea-towel, and opened the radiator to put some cold water into it.

To say it exploded is only a slight exaggeration. Filthy, boiling water fountained up from the engine with enough pressure to soak the roof Because Rusty's engine was inside the cab, it also soaked the dash, the windscreen, both front seats, and had a damn good go at ruining our new chairs, too. All I can say is, thank the Goddess I wasn't leaning over to look inside at the time, or I'd have been in hospital with third degree burns to my face.

"SHIT!" said Gill. Understandably.

"I know! Fuck me!"

"No, I mean I've just remembered the first rule about what to do when your car boils up."

"Oh yeah? What is it?"

"DO NOT open the radiator."

"Great. Thanks for that."

"You're welcome."

We made it back to Margaret River before evening, so we didn't have any suicidal kangaroos to cope with. It was much easier getting the chairs back out again, and in less time than it takes to tell, our little world was transformed.

Gill nipped off to the fire pit, and came back with two un-burnt logs. We laid a short plank across them, and I strung up the extra hammock I'd acquired.

And this was our set-up for the rest of our stay.

It did look quite out of place in the middle of a forest, and it caused quite a few double-takes when new people arrived. They'd drive in, past tents, toilets, a fire pit, a kitchen… and then pull up short with a "Holy hell! What's that all about?"

And there would be Roo, Gill and I, relaxing around our big-screen laptop. Gill would be dozing in a hammock, Roo curled up in the huge basket chair, and I'd be on the La-Z-Boy in full recline mode – with a glass of wine, of course – right next to Gill's tent, which was glowing with all the colours of Christmas. We had lights hanging in the trees, and music playing, and a box of books for the reading of.

It was paradise.

"Bloody hell," they'd say, (when they felt they were far enough past us to do so), "I wouldn't mind a bit of that!"

And they were right to feel envious. Because our camp *rocked*.

But it was still missing a little something.

"Such a shame," Gill was heard to say, "living surrounded by all these amazing trees. And yet, we haven't got a tree house…"

The Tree House

Kevin and Shelly, the owners of the Big Valley, were fantastic sports. They came over to have a goggle at our five-star encampment, and very generously agreed to keep our La-Z-Boy when we left.

And when Gill uttered the fateful words, "We were thinking about building a tree-house," – and after they'd been crying with laughter for a few minutes and were starting to calm down – they were very open to the idea.

So long as we agreed not to hold drunken parties up there, because drunken parties and shoddily-built tree-houses are a notoriously bad mix.

This brought us to the question of building materials.

First Kevin showed us to his scrap wood pile, which contained more good quality timber than most home improvement depots, and then he led us around the back of his farmhouse and presented his junk yard. Which was out of this world.

There were cars in it. Household appliances. Farm machinery. Fence poles and mesh panels, sheet metal, electronics, tools, rusty and shiny and pointy and blunt.

"Never throw anything away, me," said Kevin. And he left us to it.

All we wanted was to build a tree-house, but as I stood looking across those piles of junk I could see far grander designs emerging.

"You know what we could build out of this stuff?" I whispered (in case anyone else was listening in on my plans).

"Anything?" Gill guessed.

"Yes! Like a *giant mutherfucking transforming robot warrior!*"

"Not particularly useful, though."

"Or a submarine!"

"Again… not highly practical."

"But… just *look* at all this stuff!"

The girls looked, and I could tell their imaginations were also running wild. But not that wild. Sometimes, I felt, the girls lacked vision.

"Let's stick with the tree-house," Gill said, "*for now.*"

"And then?"

"Then we'll see."

"Plus," Roo added, "Shelly was fine with us building a tree-house, and she's happy to let us leave the recliner with her. I'm not sure she'd be as keen about us leaving a submarine."

So, with plans for robotic domination of the known universe on temporary hold, we chose the most suitable tree for the tree-house, which turned out to be the one shading Roo's and my tent. Convenient!

We picked through the wood pile and selected a number of thick planks, and spent a happy hour knocking nails out of them. Then we tried to carry them over to the construction site, and could hardly lift them.

"What the hell? They're like… solid iron…" I gasped.

"Solid Jarrah is more like it," Roo said. "It's the best Australian hardwood. It's really dense and really, really heavy. And almost impossible to split with an axe. It burns forever, though. And it costs a fortune."

"Wow, this is gonna be the strongest tree-house on the planet!"

Two at a time, we hauled the planks over to the base of the tree. We'd picked this one because just above head-height, the main trunk split into four roughly equal boughs, all of which were chunky and strong. A metre higher they spread out enough to nest a nice little platform in-between them, which would be shaded by the tree's canopy from all directions. Perfect! I was starting to have all kinds of ideas for activities that could take place up there…

It took two full days to haul the planks up the tree, and to tie them and brace them into position. No nails could be driven into the iron-hard jarrah planks by we puny mortals, so we made doubly-sure that everything was tied securely. A framework of fencing poles added support from underneath, wedged into various crooks and forks – it was an effort to be proud of, and we christened the platform by sitting up there and watching a movie on the laptop, with glasses of wine and a big bag of crisps. We all agreed that our accomplishment had gone beyond the bounds of mere practicality, and into the realm of art.

"We could do this shit for a living," I told the others, as we climbed back to earth.

I dozed off that night fantasising about some kind of pulley system, because carrying food and drink up and down the tree meant a succession of tricky, one-handed climbs.

A ferocious storm had been building all evening, so there was a strong likelihood of work being rained off, leaving us free to lavish time on the tree-house. I slept well, as did Roo, though I have hazy recollections of waking up every time lightening struck with a deafening CRACK! It sounded as though the most violent part of the storm was right above us.

In the morning, we found out why.

The four trunks of the tree moved independently in high wind, creating a kind of scissor-like motion. This had loosened the ropes, and edged the planks over the log frame, until one by one they tipped and fell – over three metres to the ground, which they'd struck end-on with a sound like thunder.

Less than a stride from our tent.

The wood was strewn around the tree on all sides, attesting to the ferocity of the storm – but the largest, heaviest planks, had missed Roo's sleeping head by the length of our guy-ropes. My head, too, as it happened, but that hardly seemed important. All work on the tree-house was suspended indefinitely, on the grounds that a) we clearly didn't have a clue what was involved in tree-house construction, b) we felt we'd used up all our good karma on this one, and c) Shelley's insurance didn't cover death by arboreal building collapse.

"I run a campsite," she explained apologetically, "and it never came up."

It didn't look good for the submarine.

But there's a light at the end of every tunnel, as they say – even in Australia, where that light is the sun, and it's so damn hot you'd rather stay in the tunnel and take your chances with the trains.

Our glorious, glowing orb of hope was the rapidly encroaching end to all our labours; as in, our three months of agricultural work were nearly finished!

This feeling was indeed like warm sun on the face, only without the accompanying threat of surgical intervention to remove skin cancer.

In our last week, we were sent to Xanadu – no, not some mythical lost land, but in fact one of the most expensive wine-producers of an expensive wine-producing region. Xanadu had strict policies of who they would employ, and we were selected to work there because after all this time in the field – don't laugh – we now qualified as experts.

Okay, okay. You can laugh.

Anyway, we did a few days of rather laid-back grape picking. It was hard to motivate ourselves, as we had our visa paperwork ready to sign, and a rare sum of money in the bank. We'd been discussing how to spend it, and had decided that a nice little holiday was in order – to Bali, as believe it or not it's actually closer to Perth than Sydney or Melbourne.

And Bali sounded kind of cool.

So we slogged on through the grape vines, picking at our leisure, when one of the Xanadu supervisors came out with a question.

"We need a couple of volunteers," he said. "Who would like to work in the warehouse for the rest of the day?"

We got picked, of course – probably because we were all jumping up and down like we'd just won the lottery, shouting, "Pick me, pick me!"

He showed us into the warehouse, and explained that their forklift had just broken down.

"We really need these cases crated up and wrapped for delivery by tonight. Can you guys handle that?"

Of course we could. So we told him as much.

The warehouse was cool and dark, which were the ideal conditions for a nap – but we were determined to go out with a bang, and show Xanadu that we really were the kind of workers they should be proud of.

So we set to with a passion, lifting huge cardboard boxes full of wine bottles off their trolleys, and stacking them in the approved pattern on a wooden pallet.

It was hot, heavy work; each box bore a label marking its contents, and every one of them contained twelve bottles of wine, for a combined weight of sixteen kilos per box.

The girls worked up quite a sweat, as did I – but there were no slackers amongst us that day. We shrink-wrapped each pallet when it was filled, and moved on to another – and another – and another.

By the end of the day, we'd shifted the lot – and by Gill's ready reckoning, the three of us had moved over twelve metric tonnes of wine by hand.

When the supervisor came to congratulate us, we showed him a case of wine that we'd found in the middle of the pile. The box was crushed so it wouldn't stack with the others, and we'd been forced to leave it out.

"I think you should each take a bottle from that box," he said, "as my way of saying thank-you for a job well done."

"Wow! Thanks!"

So we each came forward and slid a slender bottle from the case.

"Erm, what should we do with the other nine bottles?" I asked.

"Ah, just stick 'em in the back of my ute."

Wow.

It seemed that we weren't the only ones to be getting a present.

On our last night in Margaret River, we toasted each other with our bottles of Xanadu's finest. We'd let it chill in the fridge for a few days, and we sipped it now to savour its complexity.

Or whatever it is those wine-types do.

We were trying hard to appreciate the stuff, because we'd looked it up on a trip to the bottle-o – only to find it was kept under lock and key.

Eighty-three dollars a bottle, it cost.

That was more than we earned in a day.

All three of us put together, some times.

But you know what?

It wasn't nearly as nice as *goon*.

Kuta Beach

After months spent working in the blazing heat of Margaret River's vineyards, you'd think we were mad for wanting to spend our holiday on the beach. But the deal we'd been offered on a package holiday to Bali was too good to turn down.

And to me, Bali had such an exotic ring to it – I was thinking, grass skirts and coconuts full of rum, warm turquoise waters and endless white sandy beaches.

All of which was true.

Well, kind of.

I didn't know it at the time, but Bali is to Australians what Ibiza is to twelve blokes from Blackpool on a stag do – one long, rowdy, epically-cheap piss-up.

Not that there's anything wrong with that!

I mean, booze was so expensive in Australia, it was easy to imagine people losing control at Balinese prices.

We planned to do a bit of partying ourselves, and a lot of relaxing/recovering on the beach.

Because that's what paradise is all about, right?

Our first surprise came on arrival to Jakarta International Airport, when the passport-stamping woman insisted that we had to pay for our visas. At the time, Indonesia was offering two-week visas for free – but a careful check proved we'd miscalculated. Due to a slight schedule change to our departing flight, we would be staying in Indonesia for two weeks *and three hours* – therefore, we needed to pay $20 each for the 30-day visa.

And no, they wouldn't take credit cards.

This left us in a bit of a pickle; we'd planned on taking cash from the ATM in the airport, rather than risk getting ripped off by one of the dubious exchange booths in Perth. Now though, we needed that cash right away – before they would let us clear immigration – and the only ATM's in the airport were on the other side, in the terminal…

After much rolling of eyes and throwing up of hands, one of the Indonesian customs officials called up a security guard, and allowed him to escort me through miles of winding corridors to an ATM in the departures building.

He kept his assault rifle at the ready the entire time – presumably in case I decided to make a run for it, risking death by machine gun rather than pay the twenty-dollar entrance fee.

Which had apparently just gone up to $25, something the customs officials had neglected to tell me.

Meaning I was $15 short.

So, back to the ATM, then.

We sprinted through the airport for our connecting flight to Bali, arriving just as it closed. A bit of fast talking and waving of passports persuaded them to let us board, in a scenario so farcical it would have been funny, were we not seconds away from tearing the heads off every uniformed Indonesian in sight and going bowling with them.

It was perhaps not the most auspicious start to a holiday.

But I figured what the hell? We were going to the beach! What could possibly go wrong?

And to be fair, on the flight, nothing did. Denpasar airport was microscopic, and so close to the sea that one wing of the plane was still over water when we landed. By way of baggage claim, the pilot slung me the keys and told me to poke around and see what I could find…

Okay, not quite – but it was a tiny, rural airport, with thatched beach huts in place of terminal buildings, and a runway in dire need of weeding.

Picturesque, is the polite word for it; I half expected dancing girls to come out and throw flowers at our feet, or the customs officers to drum us into their offices on bongos.

'Twee' is probably a more accurate description – this was every tourist's first impression of Bali, and someone had gone to great pains to ensure it matched up to the image of a rustic paradise.

We took a trio of motorbike-taxis into town and were delighted to find that our hotel in Kuta Beach, if somewhat dilapidated, was indeed in the middle of things. Almost too much – the road from the airport was crowded with bars, already doing a brisk trade in the late morning sun. Stretching away from the hotel towards the beach, the road was lined with stalls selling every kind of tourist paraphernalia imaginable. We wouldn't have to go far to buy souvenirs!

Not far at all.

And we didn't have to wait long, either.

We'd barely stepped out of the door, on our first excursion to the beach, when it began.

The first stall on our route was festooned with clothing – much like the stall just beyond it. And the one beyond that. And every stall opposite.

The guy running the stall wasted no time. He bounded up to us, took me by the arm, and tried to steer me towards his merchandise.

"You want buy t-shirts?"

"No, thank-you." I shook him loose.

"T-shirts! You want? Come, come!"

"No, thank-you very much." I was past him now, and walking away – but he was following me.

"Hey! T-shirts! HEY! T-SHIRTS!"

"NO! No t-shirts," I shouted back at him.

"Ok. You want trousers?"

The stallholders were so persistent that only serious distance would dissuade them. Well, possibly a baseball bat to the kisser would suffice, but I never got around to trying that. Oh man, did I ever want to!

The stalls lined both sides of the street, so it was impossible to avoid one row by moving further away – in practice it was doubly impossible, as no matter which side of the road we walked down – or even down the middle – the vendors on both sides targeted us with equal dedication.

To make matters worse, every stall was between two and three metres wide. The owners knew this gave them a very limited window to secure our attention, so to combat this they started early – say, when we were three or four stalls away. So by the time we'd gone halfway down the street, we were being bawled at simultaneously by not just the stall next to us and the stall opposite – but also the next two stalls we were approaching, and the last two we'd passed by.

On both sides of the road.

It was deafening. Not to mention, maddening. Shouts and screeches of "Please sir!' and "Hello ladies!" and "Come in, come in!" "You buy now!" "Like trouser?" "Want watch?" "Here-come-buy-take-look-want-ONE DOLLAR!"

And just when I thought it was all too much, and my head, under assault from all sides, may well explode – there would come the deafening cry of

"MAAAsssssSAAAAAAAAAAGE?"

It was laugh-or-cry territory, but we couldn't hear ourselves think for long enough to decide.

"Don't worry," I told the others, "it'll stop once we get to the beach."

This, to me, seemed logical.

I don't know why.

We strolled out onto the sand, dodging around tarpaulins spread with handicrafts and (inexplicably) battery-powered plastic crawling army-men. Seriously! No trip to the beach is complete without one.

We ducked through a line of hammocks, ignoring the occupants as they shouted "Taxi? TAXI!" at us – and at last, we gazed at the ocean, and the vast expanse of golden beach fringed by slightly-swaying palm trees.

"Coconut?" A shrivelled old woman thrust one in my face so violently she nearly knocked me out with it.

"Ah, no, but thanks."

So she swivelled on the spot and thrust the thing at Roo, hardly missing a beat. "Coconut?"

Oh crap, I thought. *There are three of us. We're going to have to refuse every single thing we're offered three frigging times!*

But surely, that wouldn't be the case? Would it?

Why, yes. Yes, it would.

As we spread out our towels, it was possible to look down the beach and see the queue of vendors stretched out for miles along the sand. I could literally count the order in which they would come at us – sunglasses man, massage lady, more sunglasses, coconuts, beads/hair-braiding, sunglasses…

And no-one, but no-one, was buying anything.

Because, let's face it, if you're on the beach you probably have sunglasses already. You're probably wearing them. You're sticky with that unique combination of sun-tan lotion, sand, sweat and sea-salt, and in full view of everyone, so it's unlikely you want to be massaged by a ninety-year-old woman. Who used to be a man. There are only so many coconuts you can drink, and we were being forced to refuse them at a rate of about one every three minutes; likewise beaded bracelets, whilst they hold a particular esteem in beach-culture, have a limit to their appeal; if we'd bought one from every vendor who offered, we'd be able to wear nothing but the damn things without compromising our modesty in the slightest.

Of course, we wouldn't have to go to such extremes. In between the bracelets and the sunglasses, we were inundated with demands to buy trousers, t-shirts, flip-flops, drinks, every kind of fruit imaginable, sea shells, carved wooden statues, pirated DVDs, cigarettes, drugs, lumps of coral, fresh lobsters, knives, baseball caps and sarongs, in a never-ending procession of high-volume sales pitches. It was the least relaxing beach experience of my life. In fact it was less relaxing than having root canal surgery performed with a flaming chainsaw by an untrained monkey riding a motorbike.

"You know what?" Gill said. "This beach is fucking awful! I can't stand it. Let's go."

In the time it took us to gather our things, we rebuffed two offers of henna tattoos, one of corn-on-the-cob, a huge bundle of bananas and a carved wooden crossbow.

Although…

"Stop looking at that crossbow!" Roo hissed. "He'll see you and come back!"

I've been to quite a few beaches in my time, but it's not often I get offered a crossbow on one.

With our belongings finally packed away, we set off across the main road, past McDonalds, and turned into our street…

And it began all over again.

In my desire to stay where the action was, I'd inadvertently booked us a hotel at the very end of the main souvenir street. The beach was at the other end. And there was no other way between the two locations.

"Hey Mister! Hey, Ladeez! You want t-shirt?"

By the afternoon of my first day in Bali, I was desperate to leave.

Unfortunately, we'd already paid for our rooms.

And our flight home wasn't for another two weeks.

Another Day In Paradise

I had to hand it to those guys though – they'd developed a tactic that worked. By driving us to the very brink of despair every time we set foot outside our hotel, they eventually wore us down. Day after day we fled down that road, screaming "NO! NOOOO!" the whole way – yet still they came, catching us unawares – in restaurants when we were eating, foolishly thinking we were safe; outside the 7-11, where we stood counting our change, trying to figure how much we'd been overcharged. Little by little we accumulated pretty much all the crap that was on sale – because to be honest, if you weren't swearing at vendors on the beach, or indulging in enforced shopping, there was sod all else to do.

Most of the other tourists were medicating their way through the boredom with copious amounts of alcohol; the next street over from our hotel was packed with bars, all offering free drinks, free shots, cheap cocktails and booze by the bucket. That sort of scene had appealed to me in Thailand – perhaps because I was single, I'd taken full advantage of it. But here, it felt... threatening. There was none of that peace, love and boogie-vibe I'd experienced at the Full Moon parties on Koh Phangan. Here the locals seemed intent to squeeze every last possible cent from the tourists – maliciously, almost as though it was their right to screw us over for invading their island and paving it over with nightclubs.

It was a bit gutting, as I'd really hoped to cut loose and party – something that was so expensive to do in Australia, it made my eyes water just thinking about it. But it was not to be – the girls didn't feel comfortable enough to risk drinking in public, and I wasn't going to go out on my own – I had enough trouble fending off the pimps and hookers when I was walking along next to my sister and my girlfriend!

So instead, we braved the hard-core night-time touting ('HEY mistah, you want ladeez?' 'Sir, watches! SIR! WATCHES!' 'Come in my bar, have many girl inside!') – and made it as far as the 7-11. There we bought a bottle of cheap vodka and a carton of pineapple juice, and made our own little party in our hotel – where we felt *safe*.

Where no one could try to trick us into anything.

Because if they worked this hard to sell shitty trinkets to sober tourists – God only knows what they'd try to stiff us with if we were hammered.

One afternoon we were approached by a tour guide as Roo sat having her hair braided, and he launched into his spiel for selling rafting trips. This was a first, and was something we were actually interested in – the guy was so shocked at our sudden outpouring of enthusiasm I could tell he hadn't sold many trips that day.

None, as it turned out.

Which was fine by us.

A minibus collected us and whisked us through glorious green countryside, part glinting rice paddies and part steaming jungle. It was a world away from the concrete chaos of Kuta Beach, and was my only glimpse of the promise that the rest of Bali had to offer.

As we were the only people going rafting, our friendly guide took us straight down to the river, where several eight-man rigid inflatables lay in a muddy, ragged heap.

Our safety briefing began with the guide explaining that when he shouted, "BOOM BOOM!", we had to duck; and that's where it ended, too. Safety standards in Bali weren't quite the same as those in the western world, something I'm usually quite excited about.

But they did make us wear life vests and helmets, which often signals a rather tame experience is about to ensue.

In this regard, I was to be disappointed.

Within seconds of pushing off our raft was hurtling downstream, showing absolutely no regard for the obstacles in its way.

"BOOM BOOOM!" shouted the guide.

"What di— SHIT!"

And I threw myself flat as the raft swept beneath the bole of an overhanging tree. The trunk, as thick around as my waist, cleared the top of the raft by inches.

"Holy crap," I said, as we recovered our positions, "they would *never* let you do this back home!"

"They wouldn't let you do this anywhere," Roo said through gritted teeth.

A rush of adrenaline surged through me, and I felt *alive*.

Then Gill shouted "Look out!"

"What?"

"SHIT!"

"BOOM BOOM!"

And the raft smashed into the base of a boulder jutting out from the opposite bank, hard enough to throw us on top of each other.

From then on, we watched the route like hawks; the river roared around us and the raft ploughed on, spinning in defiance of the guide's attempt at control.

Every muscle was tensed, every sense hyper aware, as we pinwheeled through churning rapids, crashing from one side of the river to the other and bouncing off everything in between.

Vines and branches lashed us when the raft scraped along the riverbanks, and 'BOOM BOOM!' was a cry we learned to obey instantly – because it generally meant we were less than a second away from being decapitated.

It was, in a word – exhilarating!

As the route got steeper and narrower, foaming water lapped into the raft at each collision. It felt a bit like sitting in a kiddie's paddling pool while it went over a waterfall – only instead of being over in seconds, this mayhem continued for over an hour.

By the end, the river was wider and slightly less frantic. A bit of the excitement had drained away, leaving us taking stock of the various small injuries we'd sustained; cuts and scratches from overhead branches, bangs and bruises from slamming into each other at unfortunate angles, and raw patches on fingers, heels, and any piece of bare skin that had been in contact with the boat.

"We are *so* doing this again," I declared – just as the guide called out one last warning.

"BIG BOOM BOOM," he shouted, "VERY BIG!"

And with that, the raft shot along the top of a fifteen-foot-high concrete dam – and launched itself over the edge.

The impact was immense.

It flung the girls and our guide skyward, folded the raft in half, and filled it to the brim with water.

For some reason I wasn't thrown up with the others; I was slammed into the base of the raft with such violence it sent a shockwave through my arse and right up my spine. And halfway along that route, something just *went*.

When the raft beached itself a few minutes later, the girls had to drag me out and carry me to the waiting minibus, and I lay flat across the back seats all the way back to the hotel.

I never found out what damage I'd done, but it was serious enough that I spent most of our second week in Bali flat on my back with my head hanging off the bed, watching pirated DVD's upside-down.

We'd bought about a hundred of the buggers – most of which turned out to be broken.

On our last day in Bali I managed to venture out again. There was a leather jacket I'd tried on a week ago that looked gorgeous on me. I'd umm'd and ahh'd over buying it, because even though it was handmade, and softer that a kitten's soft bits (which in hindsight is quite likely what it was made out of) – it was still eighty dollars.

The girls supported me as we took the quickest route to the leather jacket shop – conveniently located on the leather jacket shop street. One long, boring day early in the holiday, I'd killed some time going in and out of all of them. I'd found the perfect jacket, and the shop staff had told me they'd keep it for me. It seemed a bit pointless, being as how I was the only tourist in any of the shops on that street, and I'd been there for most of the day. But I guess, perfect jackets are few and far between. Mine had been sold, but the staff had made another identical jacket – just two sizes bigger.

They even offered to tailor it to fit me, free of charge – which would have been great, except that I was leaving the country in a few hours.

But I was pissed off and in a lot of pain, so I bought the damn thing anyway so that we could go home. I still have it. It's still absolutely gorgeous, softer than my own skin and twice as supple.

And it's still two sizes too big.

And then, counting down the hours until our taxi to the airport, we decided to watch a movie together. We were sitting around the laptop, about to press play, when it exploded.

To be less dramatic about it, the charger exploded – well, the parts that didn't melt exploded – while the computer itself merely gave a brief puff of smoke, and died.

A thousand dollars worth of laptop.

Gone.

With my book on it.

Again.

I was starting to think that someone up there didn't want me to publish the damn thing.

When we got to the airport, having spent and given away the last of our Balinese currency, we discovered there was a departure tax – of 150,000 Indonesian Rupiahs each. And no, they didn't take credit cards. *I've been down this road before,* I thought, as I hiked across the airport to the ATM's. But at least this time I didn't require an armed escort.

All in all, I've had more successful holidays.

In fact, I don't think I've done anything less successful since I was sixteen years old, and I applied to be the Assistant PE Teacher at an all-girls high school.

Bali stands apart in my memories as the only time I've ever been happy to be so severely injured that I couldn't leave the room.

I am never – EVER – going back there.

Because you know what? You can't even bring crossbows into Australia. Something to do with them being made of untreated wood.

They confiscate the bloody things at the airport.

The bastards!

When we got back to Perth, we ran into a wall of concern from our friends and relatives. The news of the day was all about Bali; while we'd been in Kuta, a bunch of tourists had died there after drinking the free alcohol on offer in one of the bars. It was Arak, a potent Balinese liquor, that had been brewed illegally and watered down with poisonous methanol (anti-freeze).

I felt terrible for the families of those unlucky tourists – whilst simultaneously feeling rather glad I'd been talked out of going clubbing.

So it may not have been the greatest of holidays, but you know, it could have been worse.

Life Underground

Arriving back from Bali presented us with a series of dilemmas.

Once again, all three of us were broke.

Once again, we had nowhere to live.

But perhaps the strangest thing of all, was this: we had no plans.

For my whole time in Oz so far, there had always been a goal in sight. Travel up north in Rusty. Rescue Rusty from where we abandoned him up north. Complete the three months agricultural work we needed to extend our visas. Take a holiday.

And now, for the first time, we had no pressing deadlines, no requirements beyond living, surviving, and having fun – and, consequently, we didn't have a clue what to do.

We moved back into the Underground backpackers hostel, and had a lucky break; paying for three beds in a four-bed dorm, we checked out our room on the second floor to find there were only two beds in it – a double, with a single bunk above it.

Perfect!

Well, the lack of privacy from each other wasn't perfect, but separate rooms at these prices were simply out of the question.

So, with our amazing holiday just a disappointing memory, we had to start planning anew. What would we do, in this vast land of Australia? Where would we go?

Mum had given us the germ of an idea. She was saving up for a trip to visit us, and after a bit of discussion we decided the best place to meet her would be Sydney. Perth is so remote, and although we loved the place it would be a shame for Mum to make a once-in-a-lifetime trip to Oz, and not see all the famous sights.

This gave us a rough direction; east, and a rough timescale of four months to get there.

That had to be enough time! So long as we could find jobs...

While we waited, Gill and Roo did a few shifts for the Canning (toilet) Cleaners, and I listened intently for the hostel pa system. Any time workers were needed, either by the hostel or by someone coming in and asking for them, the call would go out on the loudspeaker – and I regularly ran right over the top of people to be the first warm body on the scene. I was so eager for work, and put so much effort into the jobs I got, that pretty soon the hostel managers stopped advertising in-house jobs, and simply knocked on our door.

They often put me to work under the supervision of the hostel handyman – a silver-haired ex-con known as Mex. I reckoned Mex to be in his early fifties, but he looked about eighty-five. His scrawny arms were covered in tattoos, all homemade, obviously done at school with a biro and a compass needle. Well, assuming biros were invented when Mex went to school…

Mex was a crook.

He was constantly telling me to slow down, so the work wouldn't run out. He nearly had a heart attack when they called me on his day off and asked me to shovel building rubble out of two old bathrooms. They were being turned into new dorm rooms, and were ankle deep in old bricks and plaster. Gill and Roo pitched in, and between us we cleared the lot in a morning; I think old Mex had planned on taking a week. Maybe two.

That crafty bugger 'supervised' me as I put together bunk beds and office cabinets, laid carpet and tiles, cleaned, painted, shovelled and sprayed. Because the work I did for the hostel was in exchange for money off our room, it got to the point where I'd built up enough free accommodation to keep a roof over all our heads for a month. Then Mike, the manager, started paying me in beer vouchers; soon after that I got my first bit of cash.

But it wasn't a real job. The girls were getting a couple of shifts a week each, and helping me with odd jobs around the hostel in between times. We were getting by – just.

It was frustrating, as the weeks slipped past, to know that not only were we not saving any money, or making any progress towards our goal of driving Rusty eastwards, but we weren't even living comfortably. Hell, we couldn't even afford to drink!

Along with a pool in the courtyard and an underground cinema room, Mike's hostel had a bar. It made for a great place to hang out – for wasted Irishmen – and a great way to squeeze a bit more cash out (of wasted Irishmen). But for those of us whose plans included something other than sitting around the pool getting hammered from 10am onwards, it was a bit of a headache. We all like a drink, you see; we just couldn't afford the bar's prices. I had so many beer vouchers we could have taken a bath in the stuff – only, none of us liked beer. Everywhere else we'd stayed, we'd simply bought a cheap box of *goon* from the nearest bottle-o, and that would satisfy all three of us for days. But with a bar in place downstairs, it was now illegal to bring booze from the outside, in.

So we enacted a plan so sneaky it could have been dead for the whole movie, and you'd never have known it until the last five minutes.

Way back when I was learning to sail, I was given a very colourful piece of string to practice my knot-work. I have travelled with it ever since, out of a misplaced belief that always having a piece of string handy somehow transforms me into Bear Grylls. I've never used it. Firstly because it's not much longer than a shoelace, and would never hold my weight. Secondly, because I'm not Bear Grylls – so I encounter very few situations where a piece of string could mean the difference between life and death. And thirdly, because if such an emergency ever does arise, my piece of string is perhaps a bit too colourful to be appropriate. Purple and yellow and green… rather gaudy. As in, Bear Grylls would rather die than admit to owning such a thing. So it stays in my bag most of the time. It's there right now, in fact.

Coincidentally, my sister has always travelled with a short length of red rope, which just *might* be due to the sage advice of her travel-hardened older brother. As far as I know, she has never used it either. I do seem to recall though, that it started life as a belt from one of her cuddly toys…

Anyway. Once in a lifetime there comes a situation tailor-made to provide vindication for people like me. A time to prove that carrying a very pretty piece of string from one side of the planet to the other says more about my preparedness than it does about my sexuality. And that time, was now.

Our room on the second floor had a window overlooking the street. It also overlooked Roo, as she loitered on the pavement outside, trying her best not to look suspicious. Which was tough, as she'd insisted on putting the *goon* we'd bought inside her jacket as we walked past the front door of the hostel. "Just in case…" So, tall and skinny, with a dramatically protruding, perfectly square stomach, she was nervously hopping from foot to foot whilst glancing upwards and hissing "…hello?" – it wasn't the most convincing of disguises, it has to be said.

I strolled inside after Gill, doing my best 'casual' walk (which someone once said makes me look like Shaggy from Scooby Doo). We sauntered up to our room, flung open the window, and deployed our pride and joy; two rather colourful lengths of string fastened together, with three pillowcases knotted on for additional length. We heard a curse from Roo as her nervous fingers struggled to tie the end around the cask's handles. And just like that – with a swift, double-handed yank from Gill and me – we had the booze up the side of the building and into the room. It was very nearly the perfect crime! Only a handful of people had walked past during the operation, and they'd stood on the corner watching our process with much amusement. Likewise, the people occupying the room below had thought it funny, rather than threatening, when four litres of cardboard-clad wine had bounced off their window on its way up the wall. A few other heads had appeared, protruding from nearby windows, as the cask made rather audible progress vertically. None of them seemed in a hurry to report us for it, though. Mostly, I imagined, they were thinking "Not a bad idea, that…"

I'd never seen anyone winch booze in through a hostel window before this, but I saw it happen plenty of times afterwards. The outside of The Underground resembled a row of well-used freight elevators for the next couple of weeks, until some bright spark asked the off-duty receptionist to hold his six-pack while he went up to let down a rope made from his duvet cover. No-one else had string with them, of course! I can well imagine it puzzled the laundry staff, why every time they collected dirty sheets from the rooms facing the street, they were always tied together…

There was a final moment of irony. Mike never knew of this scam we were pulling, and in any case he'd given me so many free beer vouchers I could nearly wallpaper the room with them. It was a bit of a bugger that none of us liked beer. But living in the Underground was expensive, and it was far from ideal. Roo and I craved some space of our own, and none of us could hold down a steady job while we lived there. So when rooms became available in a house owned by the hostel, we jumped at the chance. Figuring we probably wouldn't be back, I spread my beer tokens liberally around the hostel; waste not, want not.

The Irish contingent thought I was Father Christmas.

Shit, they were so pissed they probably thought I was a tap-dancing unicorn.

Anyway, we packed all our gear back into Rusty and made a short trip across town, to the considerably more up-market neighbourhood of Subiaco.

But just before we left Mike came to me with a proposition.

"I need a quick word with you," he told me, so I braced myself for the worst.

"I need you for a proper job," Mike said. "How would you feel about running a bar?"

Getting Barred

It was a hard request to say no to.

But I couldn't tell if he was messing with me, or if he was serious.

"Well, I've had a bit of experience," I said. "The last time I was in Perth, I worked at The Shed nightclub."

This was true; it had been during that difficult period, after Roo had flown home from Kununurra. Gill and I had tried all sorts of things before we landed jobs with Lindsey.

Of course, I cleverly left out the fact that I'd worked there four nights a week for exactly four weeks – during which time I'd been disciplined for being too slow at serving drinks, demoted to glass-collector, disciplined for being too slow at glass-collecting, and had quit one step ahead of being fired for giving away free drinks – whilst drunk – and for spending fully one quarter of my time as an employee rearranging the shelves in the stock room 'to make them neater'.

Guess I was kind of slow at that, too.

But Mike didn't seem to care.

"Here's what I need," he said. "Go to this address. It's a little pub I've just taken over. Not many customers, just a few regulars, and they all know what they want. Look after the place for me, and run the bar from about three in the afternoon till eleven. Okay?"

"Yeah sure, no worries! But, ah, is there anything I need to know? Like, training and stuff?"

"Nah, it's alright. There's another bloke there, handling the stock. Ask him any questions, he knows what to do."

And that was it – one of the least conventional job interviews I've ever had.

The pub, when I got there, looked derelict. I was pleasantly surprised to find it quite nice on the inside, all decked out in wood and carpet like a traditional English pub. It was sandwiched between two freeways, which could explain the lack of custom – as did the exterior, which looked like a meeting place for people with bodies to bury. The place had potential though. I figured that, given a bit of work and the right vibe, it could be the perfect hangout for people from the hostel – a backpacker's bar, with a free shuttle bus to and from The Underground. Yet another clever tactic to milk every last cent from those who seemed desperate to waste it. Had I only known how devious Mike really was…

I started at the bar. I checked what they had available, and restocked the fridges as best I could. There was a bottle shop attached to the back, too, and I took most of the stock from there through into the pub. "How much do I charge for these?" I asked the bloke who was doing the stock-check.

"Dunno, whatever," he replied.

"Is there a price list somewhere?"

"The locals will know what they usually pay. If they ask for anything different, just make it up."

"Oh. Okay…"

"If you have any trouble—"

"Get you?" I interjected.

"No – just figure something out. She'll be right."

And that was my on-the-job training.

Not that it really mattered – we had less than ten customers the entire time, and most of them did indeed know what they were after. I poured what they pointed at, and held out my hand for the cash. Booze is so expensive in Australia that most of them were paying with a note – so I just stood there holding it, my brow furrowed as though in deep thought, until the customer helpfully reminded me how much change they were expecting. It worked, albeit stressfully, and by the end of the night we'd very nearly taken enough money to pay my wages. I reckoned I'd been fair – undercharging the punters rather than overcharging, not that anyone would ever know or care.

Bloody hell, I could rob this place blind, I thought. Probably for the best that I'm not that way inclined.

Roo came to pick me up in Rusty, and she agreed that from the outside, the place looked destined to appear on Crimewatch as the scene of some grisly murder.

During the evening, whenever business was slack, I'd taken to compiling a list of things that could be done to improve the place. I started off with the most obvious jobs – like making the exterior resemble something other than the set of a horror movie, perhaps by replacing a few light bulbs and sweeping up all the broken glass. Removing some of the burnt-out cars and charred sofas from the car park. Cutting the weeds to below knee-height, fixing the boarded up windows, scrubbing off the graffiti and shovelling up enough dog shit and rubbish to fill a dozen wheelie bins would also help. But then I moved onto more proactive strategies – like expanding the clientele to include people who didn't store rifles in the back of their trucks. Maybe finding a few customers whose parents weren't blood relatives… By the time I'd finished my list, it was exhaustive. And quite impressive. I hoped Mike would be impressed anyway, and that he might consider letting me loose on the place for a couple of months. "Imagine what I could do," I said to Roo as she drove us back to Subiaco. "I could run the place for him, learn how a bar really works, fix it up really well, do some great deals to get students and backpackers down there… Get some theme nights going! X-factor competitions, toga parties, James Bond night! It could be huge. Massive! Maybe Mike would cut me in, or at least give me a share of the profits… I'm going to talk to him tomorrow."

"Of course," she said, letting me air my dreams without contradiction. "Just see what Mike says."

As it happened, Mike was so keen to find out how I'd managed at the bar that he found me first. He let me waffle on for a few minutes describing my shift, and then cut in with an offer. "I've been thinking about something. How would you feel if I gave you that place to run?"

"WOAH?! Really?"

"Yeah, why not? You can do whatever you want with it. I'll give you a bit of a budget, and maybe you can have some fun?"

"Mike, that's fantastic news! I was SO hoping you'd say something like that! You won't regret it, mate. I promise you, I'm the man for the job!"

"Well, we'll see. Might as well enjoy yourself while you're at it, anyway."

The conversation was going as well as I could possibly have hoped.

It was time to reveal my master plan.

"Mike, we can make this place incredible! It just needs a bit of fixing up, and a funky new paint-scheme. I can do that in no time. Then we've got to target the same people who stay at The Underground – make it backpacker's night every night! Forget food, and concentrate on drink – cheap deals and special offers. Do a different theme each day of the week – 70s, 80s, 90s. Do fancy dress parties, like Superhero Night, Vicars n' Tarts, a pyjama party! Find something dirt cheap to give away free shots of – hey, you could do punch! Cheap fizzy wine for 'champagne' prizes… And then get darts matches going, pool competitions, pop-quizzes… endless possibilities. And all based around cheap booze, aiming to sell large quantities to pissed-up backpackers. You could even run shuttle buses from here, instead of selling tickets for that Perth Pub Crawl – send the boozers to your own bar, and make it a no-brainer: so many different drink offers, they'd be mad to go anywhere else. And shuttle buses back at closing time, so they don't need to fork out for taxis. I bet they'd even pay you for the bus!"

"That's… very interesting," Mike said. "You've put a lot of thought into this."

"Yeah well, there weren't a lot of customers that needed serving! But we can change all that in no time."

"Great. Right, I'll get back to you."

I never worked in the pub again.

At first I felt slighted, and as the days wore on I spent hours going over my shift there, trying to work out where I'd gone wrong. It was incredibly unfair, I felt; not only had he given me no instructions at all, and no training, he'd given me no hint since our last conversation about what I'd failed at. The question ate at me – I'm a life-long perfectionist of the highest order (agricultural work notwithstanding), and the idea that I'd messed up so badly, without even knowing it, prickled me like a cactus condom.

It was weeks later that a chance conversation with old Mex shed some light on my mistake.

Mike had bought the pub for one reason only; the land it was on, straddling the gap between two freeways, was worth millions. Only, the land had a covenant, stating that the pub couldn't be demolished *as long as it was a viable business.*

He had absolutely no intention of redecorating, updating, reinvigorating.

He wanted to flatten the place asap and sell the land on to a commercial developer. He just needed the bar running into the ground first.

And for that, he had deployed his secret weapon: Mex.

The canny, work-shy ex-con had been given a slightly more explicit job description than I was, and from what I can gather it was his dream come true.

Getting paid to do as little as humanly possible, to piss off random people for no apparent reason, to throw customer service down the toilet, take everything that was good and mess it up, and, whenever the mood took him, to break something.

Mike never said anything about it, but he'd made the right choice.

I was so NOT the man for this job.

The Things You Have To Do

Living in Subiaco; it was the best of times, and it was the worst of times.

(I may have borrowed parts of that sentence from another book).

At last, Roo and I had a room to ourselves; and what a room! The huge, queen-size bed barely made a dent on the available space. There was room to turn cartwheels in there, which I took full advantage of by... um, turning cartwheels.

Come on, you know you'd have to try it!

The bay window at the front looked out onto a quiet residential street, on which Rusty was parked – facing down the slight slope, as these days the only way we could start him early in the morning was to push him.

Roo and I were more than happy to hibernate in that room, disappearing into it for days at a time and only emerging to visit the kitchen or the bathroom.

In hindsight, this may have been part of our problem; we never really integrated with the rest of our housemates, whereas Gill, sharing a room on the top floor with another girl, had no choice.

All our housemates, with the exception of the girl in Gill's room, were Irish.

They'd obviously met at the Underground, and had transplanted their hostel lifestyle seamlessly into the house.

Their nightly ritual would start at about eight o' clock. There'd be the six of them, sitting around in the lounge, drinking beer. None of them would move, other than to go to the toilet or fetch more beer, and they seemed to do nothing but shout insults back and forth in an Irish brogue so thick as to be unintelligible. I tried to join in once or twice to be sociable, but this was clearly not a game for outsiders. I could never quite grasp the rules, or figure out if there were rules, or even have a clue what the hell was going on; mostly though, I gave up because I don't like beer, and I was bored shitless. Because from what I could tell, they seemed to get through the entire night using a vocabulary of less than eight words.

The conversation went something like this:

"Fook you, ya fookin' cont!"

"Nah, youse can get fooked, youse a fookin' cont!"

"Fook off, ya cont! Yer a cont n' yoo nae it."

Then someone else would chime in, "Ahh, yer all fookin' conts, ya fookin' buncha fookin' conts!"

And they'd all collapse in gales of laughter.

I've never felt more painfully English than the night I edged into the middle of the room and said, "Excuse me, I'm terribly sorry to bother you all, but is there any chance you could be just a tad quieter? I have to get up for work in three hours…"

There was a few seconds of confused silence, then another massed roar of laughter. I took this as a good sign, so I made my escape, pursued by good-natured calls of "ya fookin' cont!"

Every night it carried on until around four in the morning, at which point the last participant would pass out in his chair, surrounded by empty beer bottles and puddles of vomit, and promptly piss himself.

This was another reason why we didn't spend much time in the lounge.

For the most part, I didn't mind. Just having Roo all to myself in that ginormous bed was compensation enough.

I was getting to know her rather well.

Although, every so often she still surprised me.

"Do you want to go for a walk?" she asked.

"What? Now?" It seemed an odd question, as we were lying in bed at the time. It was midnight. Neither of us could sleep, so we'd been talking about what possibilities the future could hold for us. "I don't mind. Might have to put some clothes on though."

"No, not now! No, a proper walk. Like, a hike."

"Hiking? Yeah, we could do that. Maybe."

"But what about a really big walk? A *long* walk."

"I dunno… maybe?"

I could tell she was building up to something, so I decided to shut up and let it happen. It's not often my intuition is this good, and even less common that I'm clever enough to act on it – clearly, being with Roo was having a positive effect on me.

She was quiet for a bit, thinking something over. Then she said it:

"I think we should walk the Bibbulmun Track."

"Oh? Really? What's that?"

"It's this amazing aboriginal walking trail, an ancient route that they used for migrations. It's all restored now, with little wooden huts to stay in overnight. I did a few sections of it with Mum, a few years ago…"

"Interesting. Staying overnight, eh? Where is it?"

"It's right here. It goes from Kalamunda, just north of Perth, to Albany on the south coast."

"Woah! That sounds like a long way. How far is it?"

"It's about a thousand kilometres."

"What? Are you fucking kidding me? That's ridiculous! You'd have to be out of your mind! Why the hell would you want to do something like that?"

"For Mum. She loved the Track. She always promised me that one day we'd walk it together."

"Oh. Ah. Um… great. So… I guess we're walking The Track then. What did you say it was called?"

"Bibbulmun! Oh Tony, are we really going to do it? YAY! It's going to be so amazing!"

"Yeah…"

I found it hard to share her enthusiasm right at that moment.

But the idea grew on me.

Luckily.

Roo told Gill the next day. It was our last chance to get out of this; if Gill wasn't keen, if she showed any sign of hesitation, there would be reasonable grounds to rethink the whole idea. Gill liked walking as much as any of us, but she's never been super-fit. She had bad knees too, I remembered – maybe that would help sway her decision?

Maybe…

This is how the conversation went:

Roo: "Hey Gill, Tony says we can walk the Bibbulmun Track!"

Gill: "Wow, just like your mum always wanted you to do! Great, when can we start?"

Bugger.

It looked alarmingly like I was about to hike a thousand kilometres.

The reality of the situation was that we wouldn't be setting off on any grand expeditions anytime soon. The holiday had wiped out all our finances, and doing odd jobs for the Underground was only making us poorer. I mentioned this to one of our new Irish housemates, and he had an almost instant solution; "Ys can gera job with this fella, he gis us a job nar n then. Easy stuff like, all cash-in-han'."

He dug in his pocket for a screwed up bus ticket, and copied a number out of his phone onto it. "Here. Jus tell im ys know us," he said, generously.

Which I probably could have done, but I didn't because I had no idea who 'us' was.

It took me two days of ringing that number to get someone on the other end of it, which in hindsight should have been a warning. But we were desperate for cash, desperate for jobs – and the further into the phone call I got, the better this one sounded.

It was with a company called Global Gardens, doing unskilled landscape labouring; in other words, shovelling soil. Trevor, the owner, manager and HR department all rolled into one, told me that we could start straight away.

"There's three of us," I explained, "My girlfriend, my sister and me."

"Yeah, no worries. You got transport?"

"Ah, yes, after a fashion. We've got a… van."

"Great. I'll pay petrol for yer, and it's a hundred bucks a day. Cash in hand. How does that sound?"

"Fantastic! Thanks so much!"

"Right, I'll give yer the address, and – oh, have you got yer Blue Cards?"

"Ah…"

At this point my acting training kicked in. Specifically, the part of it where we'd been told, at audition, to say yes to everything. Can you horse-ride? Sky-dive? Speak Sanskrit? Just say yes. Get the job. Then you can worry about how to leap from a plane onto horseback whilst chanting the *Upanishads*. Honestly! Check out the quality of my training, and then wonder why I never became famous.

"No. I'm afraid we don't have those… things."

"Blue cards. Gotta have 'em for Health and Safety. No worries, you can get 'em online, takes a couple of hours to do the exam. Costs about ninety bucks."

"Woah! That's quite a bit. Will we definitely have jobs? All three of us?"

"Yeah, no worries. And I'll pay yer back for the Blue Cards. Just let me know when you've got 'em."

"Alright! We'll go and do them now."

And so, credit card in hand, we legged it to the nearest internet café.

Trevor was dead right. For ninety-five dollars apiece, we could take the 'Western Australia Health and Safety at Work Exam – or 'Blue Card' – right there and then.

What's more, there was no time limit, unlimited re-tests were allowed for the same one-time fee – and it was almost entirely multiple choice.

In other words, it was a qualification in name only. In fact, it was barely that. Everyone knows that multiple choice tests always have one very obviously wrong answer. I could already envisage questions like:

13) What colour is a safety warning light?

a) Yellow

b) Red

c) Broken

d) Brachiosaurus, in the late Jurassic period.

I shared my suspicions with Gill and Roo, as they sat down at computers either side of me. "I think it's some bullshit red-tape they've introduced so that some government department can cover its own arse," I said.

And I was right.

Demonstrating a level of teamwork any boss would be proud of, Roo and Gill looked up the answers on the WA Health And Safety website, while I wrote them into the downloaded exam form.

Then I submitted it, re-opened the same document, changed the name on the top and a handful of words in the 'explain' sections, and submitted it again for Gill.

And again for Roo.

In less than an hour we were almost three-hundred dollars worse off – but could at least console ourselves with the fact that the average time taken to complete the test was two hours.

A day later, we had our results back; a one-hundred percent pass-rate, times three. It was a miracle!

Trevor actually sounded impressed when I told him our scores. Was that another warning sign? No, surely not…

And so, at 5:30 the next morning, we got up and donned the crappiest clothing we owned. Doubtless before long we'd be covered in mud from head to toe, and sweating like three fat swingers in a sauna. It was still dark outside, and we shivered as we climbed into Rusty for the hour-long drive to our new work place.

"Don't worry!" Roo said. She was surprisingly upbeat for that time of the morning. "We won't be doing this for long. Just think about *why* we're doing it. In a few weeks we could be starting off – to hike the Bibbulmun Track!"

Now, I was getting on really well with Roo at this point, and was starting to develop deep feelings for her. But I tell you what, she was absolutely crap at motivational speaking.

Lies That Trevor Told Us

These lies were numerous, and included the following:

"I'll pay for your Blue Card exams,"

and "I'll pay for your petrol,"

and "I'll pay you."

Trevor did none of these things.

He was a small, wiry man with a moustache any 70s porn star would have been proud of. He was spectacularly weedy for a landscaper, but he made up for his lack of physical presence with his personalities. All six of them.

On our first day he showed up around noon, by which point we'd given up standing around and had pitched in carrying wheelbarrows full of soil. Apparently Trevor liked to stage his site visits at random, so as to keep his work force on their toes. For this reason, they all hated him – and it might have had something to do with him being a rude, paranoid, obnoxious prick.

Although – was he paranoid? Because everyone really was out to get him.

On our second day he refused to speak to us, so we carried on doing what everyone else was doing.

On our third day, he cornered us by a cement mixer and demanded to know what we'd been saying about him.

"I know it's you three," he told us. "I've got ears all over this site!"

And presumably on a necklace somewhere, I thought.

On the fourth day he came to us and complained that we weren't working hard enough. He'd never seen us work; more to the point, he'd never seen any of his other workers work, and even we had seen precious little of that. I was starting to see the pattern – when Trevor showed up, a 'look busy' mentality electrified the site, and any lack of progress, complete with attendant belly-aching about our boss, was being laid firmly on our doorstep.

Presumably by the same assholes who spent all day complaining when they should have been shovelling.

Trevor told me that he didn't hire girls.

I told him he'd been perfectly aware he was hiring girls, and that both of them were working harder than any of the blokes on site.

Trevor said that, even if that was the case, he wasn't really happy about hiring *two* girls.

So Roo quit on the spot and went to sit in Rusty; later she went back to work at the Underground, cleaning the place from top to bottom every day.

I told Trevor he could give her pay to me, when payday came around.

Which it never did.

We quickly discovered that the vast majority of Trevor's workers were lazy, mean, back-stabbing idiots – but worst of all, they were incompetent.

The gardeners would complain at the pavers for driving brick trolleys through all the flowerbeds, ruining several days worth of planting; the pavers would go ape-shit at the gardeners for pushing muddy wheelbarrows full of mulch over their clean, freshly-laid patios. Nothing was done in the order it should have been, and overseeing all of it from a distance – badly – was Trevor. In our second week, he gave Gill and I a job levelling the driveways to a street full of houses. We had to make them flat and smooth, and on a precise slope so that when concreted, they would meet the edge of the garage slab. It was a ridiculous task, and we spent half a day on the first drive, getting it perfect at the top and smooth, but too low at the bottom, and vice-versa.

This was when we first met George. We'd already heard him; George was the resident bobcat (mini-digger) driver, and there was only one noise more noticeable on site than the roar of his engine; it was his chatter. George was the exception that proved the rule; an excessively friendly, larger-than-life character of aboriginal descent. He referred to himself in the third person whenever he was talking, which was pretty much the entire time. He moaned about the job and the boss, waffled on about his plans for the future – and when there was nothing else to talk about, he simply narrated his every move around the site, as though his internal monologue was spilling from his mouth with no attempt to regulate it.

"George is coming round the corner! George's bucket is very full this time!"

It made him very easy to like, although it was a nightmare to get any work done around him. Workers from all over the site were constantly shouting at George to come and do things for them. He typically sat there with his bobcat running, chattering away at someone who wasn't listening, until whoever wanted something doing actually came over to get him. Then he'd speed off quite cheerfully, achieve whatever task they required in almost no time at all, and find someone else to talk at.

After discovering that Gill and I both listened – and answered him back – he became our new best friend, and tried to help us with every job we were given.

Starting with the driveways.

George drove his bobcat right through the pile of sand we'd been painstakingly sculpting for the last four hours, up to the top of the garage slab. Then he put the machine in reverse, and pushed down with the digger bucket as he backed onto the road – result: instant, smooth, perfectly graded slope. Total time taken: eleven seconds.

"Holy crap! And Trevor asked us to do the other fifteen driveways in this street as well."

"No worries, George'll sort 'em out! Back in a tick."

And off he trundled, spinning into each driveway in turn and accomplishing in minutes what would have taken us most of the week.

We could see now why the rest of the workers overlooked George's idiosyncrasies – in the world of landscaping, George's control over his machine gave him God-like abilities.

It was like someone rocking up in Ancient Egypt to help them build the pyramids – with a tower crane.

We could also see now that Trevor, the cunning bastard, was stitching us up. Setting us an impossible task, presumably to give him an excuse to fire us. I can only guess that he was sick of me asking him for money every time he came to site – finally, after two weeks, being forced to choose between eviction and starvation made me bold. I *demanded* the money instead of asking for it, and Trevor got all nervous and started digging in his pockets. He surrendered enough grubby banknotes to cover almost half of what he owed us – for the first week – and as I walked away, shocked by the effectiveness of my tactics, the other workers began to circle Trevor like sharks. I guessed they were all in the same boat – but working cash-in-hand, which is illegal of course, is always a risky business.

You've got to take what you can get, sometimes.

And at least now we could pay our rent…

And then, in our hour of need, something came to us.

We were strolling through Northbridge, the clubbing district of Perth, after picking Roo up from the Underground, when we found it.

It was a wallet; an unassuming brown leather bill-fold, sitting on the road by the curb as though it was the most natural place in the world for a wallet to be.

Roo's eagle eyes picked it out of the background milieu of cigarette butts and McDonalds wrappers.

Nothing was parked in that space. The nearest cars were a good way down the street in either direction. Foot traffic was light too, but as any good wallet knows, if it lays in the street for long enough, it's bound to get picked up.

So I picked it up.

And opened it.

And inside was one-thousand, five-hundred dollars, in a mix of fifty and hundred-dollar notes. I'd never even seen a hundred-dollar note. I was quite surprised to find they were green.

"HO. LEE. SHIT," I said, as the others clustered round to see. "If we were the kind of people that would keep something like this, just imagine what we could do with that money!"

"We could eat!" Gill said immediately. I felt bad to have put her in this position, but the truth was we hadn't been eating much. Rationing had come into effect, on account of our dire financial situation.

"We could get pizza!" I enthused.

"We could leave here right now, and start the Bibbulmun Track," Roo said quietly.

Which was true.

In our hands we held limitless possibility. More than anything else, we held the power to escape. To set off on the next leg of our grand adventure, to see things and go places that few people had, or ever would. I'd slowly come around to the idea that this epic hike could be our crowning achievement in Western Australia. I mean, not many tourists even bother visiting Perth; I'd never met another soul who had done what we were planning on doing. Hell, I'd never met anyone who didn't think we were insane just for thinking about it.

One-thousand, five-hundred dollars.

"That is A LOT of pizza," I reminded the girls. "We *could* keep it. I seriously doubt there's a single person anywhere along this road, that would find something like this and not keep it."

"We're in Northbridge," Roo shrugged. "Everyone here at this time of night is out to get wasted."

"They'd do what they did to our shared wallet," Gill added. "Take the cash and ditch the wallet in a bin somewhere. This bloke… 'Akmed'… would have to replace his driver's license, all his bank and credit cards, everything."

"Just looking at it makes my stomach rumble," I admitted.

We gave it back, of course.

For a few minutes, walking across Northbridge, we felt like royalty. We could go anywhere, into any of the posh restaurants lining the café strip; we could eat expensive food, and drink real booze from a real pub; we could live, in short, like pretty much everyone around us was living.

Comfortably.

It was a pleasant fantasy.

Then we arrived at the police station and gave the desk-sergeant the shock of his life when we handed him a wallet filled with money.

"And you've giving this *back?*" he asked, sounding incredulous.

"Yeah, sure. Why not?"

"I've never had that before," he admitted. "Do you want to leave your contact details? In case there's a reward, or the owner wants to say thanks?"

"Yeah, sure. Why not?" I was stuck repeating myself. Perhaps it was the shock of being parted from fifteen-hundred bucks.

I scrawled my email address and phone number on a form for the cop to include with the wallet, and just like that it disappeared from our lives.

I'd like to say we got a reward, or even a thank-you from a grateful owner, but we didn't.

It just goes to show, having a fat wodge of cash doesn't necessarily turn someone into a nice person. And not everyone is as honest and as considerate as my two travelling companions were.

But I was glad they were. It was the right thing to do.

Even if it did cost us a shit-load of cash.

And so, the next morning, instead of quitting our jobs and running around the streets crying "FREEDOM!" – Roo returned to the Underground, to clean the fetid dorms and vomit-stricken toilets, and Gill and I headed back to shovel soil for a paranoid, schizophrenic, misogynist asshole.

It was enough to make anyone regret their honesty.

George Gets Pushy

It was around this time that Rusty developed a fault on his lights. It was called Gill leaving the damn things on all the time. It wasn't really her fault... no, sod that! It *was* her fault. Even though I denied it strenuously at the time, to avoid making her feel bad. It bloody well was your fault, Gill!

Because it was still dark when we left for the ridiculously long drive out to the job site, we needed the lights on; dawn would overtake us on the road each morning, and by the time we arrived at work we were bathed in full daylight. This made it hard to spot the lights being left on, and as we were always in a rush – and Rusty wasn't advanced enough to have any kind of alarm or signal – the lights, quite often, stayed on.

The result being, when it was time for everyone else to go home, it wasn't for us. Because we lived nearly fifty miles away, and our car was dead.

The first time it happened, Roo was still working with us. As the building site was on slight slope, we simply pointed Rusty's nose downhill, and Roo and I pushed him while Gill sat in to get him started. We were lucky enough, on that occasion, to have him belch a cloud of foul black smoke and shudder into life before we came to the perimeter wall – because that meant his brakes started working, too. That's always useful when you're pushing a car downhill towards a rather large brick wall.

We weren't always so lucky.

Several weeks later, after a long, trying day, we sagged into the car seats, worn out in body and spirit. Then Gill summoned up the energy to put the key in and turn it.

'CLICK'.

And nothing.

Ohhh... crap.

Gill reached up and flicked off the headlights – sadly about ten hours too late.

As usual, we were the last vehicle in the car park. Not that any of the other workers cared enough about us to help, even if they'd been there to ask.

I sighed, climbed wearily from the van, and assumed pushing position. Gill opened her door and took her own stance, one hand on the wheel – we were so used to this, it barely required communication.

"Go," Gill said, and we both leant our bodyweight forward, pitting ourselves against Rusty's steel-framed inertia. With three warm bodies, this was difficult, but doable. With just the two of us, uphill, it was borderline impossible. Inch by foot we forced the ungainly vehicle out through the car park entrance, and turned him so he faced down the slope. Gill climbed in, and got ready.

"Ready!"

And off I pushed. Downhill, faster and… not faster. Slower, in fact. Thick mud sucked at Rusty's tyres, fighting me for his momentum. I wheezed and panted, throwing all my effort into moving the van, but Rusty plodded on. Gill made a few useless attempts at starting him – a few clicks and a lurch – and then we were finished. Facing the wall.

We were struggling with the impossible task of pushing him back up the hill – backwards – when George the bobcat driver wandered up.

He came to help straight away, monologuing about his reasons for still being here – most of which boiled down to him spending so much time talking he hadn't finished his day's work yet. Unbelievably, we'd pushed Rusty almost halfway back up the hill before he thought to ask what the problem was.

"Flat battery," I told him, and explained the difficulties with push-starting him over muddy ground.

I should have known that such a helpful chap would have a solution.

And I could have guessed I wouldn't like it.

"No worries! George can sort it out. I'll give you a push with the bobcat."

"Eh? How… um, how?"

"I'll just use the bucket, eh."

Gill and I exchanged glances. I could see she was thinking the same thing as me: *Is this guy a fucking lunatic?*

But you know what? It didn't matter. We weren't getting home without him. It was an hour's drive, for gawd's sake. There was no way in hell we were walking.

"Ah, okay George," I said. "We'll just sit inside, then?"

"Yeah, no worries! Bobcat'll sort it out. Too easy!"

It was a tense few minutes, as we waited for George to get back to his beloved bobcat. Gill went over and over the procedure for push-starting Rusty. It was something we'd done many, many times already... but never whilst being pushed by an earthmover. We had no idea what George had planned, but I was hoping I'd be able to convince him to try something less extreme. Like towing us back to the top of the hill, and then lending us a shoulder to help push Rusty back down?

Surely that was the wisest course of action. I resolved to tell George exactly this.

We heard him coming long before we could see him. The bobcat's engine roared loud and throaty, as it skidded around the corner. George must have decided that taking a run-up was the best course of action, as he wasn't slowing at all as he approached us.

"SHIT! Gill! He's going to ram us!"

"I know! What do we do?"

"Fuck knows!"

George was on the approach, barrelling towards us up the incline. I braced for impact, pressing so hard against Rusty's floor panel that I was half afraid I'd put my feet through it. We both clung to the handbrake lever, as though it offered some kind of magical protection against onrushing maniacs.

The bobcat bucket was lowering as it came. I'd seen bad guys dispatched this way at the end of action movies.

But George, never subtle, was still a master of his tools. He dropped the throttle a fraction as he came into contact, and the tiny lull in speed, coupled with the uphill gradient, caused the bucket to clang hard into Rusty's front bumper – without crushing right through it and decapitating his occupants.

I was quite glad of that.

That impressive forward momentum now transferred to Rusty – at least, once Gill had unclenched her hand long enough to release the hand brake – and Rusty lurched into sudden, violent, motion.

Backwards.

It was a little unnerving, to say the least. The bobcat steamed forwards, shoving Rusty along at break-neck speed. Gill, her eyes the size of dinner plates, was steering frantically with her gaze fixed on the rear-view mirror.

"Pop the clutch!" I yelled at her.

"What?"

"Just start the frigging car!"

"Oh, right!"

Rusty lurched as Gill slammed him into reverse gear, and our speed definitely slowed – but nothing else happened. Gill's leg was going up and down, pumping like mad, while she turned the key hard enough to break it.

Nothing.

We slowed to a crawl, then stopped, having reached the crest of the hill again. George was winking at me in a most unnerving way from above the digger bucket – he wore a grin that seemed to say 'not bad – let's give her one more go…'

I shuddered at the thought.

But Rusty was going nowhere.

"No worries, George will sort it," he said. "What we'll do is swap out the batteries. Put the bobcat battery in this – that'll get her going!"

I collected my thoughts. I'd just won a ten-minute argument against repeating the process we'd just been through – downhill – "only faster!" By now I was having serious doubts that any amount of molestation would convince Rusty to start, and this seemed like a particularly stupid way to die. Even for me.

This next plan, though? Did it have merit? Not for the first time (and certainly not for the last), I wished I had any kind of mechanical knowledge at all.

"If we start it, won't it stop when we take the battery out?" Gill asked. "How do we swap the batteries back?"

"Nah, she'll be right," said George.

"But George… how do we swap the batteries back?"

"Just keep her running, keep your foot down."

"Can you take the battery out like that? Won't you get electrocuted?"

"Nah. No worries!"

That seemed to settle it. We tipped the driver's chair forwards to access the engine bay, realising at that point that to keep Rusty running at the same time as having access to the battery compartment, one of us would have to sit in the passenger seat and keep a foot on the accelerator from the opposite side of the van.

Difficult. But not impossible.

The whole scheme though? That seemed impossible. Just a bit.

Especially when George beckoned us over to look at his battery.

Bobcats are quite a mean piece of kit, so it was no surprise to find it was equipped with a battery the size of a bar fridge.

"She's a beauty, eh!" he enthused.

But one of those embarrassingly over-sized beauties that didn't really *fit in*.

"Thanks anyway, George."

"No worries! Guess we'll have to jump-start her after all, eh."

"But we don't have any leads. Or we'd have tried that first, remember?"

"No problem! George can sort it out. There's brick ties everywhere. I'll just grab a couple of those, and off we go."

"Brick ties? You mean those bits of wire?"

"Yeah, too easy! There's some."

And he picked out of the dust a pair of steel wires, slightly thicker than coat hangers, and started to untwist them for added length.

"Um, George, I don't think that'll work mate."

"No, George can sort it out! Bring the van closer, so I can reach the bobcat."

And this was where we felt we had to pull the plug. Before a friendly, somewhat eccentric bloke gave himself a lethal electric shock on our behalf. It just wasn't worth it.

I let Gill talk George down this time, as the continued failure of his schemes seemed to be spurring him on to come up with even crazier ones.

We stumbled through the front door, exhausted, more than two hours later.

Roo, bless her, had been worried sick.

Telling her the story was almost as traumatic as living through it.

Finally, George had agreed to call the RAC. He'd told us he was a 'platinum member', and that they'd be obliged to fix our vehicle just because he was with us.

That had sounded suspiciously like a load of bollocks – and had turned out to be just that. But George, in utterly inimitable style, had simply *talked* his way around it. He hadn't convinced the RAC man he was a platinum member – probably because the RAC man knew that platinum membership didn't exist. George's card was silver – and it had expired. He also hadn't convinced the bloke that Rusty was his van – that he'd bought him (in spite of the acid-trip exterior) to ferry his labourers to work. Not by a long shot. But he stuck to his story – and repeated it – and repeated it… and in the end, he talked so much, and for so long, that he wore the guy down. After listening to George's bullshit for three quarters of an hour straight, the poor RAC bloke decided discretion was the better part of valour. Or something like that. He'd stuck his machine onto Rusty, super-fried his battery, started him up – and then fled.

Against all the odds, George had, in fact, sorted it out.

And that was when we'd fled, too.

A few weeks later, we fled Trevor's employ completely. We now had just enough time to complete the Bibbulmun Track – if we really pushed it – and still get over east to meet Mum.

Trevor owed us nearly a month's wages by this point, so I had to get tough; I called him, and threatened to report his reliance on illegal labour to the Australian Taxation Office if he didn't cough up some dough.

This had the desired effect; at our last meeting, he gave Gill and I fifteen-hundred dollars *each*.

He promised to pay the rest of what he owed us by bank transfer the following week.

He never did, of course, but we knew that would happen.

To be honest, we were so glad to be rid of him that even hiking a thousand kilometres sounded like a relief.

"I need to lay down," I said to Roo after making the phone call.

"Don't worry, there'll be plenty of time to rest on the Bibbulmun Track," she said.

From this brief exchange, I got the impression that our concepts of 'rest' were somewhat different.

Be Prepared

Leaving Trevor's employ had a galvanising effect on us.

The clock was now ticking – with no more money coming in, we had to get ready and get gone before our next rent cheque was due.

Being deliciously, gloriously unemployed again after weeks of tough, thankless slog was such liberating experience it more than compensated for any misgivings we had. Amazingly, I'd come to *fantasise* about having nothing to do all day but walk – all three of us were unerringly positive about our chances of success, and our gear-shopping trips had an air of celebration about them.

Going from op shop to op shop, we quickly amassed a variety of technical 'outdoors' clothing. I have a theory about this: because that stuff is so utterly, ridiculously, unnecessarily expensive, most people who buy it do so purely for that reason. Rather than putting the gear to its intended use in the jungles, deserts and mountains of this planet, they go shopping in it – only to realise, shortly after buying it, that it doesn't look nearly as good as a nice pair of jeans and a t-shirt. So it sits in the back of the wardrobe for a year, then goes to the op shop the next time they have a clear out.

Honestly – there are more pairs of moisture-wicking quick-drying insect repellent SPF 30+ breathable membrane 'WindBreaker™' technical trekking trousers sitting in charity shops than there are wrapped around hiker's arses the world over.

"Wow! These fit great, and I'm pretty sure they're waterproof," Roo said, holding up some grey hiking trousers. They still had the Nike shop tags hanging off them.

"They're like the plastic-y part of tracksuit bottoms, but without the lining. What else can they be?"

Sold! For $8.

We made one trip to a branded outdoor clothing supplier, where Gill and Roo bought hiking boots. While they were being fitted, I wandered around the store, boggling at the prices of things as simple as a plastic knife-and-fork set.

Gill came up to me with her trademark mischievous grin. "Tony, Tony! Look!"

And she held up a tin kettle, of the whistling, stove-top variety. She pressed a button with her thumb, and the lid flapped open and closed like a mouth. "Listen!" she waggled the button in perfect lip-synch to her sotto-voice; "Oh *myyy*, darling, do behaaaaave yourself!"

"Eh?"

"Don't you get it? Tony, it's a *camp kettle!*"

"Oh. My God. That's it – we're leaving."

"No, wait! Don't you want to see my impression of a 'camp stove'?"

Next it was my turn. I'd been putting off buying boots, as the cheapest pair I'd seen so far was $250. And they say never to buy the cheapest of anything – especially when you're going to depend on them for two months straight.

Amidst reminders that if I didn't buy some soon, I'd be doing the hike in flip-flops, I entered a store that sold work wear to the average Aussie tradesman. This was my last chance to find a pair of reasonably priced boots, and there were plenty to choose from. With or without steel reinforcement.

"A size bigger?" I requested of the shop assistant. I'd read somewhere that wearing two pairs of thick socks was the most effective way to prevent blisters, and I was keen to size my boots accordingly.

She brought a huge yellow box out to me and answered my questions as I tried on its contents.

"Of course they're waterproof," she said at last, "they're leather."

Well then. That seemed to end the debate.

I left that shop $120 poorer, yet celebrating my win. I'd scored a moral victory against the purveyors of ridiculously over-priced hiking gear.

So what if it meant I'd be hiking in work boots?

With that done, we were one-third of the way through our list of essential pre-hike missions. The two remaining ones were to pack (which was bound to be easy, so we left that until last), and to arrange our free 'Organisational Meeting' with the Bibbulmun Track Foundation. We were lucky again; they had an appointment open for us, at whatever time suited us. Because apparently "not many people walk the Track at this time of year…"

Well, that just *had* to be good news. Didn't it? No crowds on the path, no jostling for space in the shelters.

Jim, the veteran hiker assigned to guide us through the planning process, was in complete agreement. "It's lovely to walk at this time of year," he told us. "It makes everything a bit different. It's good to have a challenge."

This, coming from a man who'd completed the hike himself more than a dozen times. "But never in winter," he explained, "so I'll be interested to find out how you get on."

His optimism was infectious, so we sort of glossed over what a less positive person might have called 'the downsides'.

"I think it's a wonderful idea that you're all doing this together," said Jim.

"Yeah, we all get along well enough," Gill said.

"And if not, I just overrule everyone else and we do what I say!" I added.

"No we don't," said Gill. "Not *ever*."

"Riiight," said Jim, "moving on, then. Let's talk about food. You'll each be carrying enough for eight days, because that's the longest time between resupply opportunities. This time of year there'll be plenty of rain water in the tanks, so you should be able to fill up your water bottles at each shelter. So long as you don't mind a few wrigglers!"

"Wrigglers?"

"Mosquito larvae. They're in all the tanks, but if it bothers you, you can take a water filter with you to screen them out."

"Nah," I said. "More protein!"

I could see Gill making a note on the back of her diary. I suspected it read something like: '1) BUY A FUCKING WATER FILTER!'

Which of course we didn't.

Jim continued; "The best thing you can do is to take ready-made, dehydrated meals. They sell them in all the camping shops."

"Yes, we saw those, but they're a bit out of our budget," I confessed.

"Yeah, it's expensive stuff! A good alternative is to dehydrate your own food. My wife usually does mine. It takes several weeks to make enough, but there's a machine you can buy to speed up the process. It is an investment, but well worth it."

I held my tongue. We'd made a decision, before coming in, to avoid mentioning that almost all our gear so far had been acquired second hand, from charity shops. This seemed like a suitable moment to unburden myself, but I held firm against the temptation.

"Your food is the single most important thing to consider," Jim explained, "it's vitally important that you eat as balanced a diet as possible. You'll be working your bodies hard, and you have to have the right mix of nutrients to keep going."

"Hm... yes, I can see what you mean..."

"So, are you going to consider dehydrating your food?"

"No. We've bought about fifty packets of instant noodles."

"Oh."

I thought I'd finally managed to faze him – which is probably not the best thing to be shooting for in a meeting like this, but it did have a certain appeal. Horrify the experts with our slapdash approach, and do it anyway – thereby proving, beyond a shadow of a doubt, that we can accomplish anything!

Well, so long as we accomplished it.

Otherwise, we'd look like... well, exactly what we were. A bunch of idiots.

"So you're going the whole way, and you've got how many days?"

"Two months. Sixty days."

"That's pretty quick for your first time, but it is possible. You'll have to double-hut it a few times – you know, walk two sections in one day. That could be twenty-five to thirty kilometres on those days. Think you can manage that?"

I spoke for all of us. "We'll try."

"Okay," said Jim, "so let's talk about your preparations. Are you doing much walking at the moment?"

"Ah... no. Not really."

"Any of you?"

There was a consensus of shrugs and head-shakes as he glanced around the group.

"Okay. I usually advise people to do a few k's every day for the first week, and see how you feel. Then you can up it to 10k's, as often as you can over the next couple of weeks. And then start loading up your rucksacks, trying to walk with a little more weight each time."

I think he could tell by the slight shifting in our seats that he wasn't really selling this idea to us.

"Okay. So when are you actually setting off?"

The three of us looked at each other.

"Tomorrow," Roo said.

"Ah."

"But we're quite fit," she continued.

"And we'll get fitter as we walk," I added.

"Yes…" Jim's reply seemed to have lost some of its conviction.

"Don't worry about us," I said to him, "we'll manage."

At this point Jim excused himself for a moment. I like to think he walked out of the office onto some sort of balcony, shook his fist at the sky and called out, "Why God, WHYYYYYYYYY?"

More realistically, he was putting in a call to the state Fire and Rescue Service, telling them they'd most likely be needed in the next couple of days.

And probably starting a betting pool on how long we'd last on his way back through the office.

But the meeting wasn't a total waste of time.

For starters, we met Jim – who was a veritable mine of information, all of which will be very useful the next time we decide to walk the Track.

I'd also like to point out that he was absolutely right, in every piece of advice he gave us. He was, in fact, a *bone fide* expert.

The fact that we completely ignored it all says more about us than it does about him. Actually, it says everything about us; criminally unprepared, fiendishly overconfident, and blissfully ignorant of both inadequacies. Ha! Story of my life. Anyway, I think it's safe to say that the world of long distance hiking had a new lowest standard of competitor.

Jim also sold us two small guidebooks, which he considered essential. We grudgingly forked out $16 for the pair of them, more to make him feel better than for anything else. As far as we knew, the track was signposted; surely we just had to follow the yellow triangles, and we'd get there in the end, right?

Wrong.

Those two books turned out to be every bit as essential as he suggested. They actually saved our lives on several occasions, and kept our sanity together throughout the entire trip. The mere thought of doing the Track without those guide books makes me go cold all over. It almost makes me wonder what difference dehydrated food would have made…

Ah well! We'll never know. Because it was far too late for that; we'd done our shopping, and spent the rest of the evening separating it out into our backpacks.

We'd bought chocolate, fruit, corn flakes, bread and nuts, tuna and pasta, jam and butter, and noodles, noodles, noodles.

We planned out three meals a day, for eight whole days. We matched up our supplies to this before dividing them up to carry, and put another eight days worth into a pair of plastic crates. These would be delivered to us by a friend of Roo's, at the first place the Track crossed a road – and hopefully before the stuff we had with us ran out.

At last, the packing was done.

My rucksack positively bulged. I'd had to strap the tent to the bottom of it, as there was no way it'd fit inside. "I wonder how heavy it is," I mused.

I tried to lift it.

And failed.

"It's stuck to the frigging floor!" I moaned.

But it wasn't. It was just very, very heavy.

"I can almost lift mine," Roo said. Helpfully.

Gill squatted down and tensed her whole body, as though she was struggling to squeeze out a long-overdue turd. Her face went red with the effort, but hugging her rucksack with both knees and both arms, she hefted it a few scant centimetres off the floor. Then she collapsed against it, breathing heavily.

"This isn't going to work," I said.

"No shit," said Roo.

"Either we get dramatically stronger overnight – or we're going to have to do a little repacking…"

First Steps

The following morning, bleary-eyed from lack of sleep, we dropped Rusty off with Roo's family and caught a lift with Sonja up to the start of the track.

It was a hot day, and we sweated and swore as we manhandled our ridiculous rucksacks into a Sonja's beloved Morris Minor 1000.

Three passengers was quite a squeeze for the antique car, even before considering that our luggage outweighed us… and the windows didn't open.

The sun beat down, raising the temperature in the back of the Morris from 'uncomfortable' to 'molten lava'. Sweat dripped off Roo's forehead, onto mine (as we were quite oddly positioned), and we sweltered and steamed all the way down the freeway from Perth to Kalamunda – making the trip in exactly the same length of time as it takes to roast three large turkeys.

Popping like corks from the car, we hauled out our rucksacks and dragged them into the shade of a small log pagoda. This was the Northern Terminus of The Bibbulmun Track, which sounded rather grand for a few planks of wood with a map nailed to them. But it kept the harsh midday sun at bay, as we psyched ourselves up for our biggest challenge so far: putting on our backpacks!

It took all three of us in careful coordination to hoist one bag up and attach it to its target. By the time we'd done this three times, we were already knackered. My back was aching, and I was finding it difficult to take a full breath. Gill was panting and staring at the ground, and Roo had propped herself upright against the Northern Terminus, using it to take some of the load off while she hauled futilely on the various straps and buckles. It was a brave effort, but the reality of the situation was that no amount of rucksack adjustment would stop the things weighing well over twenty-five kilos apiece.

But task one was complete! All three of us were standing, mostly upright, and almost all under our own power. We'd done it! Surely that meant the hardest part was behind us.

All we had to do now was maintain this position whilst walking forwards for the next two months…

Beyond our miniscule shelter, the sun still blazed. The first stand of trees, our entry point into the vast jarrah forest that would dominate the northern section of the track, shimmered in the heat-haze.

I remember thinking, what a beautiful day for a walk!

And for the next five minutes, it was.

As we hugged Sonja and said our goodbyes, the clouds rolled in. Then with a flash and a rumble, they split open and pissed all over us. By the time we'd finished fiddling with our packs, the rain outside the shelter was so intense it was making it hard to see the trees. The sound of it on the tin roof was deafening. Sonja had to shout as she explained she wouldn't be leaving – if we changed our minds about the whole endeavour, she'd be here to take us back. She had no choice; the sudden downpour was too heavy for the tiny windscreen wipers of her Morris. She couldn't drive home.

But we were not deterred.

Well, some of us were deterred, but were dragged along anyway by those less deterred.

"Should we wait for it to go off a bit?" I suggested.

"Nah, we're all wearing waterproofs!" came the reply.

So we marched off, into the deluge.

Instantly, we were soaked.

At first, we could cope with it. Despite the crippling weight on our backs, we were cautiously optimistic about our chances. After all, how bad can a bit of rain really be?

An hour or so later, we'd realised the truth about 'waterproof' gear. Which is that the vast majority of it isn't.

And the rest of it might as well not be.

Because, when it rains heavily enough, water forces its way into anything. When it meets an impermeable something, it simply finds another route. Waterproof shoes lose their appeal as soon as the rain soaks through to your socks, wicks down to your feet, and turns them into a pair of shoe-shaped swimming pools. Jackets ride up, exposing your soft undergarments, which absorb enough water in a few seconds to make it feel like you've peed your pants. And the bit that stays waterproof? The torso, heavily protected by all that costly Gore-Tex™? Well, when you're hiking at speed through difficult terrain whilst carrying something the size and weight of a dead rhino on your back… let's just say, what the rain doesn't do, the sweat does in spades. Only it's smellier.

After a few more hours, we were all getting a bad case of the 'are-we-nearly-there-yets'. It was at this point, consulting our miniature guide book for the first time, that we realised a) our miniature guidebook was ruined, and b) we *were* nearly there – so long as the halfway point counted as 'there'.

We stopped for a soggy sandwich, and what little conversation there was revolved around how to make our gear more waterproof.

Personally I was hoping we'd be talking about going home. I mean, this was ridiculous, right? This rain was too much! It's one thing to nip out to the shops and get a bit wet crossing the car park, but this was something else. We had nowhere to go and nowhere to hide. We were walking through something approaching a biblical flood, for no greater purpose than to carry on walking. We were headed to the middle of nowhere, with no plan more gratifying than to repeat the process the next day – and no reward stronger than a bowl of instant noodles at the end of it.

And yet, with the sandwiches consumed, we struggled back into our bags and carried on. Walking.

There seemed to be a lot of walking on this… walk.

Darkness overtook us as we struggled on towards our destination. Night-time in the forest comes swiftly, and results in much blundering into stupidly-positioned trees. We'd hoped and planned to arrive before dark, but we learnt several important lessons that evening. One was that planning, however detailed it may be, is utterly useless if you know nothing at all about the trip you are planning. Likewise, hope is about as much use as a non-waterproof torch buried at the bottom of a soaking rucksack. Or three such torches, in fact.

Finally, just as we began to panic, a tiny pinpoint of light appeared through the forest ahead. It was in the direction we were heading in, which comforted us; we hadn't been wandering lost for hours, as we'd imagined. It had just taken us a bloody sight longer to reach the campsite than we expected. Gratefully we waddled towards the light, finding its glare outlined a small, three-sided wooden hut – not unlike the shelter we'd set off from. Kind of like a medieval bus stop. A tin roof and walls of rough planks, and a raised platform of the same for us to sleep on – this was our lodgings for the night. And the night after that. And… well, it'd be a while before I'd be seeing a double bed again, that's for sure.

We crawled into the shelter, made somehow inviting by the torchlight of a hiker who was already tucked up in her sleeping bag. We shed our wet outer layers, keeping our wet underwear on because we didn't have much choice. All we had to do was find our stove, set it up, find our food, prepare and cook a meal, eat it, dig out all our sleeping bags and mats and arrange them, hang up our wet clothes somewhere, and then we could do the one thing we'd all wanted to do since about ten minutes into the walk: crawl into bed and go to sleep.

But all that had to wait. For now it was freezing cold, and we were mostly naked. I squeezed my undies against myself to wring the worst of the water out of them, and fumbled around inside my backpack for my tights.

What?

Don't judge me! I acquired my gear exclusively from charity shops, remember. There wasn't always much choice in the thermal base-layer department. Not in the men's section, anyway. So... I bought leggings. Beige ones. Size 16, as I recall. They were quite comfy.

It took considerably longer to cook the noodles than to eat them. I was left thinking that a second portion of about the same size would have been nice.

And a steak.

But the rest of the noodles would be needed for the rest of the week. As for steak... well, I could always kill and skin a kangaroo? Except that most of them were substantially bigger than me, and I was armed only with a plastic spork.

Steak looked about as likely as duck á l'orange, which is to say, not at all.

Part way through our list of chores, we received our final lesson for the night, from the solitary hiker sharing our hut.

"You should try to arrive before dark," she said, "it's not safe to walk at night."

This was followed by an apology – then her torch was switched off to save the batteries, plunging the hut into blackness.

To be perfectly honest, I was pretty sick of hiking.

Staying On Track

We woke to the sound of rain.

Heavy rain, pummelling the wooden roof of the shelter, filling the view through the gap where a front wall would have been in a house.

"Holy shit, that looks miserable," was the first thing I said.

"Maybe it'll stop by the time we're ready to leave?" Gill suggested. "Surely it can't keep on like this!"

She was wrong, of course.

It rained almost without pause for the next two weeks straight.

Getting out of bed – when bed has been a sleeping bag on a wooden plank – is probably the second most miserable experience I encountered on the Track.

Every morning I awoke feeling as stiff as the board I was laying on, muscles screaming from a day of serious abuse followed by a night of extreme discomfort.

I felt broken as I struggled to sit, and instantly regretted the decision to stand – because this meant getting out of my sleeping bag, and the world outside of my sleeping bag was freezing cold, depressingly grey and unfairly moist.

The first most miserable experience was the one that came next: putting on the cold, sopping wet clothes from the day before. They'd been hung up in the shelter overnight, but had less chance of achieving dryness than an insurance commercial has of making you buy insurance. The feeling of soaking, frigid material pulled on over cold bare skin is something I'll never forget. Especially when it reached the more tender parts of my anatomy. There was a chorus of shrieks and wails as we variously dressed ourselves, followed by a frenzy of activity as we all rushed around doing anything we could think of to take our minds off the disgusting, clingy sensation of wet technical-wear.

Breakfast was next, and was devoured with a desperation that belied its modest components; corn flakes from a zip-lock bag we each carried, and powdered milk from another. Our rucksacks were festooned with zip-lock bags, and they were one of the few bits of equipment that actually did what we expected of them. We quickly learned to divide our foodstuffs into three plastic shopping bags, each corresponding with one meal, so that when we stopped for lunch, but the rain chose to carry on, we could locate everything we needed to eat in one quick move.

And then it was time to head off, into the deluge.

The northern-most section of the Bibbulmun Track takes walkers "through towering karri and tingle forests, down mist shrouded valleys, over giant granite boulders," sayeth the guide. It sounds so beautiful.

I wish I could've seen it. The relentless ferocity of the weather reduced visibility to a tiny patch of saturated foliage about the size of the eye-slit I left in my hood. All three of us squelched along in disbelief that this much water even existed in the world. For us to get all of it, right through our rain jackets, seemed unfairly generous when so much of the world is in need.

Regularly as I walked, I cursed the woman who'd told me my boots were waterproof. They'd lasted about twenty minutes.

Wet feet, however, were a comparatively minor inconvenience.

How does that expression go? Something like "Does the Pope shit in the woods?"

Well, honestly I don't know.

But in case you've ever wondered, a Tony most definitely does.

It's not like I had much choice!

And for anyone that wants to know, a human poo, passed naturally in the wild, curls around and around in one long, delicate spiral – looking rather like a walnut whip, when it's finished.

For anyone that doesn't want to know, you should probably avoid reading the above paragraph.

Bodily functions were a frustratingly regular occurrence on the Track. They took so much time and effort to perform, I'd have gladly gone without, were it possible – but no. Inevitably, every couple of hours, one of us would utter the dreaded phrase; "Uh, sorry guys, but…"

And so it would begin. First, we had to stop. And stop in someplace suitable. And stop without falling over, which was particularly difficult, as we were generally relying on our forward momentum to keep us upright.

Next it required the Removal Of Backpacks. This was a team manoeuver worthy of recognition by the Arts Council; it evolved daily, and by the end of our first week had been refined into a form so beautifully efficient that it rivalled ballet.

Say for example, Roo had to go. (She tried hard not to, bless her – displaying camel-like qualities of water retention – but in the end it was unavoidable.) Upon hearing the dreaded words, I would take up position behind her and clamp my arms around her rucksack. Feeling me firmly attached, she would then unfasten her waist-belt and shrug her way out of the shoulder straps, leaving me supporting the thing. Then she'd spin around, grab a hold herself, and between us we'd lower the bag to the ground. I would be next; Roo would take the weight of my pack momentarily, while I slipped out to help her; and then there would be two bags on the ground. At this point, if she was desperate, Roo would vanish into the bushes, while I relieved Gill of her bag; it was a necessary evil, as standing around fully-laden for the time it took one of us to pee, simply wasn't an option. By the time Gill had stretched and managed to fill her lungs to capacity once or twice, Roo would be back – and the whole process would begin again, only in reverse.

Now, there were exceptions to this procession of events. Occasionally – and I stress, occasionally – I would feel strong enough to attempt to pee standing up – with my backpack still in place. This was dangerous in the extreme, as falling flat on my face in a puddle of my own piss was not only undignified, it could also be quite damaging; sort of like lying in a puddle of piss while someone drops a piano on you.

Washing clothes was also not an option, so anything I did choose to lay in was going to be keeping me company for quite some time.

But the other deviation from the standard pattern for toilet breaks came not as a result of strength, but of weakness. Because after spending most of the day hiking up mountains with half a sperm whale on your back, your legs tended to get a little… trembly. It made crouching somewhere between difficult and impossible.

So more often than not, on the last few toilet stops of the day, I would have to follow Roo into the bushes – and hold her up by the shoulders while she peed.

That, ladies and gentlemen, is the kind of sacrifice you make for love.

I can only thank God that Gill, with her shorter stature and thighs built up by pushing Trevor's wheelbarrows, never required this kind of assistance.

The other major reason for stopping was more appealing; it was the thing we looked forward to all day, every day. And for most of the night too.

It was food.

We'd planned our first two weeks of meals very carefully before setting out, but to keep our spirits up – and our bodies alive – we scheduled an extra stop mid-morning, which came to be known as 'Chocolate o'clock'.

We'd packed one chocolate bar per-person, per-day – no more, because we couldn't take the extra weight, and no less – because honestly, if any of us had to face a day on the Track without chocolate, there was a good chance we'd have committed suicide.

Lunch was less exciting, but equally vital – and whoever said that hunger is the best seasoning, was bang on the money. We'd started out with a loaf of bread swinging comically from each of our rucksacks. Your average loaf gives you around twenty-odd slices – which meant three slices a day, for a week. If it was more than a week before we hit the next town, we'd have to resort to crackers. But three rounds of bread doesn't make a lot of sandwiches – especially when you're burning about 6,000 calories a day. We tried ways of making them last longer – like breathing between mouthfuls – but the reality of the situation was that by 1pm we were absolutely ravenous. In the end we developed a desperate way of making it feel like we were eating more food – we invented the 'open-topped' sandwich, more commonly known as a single piece of bread with filling on top! This cunning ploy allowed us to feel like we were eating three separate sandwiches, each covered with jam or cheese, which made lunch times a much more satisfying experience.

It didn't actually change what we were eating though, with the result that, over the course of the first couple of weeks, we all shrank dramatically.

Gill got skinny.

Roo became skeletal.

And I discovered my hip bones, and ribs, and the nobbly-bits of my spine.

All of which made sleeping on a plank even more enjoyable…

Oh yes! Those first two weeks. They were a killer.

Then, one morning, I woke feeling grumpier than usual. I couldn't quite figure out why, until…

"Happy Birthday!" the girls chorused as they sat up.

Ah yes, that was it.

"You owe me a donut," I growled at them.

The girls had outdone themselves, though. Somehow, without me noticing, they had smuggled an extra item with them all the way from Perth: a bag of marshmallows!

That evening we clustered around our miniature camping stove, toasting marshmallows on sticks to the amusement of a pair of elderly ladies who were also in the hut.

They were doing an overnight hike, and when Gill stuck a match in the top of a marshmallow and gave it to me as a surrogate birthday cake they came over and offered us something better. Unbelievably, it was a tiny birthday candle! They were travelling with a whole packet of them in lieu of proper candles. This was the kind of revolutionary idea we'd probably had learned from Jim, if we'd had time.

With the lit candle in the top, the marshmallow made an admirable imitation of a cake – so as the two octogenarian women sang Happy Birthday to me, I blew it out and made a wish. Actually I made two; *Please, God,* I thought, *'let me be in a better place this time next year. Or tomorrow morning, ideally. And more than anything, tonight let me sleep…'*

The marshmallow itself I decided to save for breakfast.

I slept remarkably well that night.

In the morning I was still in the same place – but the sun was shining! It was a phenomenon I thought I'd never see again. And deep down, I knew that something else had changed too.

It was the marshmallow.

I'd placed it next to my tiny travel pillow as I slept; mere inches from my nostrils, which were the only part of me that dared protrude from the sleeping bag.

Now, weak sunlight revealed the damage; my marshmallow was half gone, having been thoroughly enjoyed in the middle of the night by some kind of rodent. I could only be grateful that the tip of my nose hadn't shared the same fate.

I picked it up by the (uneaten) candle, and stared at it in disbelief.

"The *bastards*," I moaned, "they ate my birthday marshmallow!"

"Aw, I'm sorry love," Roo said, patting my arm in sympathy. "Next year we'll try and get you a proper donut."

Supply and Demand

As we approached the first town we'd seen since leaving Perth, we realised something; it wasn't just the promise of good food and a real bed that was putting an extra spring in our step. Nor was it a sudden dramatic increase in strength and fitness, much as we may have wished otherwise. No, what we realised is this: being able to lift our own rucksacks meant that we were dangerously short of food. We were now eating almost double our starting amount at every meal, and were constantly hungry in between times.

Everything had gone well with our first re-supply; eight days and 120km into our journey we'd reached the first point where the Bibbulmun Track was accessible by road. We'd eaten every tuna-tin and pretzel we'd brought, and had come dangerously close to eating Gill – but cannibalism had been staved off by the timely arrival of Roo's friend in a car full of food.

Now, as we hiked into the small mining town of Collie, a suspicious lightness to our rucksacks told us we'd made it just in time.

We trudged wearily down the main street and stopped at the first hotel we came across. This was not a glowing endorsement of our decision making paradigm; it was the only hotel in town. It was overpriced and it was shabby as hell – and we didn't give a shit.

We checked in and were delighted to find that the rooms had heating. In fact we very nearly collapsed right then and there – but somehow we dragged ourselves back out to complete our chores.

"I think we should post the tent home," Roo said. "The shelters have always been empty and we'll never use it – and it must be seriously heavy."

"It is," I agreed. "I'm going to get rid of my fire-stick too. I'm always far to knackered to practice with it. I can't believe I was dumb enough to bring it, to be honest."

We bagged up the items we were each sending back to Perth, and bought a giant cardboard box from the post office.

Gill unburdened herself of a pair of fire-twirling poi, a bottle of face-wash and the few sticks of make-up she'd permitted herself.

"What are you sending home?" I asked Roo.

"My so-called waterproof pants," she said vehemently. "I sweat so much wearing them that the inside gets wetter than the outside!"

"Ha! Great. Score one more for the technical gear. Anything else?"

"Just these…" she pulled out a deck of cards from her bag. And another one. And then a third.

"What the hell are you doing with *three* packs of cards?"

"I thought maybe we'd meet a big group of people, and they'd all want to play."

"But Roo – *none of us can even play cards!*"

"I know. That's why I brought these."

And she pulled out a deck of Uno cards.

"You are fucking kidding me."

The pharmacy was the next stop. Both Roo and Gill were suffering terribly with blisters – blisters on top of blisters in fact, so many that our limited first-aid kit hadn't been able to keep up.

Bursting them had become our nightly social activity.

Next we headed to the supermarket, and spent an hour agonizing over all the delicious foodstuffs on offer – not one of which we could take with us. In the end we bought identical supplies to the ones we'd started out with – only substantially more of them. The next hour was spent sitting on a bench outside the supermarket, opening every packet, box and tin, and repacking their contents in more appropriate containers. Tuna we bought for protein and variety; it went into a zip-lock bag inside another zip-lock bag, a lesson we'd learnt the hard way when our first meal of tuna had erupted all over Gill's backpack. We'd have lost the lot – except we were so damn hungry, we scooped it out and ate it anyway! Gill's backpack, unfortunately, retained a certain *ambiance* after this incident.

Then, when everything that had to be done was done, we could finally relax. Back to the hotel, where we peeled off clothing thick with mud, disturbingly moist and reeking of sweat. We piled them in the furthest corner of the room while we took turns experiencing that ultimate luxury – a long, hot shower each – and then we forced ourselves back outside to find some dinner.

In our pyjamas.

Walking without the bags was a truly strange experience. We felt bouncy, lighter than air, as though we were strolling across the surface of the moon. It still hurt like buggery of course, because of the torment we'd been subjecting our bodies to over the last few weeks – but it was painful and easy, instead of painful and hard.

Sometimes you have to be grateful for the small things...

And what do you know? Right there, next to the take-away, was a bottle-o!

It was as though someone up there was smiling on us, rewarding all our efforts. We nipped in while waiting for our pizzas, and bought a cask of *goon* for $10.

This was going to be a night to remember!

We bounced home in much higher spirits, anticipating the joyous revelry to come. Climbing the stairs to our rooms was a massive effort, but what a reward was waiting! Warmth and food and soft, soft blankets...

None of which mattered, because I fell asleep on the floor.

In my pizza.

We never even opened the wine.

The next morning dawned on three equally horrible revelations.

The first was, quite obviously, that we had to leave. To pack our shit and hike out of that haven of comfort and luxury, and back onto the sodden forest trails.

The second was that, because we'd been too tired to do anything about them, our clothes were every bit as soaked and stinking as they'd been when we took them off the night before; we had no choice but to put them on, and walk off in them.

And the third, was that there were four litres of wine, sitting in a box right in front of us, and we were going to have to leave it all behind.

Unless...

And so it was that we hiked out of Collie with our water bottles full of sweet white wine. It wasn't the most sensible choice we made on the Track, but it was one of the most entertaining! For the rest of that morning, whenever we paused for breath, we got a little more inebriated. By the time we got to lunch we were pissed as farts, singing and panting as we staggered along and collapsing at our chosen picnic spot in fits of giggles.

For this, I blame the authors of the guidebook.

Faced with a rather bland and unending procession of forest, they'd taken to describing many of the plants they considered to be prominent landmarks. 'To the left, about a kilometre past the wooden bridge, you will see a dense thicket of *Daftus Namus Extremus*, a lovely flowering vine that is common along this section of the track.'

I dunno. Maybe I'm doing the authors a disservice? Maybe there really are people that counted their steps from the bridge, and cast about for a glimpse of this particularly elegant plant. That grows everywhere. To us, it seemed like a bloody stupid way to mark the distance – rather like saying 'the large brown tree'. Which, as it happened, was in there too. But not for another kilometre.

"We're in a fucking forest!" I howled, as Roo read aloud the description. "It's full of fucking trees! Look – there's one! And another..."

"Drink!" said Gill. She'd been the first to notice how ridiculously redundant the plant-based reference points were. She'd voiced her opinion that they were blatant fabrications designed to fill space in the book, and had decreed that we turn them into a drinking game.

So it was her fault that by the time we finished our sandwiches, we couldn't stand up.

As we were repacking the tubs of jam and butter, I noticed something odd in the top of Roo's bag.

"Roo, what the hell is that?"

"Duh! It's my fairy tutu."

She said it in a way that suggested it was perfectly normal to be hiking with a tutu. Which for Roo, I guess it was. It may only have weighed as much as a Mars bar, but I couldn't let it slide. I mean, hello? *Mars bar!*

"I thought you were going to send that home."

"What? Are you out of your mind? Why on earth would I send this home?"

"I dunno. We were cutting down on weight, so..."

"But it's a *tutu*, Tony! It's essential! How crazy would it be to hike the entire track and not bring a tutu?"

"I. I...?"

"Exactly! Listen to yourself. Listen how crazy you sound."

"But... you never wear it."

"Honestly! Not when it's *raining*. But if you're going to be like that about it, I'll put it on right now."

So she did.

"And I'll wear it every single day, from now until we finish the Track."

And you know what? She did that, too.

Drunk in a forest is a grand place to be – so long as you don't have twenty-five kilometres to walk before dark, and a bag the size of a whale shark on your back.

It was a very sorry, if still rather sozzled group that rocked up to the shelter that evening. We were dangerously dehydrated, but at least our raging hangovers helped mask the pain from the rest of our bodies.

And ironically, the night after we'd posted our tent home, we arrived to find the shelter had been completely occupied by a Scout troop.

Bugger.

But to be honest, we were too pissed to care.

The Scouts thought we were awesome – maybe because we were hiking the entire Track, or possibly because we were doing it drunk – so without being asked, all twelve of them squashed onto one of the sleeping platforms, leaving the other free for us.

What a lovely bunch of kids!

"We could have a great night," Roo said, "if only we had a couple of decks of cards…"

And that night, despite the lack of soft beds and duvets, we slept like the dead.

Halfway Home

The mid-point of the Bibbulmun Track is a place called Donnelly River Village.

Donnelly River Ghost Town might be more appropriate – or would be, if there was a town. Hell, there wasn't even a village.

Donnelly River Ghost Post Office, I shall name the place – because apart from an abandoned petrol station and the crumbling ruins of what used to be a school, there was absolutely sod all else.

You may notice that I've cunningly glossed over several weeks of arduous walking here. I figured it was an endless, gruelling slog – pretty much the opposite of what a book should be – so I spared you the details.

I do these things so you don't have to, folks!

That might become my new motto.

Although, the lazier part of me is leaning towards, 'other people do this shit so I don't have to!'

Hm. Maybe I'll get to that in a decade or two.

The 'DRGPO' doubled as the world's most specialised shop. It sold one thing; hiking food, to one group of people; those who were a) stupid enough to set off on a two-month hike, and b) tough enough to make it this far.

A well-creased old fellow showed up after we'd been poking around the shop for about ten minutes. He was good enough to sell us supplies for the next week, even though it pretty much emptied his shelves to do so. We had to make a few compromises, and almost had a collective heart-attack when we heard the price. No wonder this place managed to survive on such a tiny client base.

"You can camp in the school," the old bloke told us, "it's the only place around here, unless you've got tents."

And as far as we could tell, there was no-one else living in Donnelly River Village.

We spread out our sleeping bags on the rickety boards of a classroom floor, and went to poke around the rest of school. It was almost entirely empty; in one room we found a wooden desk with an old electric kettle on it.

"Doesn't work," Gill confirmed, flipping the switch on and off. "I wonder what's in there, though?"

She pulled a large cardboard box from under the table. And discovered…

"Coffee!"

The box was filled with single-serving sachets. Roo rolled her eyes in disgust as Gill and I unpacked the stove and fired it up. The zip-lock bag of coffee I'd started out with had long since run out, and at upwards of $12 a jar, it simply wasn't in the budget to buy more.

"Ahhh!" Gill and I exchanged satisfied grins over our steaming mugs. "This is nice coffee, actually!"

"It is," I agreed. "Damn nice. Upsettingly nice, even. Like, almost a shame to leave it here…"

"Are you thinking what I'm thinking?"

So we spent the next two hours sitting on the floor, ripping open hundreds of sachets and pouring the contents, one cup's worth at time, into my empty coffee bag. We were at it so long it went dark around us – but we didn't run out of coffee again for the rest of the hike.

Result!

In the morning, we had another chore; no visit to Donnelly was complete without feeding the kangaroos. They were everywhere, roaming around town as though they owned the place – which in the absence of any humans, I guess they did. The old bloke at the post office sold us a few bags of pellets which the kangaroos went nuts over. I held up a handful and was instantly surrounded, mobbed by roos of all sizes. They had an appealing habit of holding onto my hand with their forepaws, while their velvety noses snuffled around for the grub.

"It's Kangaroo Happy Hour," I said to the girls, as even more roos rounded the post office and bounded straight towards me.

But Roo (the girl) was giving me a peculiar look. "Ah, Tony, that big bloke you're feeding?"

"The one in the middle?"

"Yeah. I think he likes you."

"How so?"

"Because he's got a massive erection!"

"WHAT?"

"I don't know what you're doing, but he's definitely enjoying it."

"I'm not doing anything! Honest!"

"Wow," said Gill, taking a peek, "it really is Kangaroo Happy Hour!"

It was a pleasant afternoon's walk to the next shelter, and even though we'd resupplied with a full week of provisions we managed to set a decent pace. Despite our all-noodle diet, we were clearly getting stronger.

Staying in the shelter that night was a stick-thin young Aussie bloke called Shawn, with some of the strangest gear we'd come across so far. As we boiled water full of instant noodles, Shawn was measuring out cupfuls of dried lentils from a burlap sack, and proudly displaying his collection of herbs and spices to Gill.

"I even collect some as I go," he explained, "some Dandelion, which is great for tea, and some Chickweed which has kind of a nutty taste…"

Gill was rapt.

She spent the entire evening in deep discussion with Shawn, covering their various spiritual inclinations, his vegan lifestyle, a shared love of nature and many other things besides.

At midnight we left them to it, because they were discussing internet sites that sold piano sheet music, and to be honest I needed sleep far more than I needed to hear that conversation.

"He's travelling with *lentils*," I whispered to Roo, as we snuggled up on the far side of the shelter.

"I know! What the fuck? That's got to be the least practical food I can think of. Don't you have to, like, boil them for hours, before their even edible?"

"I think so."

"And herbs and spices for flavouring…"

"Yup. He's gonna die out here for sure."

Now, there's an inexplicable habit amongst hikers which we came to call the Early Hiker Phenomenon. It seemed to infect everyone who walked the Bibbulmun Track – except us.

Every morning without fail, at about 5:30am they'd start to stir. It was as if they were receiving radio signals from some atomic clock that told them dawn was only minutes away. I'd wake to hear them stumbling around the shelter in the darkness, struggling to roll up sleeping bags, or light the burner on their stove with frozen fingers.

They would talk – and curse – in stage whispers, as though there was any possibility of not waking everyone up with the clanging of pots and pans as they made their breakfast.

Cooking and eating would be achieved in the semi-darkness before the sun made its first appearance. I'm fairly sure it was more difficult this way, but that never seemed to occur to any of them.

Then, fully packed and breakfasted, they would stride off into the frigid gloom, leaving just as the first rays of light made the ground start to steam.

Doesn't it all sound picturesque?

Well, I have one thing to say to that: Bollocks to it.

When those overly-keen nut jobs finally buggered off, we would drift back to sleep, snuggling down into our sleeping bags to ward off the cold. Sleep in the shelters was never of the best quality – mostly because we were lying on planks of wood – so we tried to make up for that with some good old-fashioned quantity.

About half-past nine, with the world ablaze in sunlight, we dared to venture from our nests. It would still be cold in the shelter – it was *always* cold in the shelters – but nothing a bit of exercise wouldn't cure. A trip to the long-drop loo, for example, was usually enough of a wake-up call to get the blood pumping. You just can't remain half-asleep on the toilet when dozens of creepy-crawlies are straining to cross the gap between the cold plastic seat and your warm, inviting buttocks.

Especially when every one of the little buggers wants to bite a piece out of them.

So. Suitably adrenalized by the early morning brush with wildlife, we made a leisurely breakfast without the need to whisper and huddle. We packed our gear whilst alternately laughing and moaning about the route ahead, using the guidebook to identify a suitable stopping point for chocolate o' clock, and for lunch.

By the time we set off, the temperature was almost civilised!

It was warm. It was light. It was 11am, but then who cared? We had only one deadline: darkness. Get into the next camp – or possibly even the one after that – before day turned to night. And that was it.

Our fellow hikers, with all their admirable motivation, tended to machine through their day's hike and be done and dusted by lunchtime.

All power to them.

Then, with sod all else to do in a three-sided wooden shelter, they must have sat around eye-balling each other for the next five hours.

Just before dusk we would rock up, make our dinner straight away, and lay out our sleeping bags with the last of the light. That warm, wearied feeling of a hot meal after a long, hard day, was just the ticket for getting to sleep in less-than-ideal circumstances – and we generally managed it not long after our arrival.

Perfect!

And then it would be 5:30am again, and the whole show began anew. We laughed at them, as we walked. What the hell was wrong with these people?

"It's a beautiful thing, dawn in the bush," one of them told me once.

"Mmm," I agreed, without conviction.

So the next morning we got up and looked at the dawn, as it broke across the wooded valley we were camped in. Mist rose up quickly all around us, turning the trees into ghostly statues and imbuing a simple trip to the toilet with all the eerie atmosphere of a Stephen King novel. Fragments of sunlight burned through gaps in the ever-shifting fog, reaching out in swirling shafts like the fingers of God, grasping towards his creation.

It was absolutely magnificent.

Utterly breath-taking.

But it was also bloody cold, so we went straight back to bed afterwards.

5:30am is a fairly magical time the world over; almost everything is quiet, like the calm before the storm; nothing seems the same, caught in the half-light of dawn, and devoid of the chaos normally associated with the waking world.

But I've seen all that shit.

And I'd still rather be in bed.

Shawn was one of those frightfully early-risers; he managed to pack, cook, eat and leave without waking any of us. The only evidence he ever existed was a folded piece of paper torn from his notebook, on which he'd jotted down the addresses of some websites that sold sheet music. He'd left it on Gill's rucksack for her, and she was secretly a little heart-broken that that was all he'd left.

Gill is one the nicest, friendliest, funniest people in the world, but she had a terribly low opinion of herself. I knew that deep down, in a place my reassurances couldn't reach, Gill firmly believed she wasn't good enough for a guy like Shawn.

It wasn't true, and it was holding her back from meeting someone, but it was something I'd never managed to help her with, even after all this time travelling together.

Maybe that's part of it, I mused. *Maybe I'm holding her back? Hanging around with me and Roo 24/7 has got to be cramping her style…*

I tried not to think too much about that, but on this kind of walk, all you can do is think. And the mind goes where it will, with nothing to interrupt its deliberation for hours and hours at a time. The germ of that thought grew, as yet unspoken, until it became a certainty.

It was my fault. I was holding her back.

But what could I do about that? How could I set her free?

I was pondering exactly that dilemma several weeks and several thousand miles later, halfway across the desert between Perth and Sydney. We'd made a stop for petrol, and as Gill got out to pay for it her journal fell out too. She picked it up, and narrowly missed leaving Shawn's note on the forecourt. Reaching down for the scrap of paper, she noticed for the first time that there was something written on the inside. She unfolded it, held it up to the light, and read;

Gillian,

Very much enjoyed our conversation last night, and events seemed to continue into my Dreams.

All the best

- Shawn

And his phone number was scrawled across the bottom.

"Oh for fuck's sake," she said, dropping the note onto her seat.

I took a quick peak. "Woah, no way! And he's probably back in Perth by now…"

"And we're halfway to Sydney. I can't believe it."

"Sorry, dude."

"It's just my luck! I meet one of the hottest guys in the world, and he likes me too. So what if we were going opposite ways on a two-month hike? I could have worked with that. But why do I have to meet the only bloke on the planet who still writes in fucking *pencil?*"

The Memory of Trees

I've always loved climbing trees, so when the Track passed right by one of Australia's biggest it was impossible to resist.

The 72m (236ft) tall Gloucester Tree had been used as a fire look-out in the days before helicopters, and it still survives as a tourist attraction. Ditching our rucksacks at the base – safe in the knowledge that only a professional bodybuilder could steal one and expect to get away with it – we set off, up a spiral of steel rungs driven into the trunk of the tree. Round and round we went, climbing ever higher, until we emerged from the forest canopy to a breath-taking three-hundred and sixty degree view.

Of trees.

It was incredible though, looking out over hundreds of square miles of old-growth woodland; just enough to take our minds off the twin facts that a) we were ridiculously exposed, insanely high up and supported only by a single tree, and b) we were going to have to climb back down...

The steel viewing platform was nice and secure, even if it did weave quite a bit in the wind. On the safety railing someone had scratched out the best line of graffiti I'd seen in years: 'Zeppelins leave every half hour', it said.

When our feet hit terra firma, we noticed the same people were still hanging around the bottom – trying to get their courage up to make the climb.

According to the guidebook, more than three quarters of the people who try it never make the top.

The forest we'd been treated to an aerial view of, and were currently slogging our way through on foot, was comprised mostly of karri trees. They gave us another fascinating insight into Australia's fire-governed ecosystem; the trees, many of them true giants, were often hollow. What we might think of as the heartwood burns away in the dozens, or even hundreds of fires such a tree would experience in its lifetime.

Only the outermost layers of wood remained, conducting moisture skywards and somehow supporting the immense bulk of the tree above. We took turns standing inside the hollow, living trees, but a camera doesn't do them justice; there is one, still living, with a blackened hole in its base big enough to park a car in.

The more immediate effects of fire were to be seen on a section of Track that was technically closed due to a controlled burn in progress. Signs were posted, and the trees beyond them were a smoking, smouldering mess. The alternative route suggested by the signs involved a two-day detour along the road, which none of us were in the mood for. In the end, Roo called it; "Looks like they've done all the burning they need to do," she guessed, and we hiked on into a forest of standing charcoal. Like the bigger karri trees, these ones were perfectly okay beneath their protective layers of charred wood; the undergrowth, however, had been decimated, reduced to knee-deep drifts of ash and enough airborne flakes that it looked like it was snowing.

Unsurprisingly, there was no-one else in the hut that night.

All three of us slept fitfully, and woke at every noise. The shelter wouldn't have been targeted directly of course, but it was slap bang in the middle of the burn area, in a clearing less than twenty metres across; and (as Roo pointed out) aerial fire-bombs aren't famed for their accuracy.

Needless to say, we woke early that morning – as far as the signs said, the fire-bombing was set to continue for the next few days, and trusting we'd be okay because we were in an area that had already been burned was possibly one of the stupidest choices we made.

But we survived!

Chalk another one down to dumb luck.

Just when we thought the Track had nothing new left to throw at us, we hit a section delightfully named 'Dog Pool' – and spent the next two days wading through a swamp.

This was one of those 'challenges' Jim had been talking about, when we first mentioned we were hiking in winter.

We'd been using flip-flops (sorry, 'thongs') as our 'indoor' shoes, so now they did double-duty protecting our feet from the rough ground underwater.

They did little to protect against the 'yabbies' though – small, lobster-like crayfish that inhabited the swamps, and loved nothing more than nipping the occasional exposed toe with their pincers.

And nothing – but nothing – could protect against the

mosquitoes. The first night we camped in a shelter on a hillock, surrounded on all sides by the swamp. It was alive with insects, and we drew our sleeping bags as tightly closed as possible; only the barest trace of flesh was open to the elements.

And that's exactly where the little buggers bit us; Gill on the forehead, Roo on the eyelid, and me lip. All three bites swelled immensely, turning us into grotesque caricatures, like cartoon mutants – man, those were some potent mozzies! We were tremendously glad when our feet hit the start of a wooden boardwalk, leading us up and out of the stinking swamp at last.

After weeks of trees, and hillsides covered in trees, and occasional gaps in the trees through which we could see forested hillsides further down the track, we were eager for a change. We weren't disappointed. Slowly the vegetation fell back, became more open and scrub-like, until the day we crested a heather-bound ridge and caught our first sight of the southern coastline. It was spectacular. Even from several kilometres away we could see the savagery of the surf. It foamed and spat as it drove into the rocks, crashing around them with violent glee. The wind had picked up dramatically and was making it hard work just to stay upright. All our efforts paid off when I tumbled down a sand dune onto our first beach. The sand was golden and untouched. Our footsteps alone marred the smooth, ageless expanse. As we strode along the water's edge and looked back at the three lonely rows of indents, it was as if humans had never set foot here before.

We'd met so few people on the journey that we felt like explorers; pioneers in a new and uninhabited land. On one of the longest sections, we'd managed ten full days without seeing another person. Only the cheerful yellow triangles marking the Track gave us any indication that this was more than a deer trail. It had been at times a wide, leaf-strewn boulevard sweeping between rows of giant trees; at times so enclosed we had had tunnel-vision. The Track was maintained by volunteers, and some of them were obviously more dedicated than others; the last stretch of woodland had been so overgrown we could have done with a machete.

We'd scrambled over boulders, negotiated giant fallen trees, crossed rivers on logs (and occasionally had to wade in places where the logs had been washed away) – and all three of us, tree-huggers of the first degree, were thoroughly sick of the forest.

We wanted to see the sky, more than a narrow, patchy ribbon far above us, and here, at last, was our chance.

The immensity of the landscape was revealed to us along with the shape of the coast. In the trees we'd been able to see at the most a few hundred meters ahead of us, and the occasional mountain-top had offered spectacular views of the surrounding forests. None of it compared to the sight of the coast though, curving around a series of rocky headlands and tiny sandy bays, the furthest of which was still several days' hike away. And to get there, we had a new type of problem to solve; estuary crossings.

The first one we came to was a bit like that riddle with the fox, the chicken and the sack of grain that you have to get across the river.

There was one canoe in a metal storage cage on our side, and presumably one or more tied up on the far bank. Each canoe could take two people and one bag, or one person and two bags. And at least one boat had to be left on each side – otherwise the next poor sod unlucky enough to turn up on the wrong side would be swimming…

So we tried to think logically, and solve the problem in the fastest, most efficient method possible. This is what we came up with:

Roo rowed across first, and came back towing an empty canoe. While she had a breather, Gill and I loaded the bags into the canoes and each paddled one over to the other side. There we unloaded the bags, and Gill stayed with them while I returned pulling her canoe. I left that one in the store-cage while Roo, sufficiently recovered, took the two of us back across in the remaining canoe.

Damn, we were good at that! Of course, I'm not mentioning the hour of debate it took us to come up with such an elegant scheme – but the point is, no-one got dunked, the bags stayed safe, and nothing got left on the wrong side of the river.

As far as we know, anyway.

We braced ourselves for a trickier crossing a few days later. We'd met an older couple hiking in the opposite direction, and they'd told horror stories of wading through chest-deep water with their rucksacks held above their heads. Not all the inlets were deemed worthy of having canoes – or else, like this one, they were too close to a town to risk leaving a bunch of canoes tied up on the riverbank.

But we were saved from a dunking by an intense bout of laziness and gluttony; we slept in late and lingered in town for a delicious breakfast of pastries from the bakery. We reached the inlet to discover it was tidal – and midday was apparently low tide. So we pulled off our socks and boots, and strolled casually across through the ankle-deep water. Yet again, the 5:30am crew seemed oblivious to the torment they caused themselves.

Suckers.

The next week led through a sort of coastal heathland, with scrubby fern bushes bordering a sandy, snaking trail. The path was so narrow we had no choice but to walk single file, so with conversation cut to a minimum, I trudged along in the lead and let my thoughts run free.

Suddenly I heard a cry of alarm from Roo. I froze, scanning the way ahead, but saw nothing. So I turned carefully, to find that the girls weren't behind me any more. They were several metres back, staring at the ground with wide eyes.

I followed Roo's gaze to the middle of the path between us – and there, calmly sunbathing, was an enormous brown snake.

"SHIT!" I yelled.

"Shhh!" Roo pleaded. "Don't wake him up!"

"Oh. Okay. What are we going to do?"

"You just walked right over the top of him, and he didn't move. We could do the same…?" she didn't sound too confident.

"Should I get a stick?"

"No!" Roo hissed.

I looked around anyway, but this was not a good place for it. The scrubby bushes stretched in both directions, lining the sandy path as far as the eye could see. Short of uprooting one of them, there was absolutely nothing with which I could tackle a snake of that size.

"We're coming over," Roo warned.

And they did. The big snake didn't flinch, either too deeply asleep or quite likely not even remotely bothered by our presence. We quickly moved further down the path to regroup.

"What kind is it?" I asked.

"Dugite," Roo replied.

"Poisonous?"

"Deadly. Third most, I think, in all the world."

No-one spoke for a couple of minutes, as we all contemplated the implications of that. But I'm not good with silence, so I broke it.

"He's a lazy bugger, though."

"Yes," said Roo, "luckily."

We were quieter as we walked on – and a fair bit more cautious. I had a tendency to wander along, lost in the remembering of some past adventure or day-dreaming about future travels, but it now occurred to me that this wasn't the safest way to bush-walk. As I thought about it, the reality of the situation dawned on me. It had been a week since we'd had any phone signal. We were far from help – and when I say far, I mean several days' fast hiking. And that would only bring us to the nearest road, with the hope of flagging down a car, getting a lift into the nearest town, and then hoping the local hospital had a helicopter…

Treatment for a snake-bite involves lying still and moving as little as possible to slow the spread of the poison, whilst a friend calls for an ambulance. Out here… well, I could either ignore that advice and hike for help, or I could lie here under a bush whilst the others went to get some.

But I'd be dead either way, so it didn't really matter.

Following this revelation I started watching the path intently, and stomping my feet as I walked, which Roo advised us would scare snakes away.

I did this for about the next half-hour – and then I gave up, because that shit is *exhausting.*

And day-dreaming, though potentially deadly, was much more fun.

Point Of No Return

At long, long (LONG long LONG!) last, we crested a headland and saw the giant windmills of Albany's new wind farm gleaming in the distance.

As welcome sights go, you could be forgiven for thinking this was one of the greatest ever seen. But to be honest, we were all having mixed feelings.

On the one hand, the desperation to be back in town, to eat anything other than bread and instant noodles, to be clean and dry and to sleep on real mattresses was a palpable thing. We'd talked for days (weeks, if I'm honest) about what the first thing we'd do was, once we were back in civilization.

'Take a shit,' I think, was highest on my priority list.

On the other hand... this was it. The End. Game Over.

Sighting the graceful white windmills was a bit of a false alarm, in that we still had three days to go; for now, they were the size of daisies on the horizon, and they would continue to grow until we hiked right beneath the thirty-five metre long Kevlar blades, mounted on towers twice that height.

It meant that the end was a long time coming.

We had ample time to address our feelings; triumph, mostly, at having achieved such an impossible task; gratitude, to the Gods of Fate, that had somehow allowed us to escape serious injury the entire time. And regret, because no matter how difficult, and how painful this journey had been, we still didn't want it to be over.

Because, what do you do, after hiking for over six-hundred miles?

Where do you go?

Other than to the pub?

"Anyone feel like turning back?" Roo quipped, as we hiked past a signpost. It was a rare distance-marker, pointing back in the direction we'd come from. 'Kalamunda – 952 km' it said.

I think that was when it first hit us, that this whole endeavour was nearly over.

"Remember Cardiac Hill?" Gill said.

We all had a chuckle. About three weeks in we'd started hearing about this monster from people coming the other way, and had been psyching ourselves up for it for days. Everyone we met complained that it had nearly finished them off, a slope so long and so steep it had earned its name by giving several people heart attacks.

Then one day we'd started descending, and descending, doing a solid two hours of serious downhill gradient. It wasn't until right at the bottom that it occurred to me; "You know what folks… I think that was Cardiac Hill!"

And it was. Lesson learned: *never* try to do this hike in the opposite direction.

"I'll miss climbing mountains," Roo commented. We'd summited several peaks on the course of the hike, our biggest accomplishment being two in one day – and a beast of a day it was, owing to our decision to double-hut. We'd been unofficially racing a group of loud-mouthed army cadets for a couple of days; they'd been doing a week-long section of the Track for 'training', and were walking in head to toe camouflage, toting all the expensive bits of gear we couldn't afford. There were three of them, and they marched off at speed, while we sauntered – but somehow we always seemed to catch them up, which became slightly awkward after a while.

So we studied our guidebook, and planned a coup. Up the highest mountain on the Track we climbed, puffing and blowing, to find the army boys waiting for us in the shelter at the top.

"Thought you lot weren't gonna make it," the loudest bloke said. Then he generously offered us one of the three rooms in this unique stone shelter, being as how him and his mates had arrived first and occupied the other two.

"No, that's quite alright," I told him. "We're not staying in this shelter. We're hiking on to the next one."

And after scoffing a chocolate bar each, that's exactly what we did – leaving him standing there, open-mouthed in disbelief.

Thirty-four kilometres we made that day, arriving at the second campsite long after dark. That's twenty-one miles. It doesn't sound that far actually, but we did climb *two* mountains, adding almost a thousand vertical metres up, and the same again coming down, to our total.

"What about you?" Gill asked me. "What will you miss most?"

"Strangely enough, I think I miss the trees…"

I could feel the black look she fixed on my back. "Pah! If I wasn't too knackered to bend over, I would totally find something to throw at you right now."

Roo started the next obvious thread of conversation. "So what won't you miss?"

"These bloody boots!" I moaned. "Buy a size too big, they said. But then the wet socks compress to nothing, the shoes expand with wear, and every time I walk up or down hill I slide around in them, bashing my heels or my toes with every sodding step! Worst. Advice. Ever."

"At least you didn't get blisters," Roo countered. "How many do you reckon we've burst, Gill? Three or four a day, for the first month?"

"I've still got a few," Gill admitted. "You know what I'll miss least of all, though? Having to get up in the middle of the night – in the freezing cold, the dark, and the frigging rain – and put soaking wet shoes on to scarper to the loo. And worst of all, no matter how cold I was, or how desperate for a wee, I still had to spend ages running the torch around the toilet seat, checking for redbacks!"

Roo shuddered. "Ugh! Yeah, checking under the rim of the seat was the worst! I saw things I can never un-see. I'm mentally scarred! But still, it was better than dying in the wilderness of a spider-bite on the arse."

Hearing all that surprised me a bit. "So you guys checked the toilet seat for spiders every single time you went? Even at night?"

"Yeah, we had to use a bloody torch! Why, didn't you?"

"No. It never occurred to me."

A day later we passed under the windmills, and strolled casually down the side of the main road into Albany. We were stronger – mentally more than anything, having overcome a desire to quit so strong that some days it was the only thought in my head. But physically also, particularly the girls; looking back, I'm blown away by what they achieved. At times I thought that hike would kill me – but both Roo and Gill handled the whole thing, ignoring the pain and carrying on (or on occasion, crying with the pain, and still carrying on). They'd been directly responsible for me completing the Track; I'd never have made it without their example of tenacity and relentless positivity, shaming me into carrying on even when every fibre of my being screamed at me to give up.

Ladies, I salute you!

In Albany we encountered nothing of note. No fanfares, no celebrations, no crowded streets welcoming us back to reality. We were just three tired hikers, hobbling in on battered boots, covering the last few steps of a long and lonely road.

So after we collapsed in the youth hostel, and ditched our stinking clothes, we made two forays – once more in our pyjamas.

First we went to McDonalds, and ordered everything on the menu. And then found out our stomachs had shrunk so much we could hardly finish a meal between us.

Then, we went to K-Mart, and bought three plain white t-shirts and a packet of marker pens.

'I Just Walked 1,000 Kilometres!' we scrawled across the t-shirts, in a variety of styles.

And the next day, when we roused ourselves after fourteen hours of blissful sleep, we wore the t-shirts all around town. A few people smiled and waved at us, and then a photographer from the Albany Advertiser spotted us.

Our vindication came in the form of an article, printed the very next day, alongside a photo of us looking considerably cleaner than we had in months.

'The Big Trek Is Done', the headline announced.

The article was one paragraph long.

108 words.

Including the title.

"You know what would make the whole thing more interesting?" Roo said.

"I dunno. If one of us had died?"

"No! Next time we should do it for charity!"

I gave her a long, hard look, and tried to inject every ounce of defiance I could muster into my reply.

"*Next time?*"

To this day, I count completing the Bibbulmun Track as one of the foremost achievements of my life.

But it's impossible to tell people about it.

Every so often, just for a laugh, I give it a go.

"I hiked a thousand kilometres, once," I'll chuck casually into a conversation.

"Woah! Really?" will be the response.

"Yup."

"That must have taken *ages!*"

"It did, actually. It took two months."

"Wow, that's so cool. Hey, did you ever see that movie about the climber that got trapped by his arm? He had to bite his own hand off!"

And that's as far as it goes.

I could launch into an hour-long tirade about wet feet and crippling shoulder pain, about the dangers of downhill acceleration over rough terrain when you've got twenty kilos on your back, about cold and hunger, gigantic trees and lonely beaches, about mental barriers erected and demolished, and noodles, noodles, *frigging noodles*.

But no-one really cares.

I mean, why would they?

No reason to make a big song and dance about it.

All I did was go for a walk.

Desert Crossing

Something I've just realised about the Nullarbor: the name, Null-Arbor, literally means No Trees.

So, to call it featureless may actually be a misnomer; it is a landscape clearly defined by its complete lack of features.

Like trees, and shade.

And water. And life.

To me, the incredibly flat, arid wasteland looked about as devoid of life as anyplace on Earth.

But I was wrong about that once more; aside from spikey grasses and countless flies, there were things that lived in this desert. Lizards, like the racehorse iguana, and marsupial mice (that's right folks – kangaroo-mice!), the ubiquitous kangaroos, plus snakes, spiders and scorpions (everyone's favourite trio of desert-dwellers) – and wombats, apparently.

"So what do wombats look like?" I asked Roo. Chatting about the peculiarities of Australia, and in particular their wildlife, was one of my favourite ways to pass the endless hours we spent in Rusty.

"They're gorgeous!" Roo replied. "Like big fat balls of fur the size of a dog, with a smushed-up face. Like a giant version of a chinchilla, actually. They've got a pouch, but – how clever is this – it faces backwards, so they don't fill it with soil when they're burrowing!"

"Wow, that is cool. I could never remember out of 'wombat' and 'numbat', which was the real animal and which was the insult."

"Ahh... they're both real. You know that, right?"

"Eh? No? You're kidding me! Then what the hell is a numbat?"

"It's like a tiny, stripy ant-eater. With a pouch. Only, it eats termites."

"No way!"

"Yeah! They're adorable. But they're practically extinct. We used to breed them at Perth Zoo, but all the wild ones get killed by foxes."

"That sucks."

"Yeah. Foxes kill everything here. All the numbats and bilbies and quokkas."

"Honestly, it's like you're speaking another language sometimes. All I hear is 'Willa-billa-balla-bong'."

"You're just jealous because your frogs don't whistle."

We'd been advised not to risk free-camping by the side of the road on the Nullarbor; aside from the danger of careless drivers passing in the night, there were more sinister stories that we honestly couldn't decide whether or not to give credence to. We'd heard around campfires in Broome that gangs of disaffected youths sometimes prowled the desert highway at night, looking to cause trouble. Horror stories of cars being torched with their owners still asleep inside were enough to give us pause – even though a bit of cautious Googling hadn't returned any evidence of such crimes.

We'd seen enough burnt-out wrecks on the drive through Halls Creek to make us a little paranoid – so we limped into a different road-house every night, pitching our tents on gravel car parks and shivering through the frigid desert night.

Rusty was struggling, as expected, and the intense daytime heat and complete lack of shade did little to help – so we made small hops, from rest-stop to gas-station to road-house, refuelling every time (which was sensible), and scraping the coating of dead bugs off the windscreen every time (which was essential). Hours were spent every day waiting for Rusty's radiator to cool down enough for us to open it and add more water.

On Australia's longest straight road – ninety miles of tarmac without the slightest curve or bend – we boiled up a total of three times. But there wasn't much we could do about it – we'd tried to get him looked at by a mechanic in Subiaco, before we left Perth. Perhaps it wasn't the wisest move to drive a crippled old van decorated like an explosion in a paint factory into a dealership filled with gleaming Toyota Prados, but it was the only place with an appointment at short notice. We'd been a bit embarrassed, but had left Rusty parked amongst the Lexus SUVs and the Jeep Cherokees and wandered the markets of Subiaco while we waited for a verdict.

It hadn't been kind.

"I reckon you should drive this van to the nearest scrap yard," the mechanic had said.

"Yes?" we chorused.

"Then push it through the gates and walk away."

"Oh."

"Because it's buggered."

And that was the last professional opinion we dared invest in, before making our attempt to cross the Nullarbor. After all, if five more mechanics had told us the same thing it wouldn't have made much difference to our plans – just to our stress levels. And to our bank balances. So we chose to believe he'd been a bit hasty, or had been trying to avoid taking Rusty on as a project. I couldn't blame him for that, even if his delivery had lacked a little tact.

Because Rusty had no air-conditioning (of course!), sweat poured off us as we chugged along with all the windows open. Once again, every pore in our skin was clogged, every fold in our clothes became filled, and every tooth and every eyelash sported a thin coating of fine red grit. I was picking it out of my nose for weeks afterwards.

I'll leave to your imagination the effect it had on my other orifices.

But believe me when I say – that shit gets *everywhere*.

I had it worst of course, because I was lounging in the back – we'd stopped making it into seats, and were basically driving with a permanent double bed in the back – on which I spent the entire drive reclining, and gathering vast quantities of dust.

Because I couldn't drive.

It occurs to me that I've never mentioned why this was, and now seems like as good a time as any.

I was given six driving lessons as a present for my seventeenth birthday. I'm still owed three of them.

You see, when I was about ten, my Dad took a fantastic new job that involved us all upping sticks and moving from Yorkshire to Lancashire, where we got a shiny new house in a quiet cul-de-sac. We'd traded one sleepy northern English village for another, and to the adults, it was just geography. But to us kids, making that shift between counties transformed us both overnight into *persona non-grata*. We were like the unclean. I don't think it had anything to do with the ancient grudge between Yorkshire and Lancashire – Gill was only seven, and I seriously doubt anyone in our age group gave a toss about that stuff. But the trouble was, *we weren't from there*. And if you weren't from there – well, then you weren't one of them.

To say we were bullied, my sister and I, is to make an understatement so dramatic it defies words. Every day at school there were torrents of abuse waiting; the kids in our new village threw stones at us on sight. I hid when I could, and took the brunt of it when there was no other option. It probably didn't help that I was so damn *weird*. Years passed this way, with home my only refuge. Of course, I thought of giving up on this life, and taking a peek at the next one. Especially whenever I was high up, on cliff tops and castle walls and the like. I could picture myself soaring through the air, letting it all just float away as I plunged, free, through the endless empty sky. Oddly enough I've never feared death; injury for sure, because that stuff bloody well *hurts*; but not death. I'm too curious for that. But it wasn't only me that I had to think of. More than anything, I knew that I would miss my family – and that they would miss me. It was our love that kept us so close, and in my darkest days, it was that love that kept me here.

Which is probably for the best, or you'd be reading some other idiot's book!

In the end, we lived for ten years in Lancashire. But we were never *from there*.

I did, however, take my first three driving lessons there. The driving instructor's son was the ring-leader of the local stone-throwers, and for no reason I could ever establish, that man shared his son's irrational hatred of me. They were cut from the same cloth perhaps, man and boy, and I was terrified of both of them. Towards the end of my third lesson, I was trying to bring the car to a halt on the side of our road. The instructor had spent the last hour berating me, and was disgusted with my ineptitude. He'd long since stopped advising me and merely barked orders, sighing theatrically when I failed the manoeuvre on my first attempt.

"Closer!" he shouted, as I nudged the car towards the curb. He seemed genuinely angry, and I half expected him to grab the wheel one-handed and do it himself, just to prove how easy it was. So I swung in as close as I dared, and was rewarded with a gravelly crunch.

"No, NO!" shrieked the instructor. He leapt out of the car and bent down to study the wheels. "My hubcaps," he said with venom, when he got back in, "you've smashed them to pieces."

I never got in his car again.

And that was why, more than ten years later, I was a backseat passenger for the entirety of the Voyages of Rusty. Strange, isn't it, how such small events in your past can make a big difference in your future?

After eight days in the blazing wilderness, with the girls driving in shifts from morning till night, we finally made it across the Nullarbor.

Sydney appeared like an oasis – at once an historic port, a

modern metropolis, and the most famous part of the country – about which we knew absolutely nothing. Sydney was an unknown quantity to all of us, and that made it all the more enticing. Once out of the desert we pushed Rusty to his limits, speeding through the New South Wales countryside right into the heart of the city. Not only were we all excited about this next stage of our adventure – but my dear old Mum, bless her little cotton socks, was waiting for us there.

She'd set out on her own little adventure at about the same time we were stuck halfway across the country in the world's least reliable vehicle.

The scene was set for an epic Slater family reunion – and we all know what happens when Slaters get together, don't we?

Mum; Incoming

Because we'd had so much trouble with Rusty, we were a bit late picking Mum up from the airport.

Three days late, to be precise.

Luckily, being a mum, she was both highly resourceful and prepared for disappointment. Having promised to be there to meet her, I was kind of expecting to look after her – but I should have know that within minutes of us being back together, she'd be looking after me again.

By the time we arrived she'd not only booked herself into a hostel and spent several days exploring Sydney, she'd also booked us into the same hostel; and now she was bored with sightseeing, raring to go, and counting on us to provide the excitement.

Personally, I was just hoping it wouldn't get too awkward.

I mean, travelling with my new girlfriend and my sister was one thing.

Travelling with my new girlfriend and my sister – and my mum – was something else.

But she was delighted to see Roo again, and overjoyed that we'd become an item.

"You'll have such beautiful children!" she exclaimed.

So, maybe a little bit awkward, then.

The first thing we tackled was the Sydney Harbour Bridge – climbing it, because… well, because it's an iconic Australian structure, of course. And because you can.

The guide made us put on suits that looked suspiciously like prison overalls, and Mum emerged from the dressing room trailing a foot of spare material from both sleeves and both legs.

"It's made for a giant," she moaned.

"Ah, what size do you normally take?" the guide asked her.

"In these? I haven't got a clue. It's not something I wear very often."

"She takes Size Gnome," I chipped in.

"Well, we can't have anything flapping," said the guide, "as it could distract the drivers on the road below. But don't worry – we've got overalls to fit every size!"

A short while later he was forced to concede defeat. "We've got every size except yours," he admitted, "so we're gonna do the roll-up thing."

All four of us took a limb, and rolled up Mum's suit like we were changing her tyres in the Grand Prix.

Then we spent some time clipping our hats, sunglasses and special-issue face-cloths to ourselves with lanyards, and practicing with the Navy Seals radio – a high-tech headset which transmitted the guide's comments as vibrations through our jaw bones, allowing our inner-ear to 'hear' them in spite of the traffic noise and the deafening wind.

"Good to go," the pit-crew boss said, and we followed him out onto the bridge.

At first we walked through the middle of the bridge's structure, suspended above the thundering traffic below on a narrow walkway of steel mesh. Looking down whilst walking made the mesh seem transparent, which was a truly eerie feeling.

A series of ladders led us up onto the bridge's main steel frame, and we followed the curve of it all the way to the top. The view, three-hundred-and-sixty degrees over the city and the harbour, was incredible – very nearly worth the two-hundred dollars each we'd paid for the privilege. Roo and I paused there for a lingering kiss, much to the disgust of three turban-wrapped men at the back of our group.

"You don't have to do that every time we stop, you know," Mum said. "It's very nice up here, but I'd like to get down sometime today."

We spent about two hours on the bridge. "I'd love to have your job," I said to the guide afterwards. "How did you get it?"

"Oh, I just walked in and asked for it. They do all the training here. It's not as fun as it looks though, you have to be very fit. That walk we just did is nearly half a mile, and sometimes I have to do it *four times a day.*"

"Wow, you guys have got it tough," I said, straining to keep the sarcasm from my voice.

"Hell yeah!"

Next on our list was a beach trip.

Assuming we'd find Bondi horrendously crowded, we decided to visit one of Sydney's lesser-known beaches. A trip to Manly Beach involved crossing the harbour by ferry, which we wanted to do anyway, so we spent the morning watching jugglers, human statues and didgeridoo players in the bay area and then headed to the dock with our bathers and towels.

I struck a suitably macho pose under the sign for Manly Departures, and then we were on the ferry, transfixed by the gleaming Sydney Opera House sliding past to starboard. It looked magnificent, in a what-the-hell-do-they-do-with-those-pointy-bits-on-top kind of way. I never got the chance to go in, but I have it on good faith that the ceilings are vaulted to match the exterior shape, rising inside to majestic peaks much as they do on the outside. Now, I've been in a lot of Australian buildings, and I couldn't help but wonder how they clean out the cobwebs up there. Once, when I left Rusty's door open to let the hot air out, I caught an ambitious spider spinning a web right across the opening! So you can bet those pointy, spirey-type things are chock full of the buggers.

And you could bet they were bigger than the ones in Roo's games room.

Maybe they keep lizards, I thought.

When the ferry docked, we sauntered off in a cheerful mix of locals and tourists. They all rushed off in the same direction, clearly ignoring the beach, leaving us staring down at it alone. It wasn't quite what I'd expected. About fifty metres wide, the strip of sand was littered with rocks and gravel, and sloped down to the same stretch of water that the ferry plied. It wasn't a particularly enticing swimming experience, but we made the most of it, stretching out on our towels and watching a bunch of local lads trying to turn back-flips off the beach wall.

Another ferry docked an hour later, sending swarms of people skittering past our empty strip of sand, all clearly too busy to catch a few rays.

"I know this isn't the best beach in the country, but I'm surprised we've got it all to ourselves," Mum said.

"It's filthy," Roo pointed out. "I don't really want to stay here. That swim left a layer of diesel all over my body! I can feel it, all slimy-like."

"Sorry love," I said. "Gill, you want to call it a day? Go find some ice cream?"

"Hell yeah I do! This beach stinks of sewage."

So we packed up, and said goodbye and good riddance to Manly Beach.

"What a shithole," I said as we walked away. "Even Blackpool Beach is better than that!"

"I dunno," Gill said, "last time I was on Blackpool Beach I found three used condoms and a syringe. And it pissed it down with rain the whole time. This beach is pretty shitty, but it's still in Australia!"

"True."

With no real plan, we drifted with the latest crowd of arrivals, past a row of shops and cafés. Mum bought us all ridiculously large ice creams, because it was Wednesday, and we sort of went with the flow while we ate them.

And that was when we found the real Manly Beach; a kilometre-long ribbon of the whitest sand, bordered by blue-green ocean so inviting my feet were in it before I knew what I was doing.

"Oh bollocks," Gill said. "No wonder we were getting funny looks from people when they got off the ferry!"

"No bugger told us though, did they?"

"Would you go up to a bunch of half-naked people our age and start telling them where to go?"

"Probably not."

We slurped our ice creams in quiet awe, scanning the hundreds of bodies sprawled across the sand, not even close to filling it. Dozens of jet skis zipped past, churning up the ocean either side of the 'Swimming Allowed' flags. Swimmers swam and surfers surfed, and it looked… exactly like the Australian beach scene I'd been anticipating.

"Shall we go for a dip?" Mum asked the others.

"Nah, I'm kind of dry now…" Gill said.

"I don't want to get undressed again," said Roo. "I stink of oil, and I'm scared that if someone smokes near me I'll burst into flames!"

"Oh. Alright then. So, shall we head back to the ferry?"

That was Mum's first beach day in Australia – and because we were having so much fun doing other things, it also turned out to be her last.

It probably didn't give her the best impression.

Mum really fancied seeing some of Australia's unique animals, so the next day Gill agreed to take her to Sydney Zoo. Both Roo and I felt we'd had enough close encounters with the local wildlife, and decided to forgo the entrance fee in favour of a rare bit of together time. No – it's not what you think!

Unfortunately.

First we did our chores – and bought a nifty new phone with a 'Skype' button, as part of a decision I'd made to keep in closer touch with my family back in England.

Then we went in search of a hairdresser.

Roo had been toying with the idea of going blonde, and she

thought a sudden change of hair colour would be a great way to surprise Mum and Gill when they got back. I had to admit, it's a tactic that would never have occurred to me.

Sydney has everything, usually many times over, so it was no trouble at all to find a hair salon with an appointment free. It only took about two hours to transform Roo's mousey brown locks into a platinum blonde bombshell.

"That's fantastic!" I said, blown away by the transformation.

"I've got plenty of bleach left if you want it," the hairdresser offered, "I mixed up way too much."

I'm a try-anything-once kind of guy, so I thought, *why not?* And told her to go for it.

My hair is obviously made of something quite different to Roo's, as after a similar length of time wrapped in cling-film it turned a shocking bright orange. I looked like one of the *Rug Rats*.

"Oh dear! That's not supposed to happen," the hairdresser said, which wasn't the most comforting thing I've ever heard in a salon. "Don't worry, let me try this…"

Two hours later I emerged with hair the colour of dirty straw.

"Well, that rules out horse-riding as an activity," I told Roo. "If I get within striking distance of a horse, I'll get eaten."

"We could get some red dye from the supermarket," she suggested.

"No thanks."

"Really? What about purple?"

I was already used to Roo's new hair by the time Mum and Gill got back, so I wasn't prepared for all the gasping and shrieks of delight.

"Look at you!" Mum exclaimed, "you're *amazing!* So blonde! So beautiful! WOW!"

Then she turned to me.

"And look at you! You're… ah… what exactly *are* you?"

"A bloody idiot?" I supplied.

She seemed to consider this for a moment.

"Yes," she said, "that looks about right, then."

Mum; Outbound

Next we took Mum on a wine-tasting tour to the Hunter Valley, where three things happened: we all tasted a wide variety of Australian wines; Rusty broke down; and Mum got thoroughly drunk for only the second time in her life.

The first time had been on a pirate ship, on an all-you-can-drink excursion we'd booked onto as part of a Caribbean cruise. She'd gone into it with the best of intentions, wanting only to keep Gill and I safe from the evils of drink-diving. We'd persuaded her to have a cup of a bright red cocktail the crew were doling out from huge vats. She'd quite enjoyed it, pointing out that she couldn't even taste any alcohol. *But of course,* we told her, *that's because it isn't really alcoholic!* And being ridiculously naïve, and already slightly intoxicated, she took our word for it and spent the rest of the afternoon drinking the stuff. When we carried her back to our cabin on the cruise liner, she lay on the floor for the next two hours, frantically holding on because she said she was spinning so much she was going to fall off! She made one long-distance telephone call to Dad, apologising incoherently for waking him up at 4am, then threw up in the sink and passed out on the carpet. It was like watching her experience a condensed version of my entire time at university.

This time however, she promised us faithfully that she would not get drunk.

Not in the slightest.

She merely became very happy, then very giggly, and then spent the rest of the evening loudly denying that she was drunk to everyone that walked past our tent.

Poor Mum was losing quite a bit of her holiday time to car problems. With Rusty boiling up almost everywhere we drove, it brought an unnecessary element of stress into every journey we made. When it happened again, only days after we'd paid a garage in Sydney to fix hoses and check the radiator, we knew straight away who to call.

We'd seen a cartoon spanner on a van driving around town, and Gill and I had erupted with laughter so suddenly she nearly swerved Rusty off the road.

LUBEMOBILE, it said on the side in huge red letters.

"What does he do, deliver sex toys?" Gill said, when she'd regained control of herself.

"I don't get it," said Roo.

Mum was similarly nonplussed.

"*Lube* mobile," I repeated, by way of explanation.

"Yeah, they have those everywhere. They're mobile mechanics. They have adverts on TV and everything."

So this time we decided to leave Rusty behind our hostel and call in the grease monkey.

"There's not a lot of room in that car park," Mum pointed out. "I hope his van will fit."

"Mum, it's the *Lubemobile!* Trust me – it can slide in anywhere."

Actually he reversed in, when he arrived, which seemed appropriate.

The mechanic was friendly, professional, and gave us a tip that he reckoned would stop Rusty having so many radiator problems in future; "Call a decent mechanic," he told us. "The last one didn't even tighten the screws!"

"Bet the Lube Mobile has no problem with tightness," I muttered, noticing that Gill was having trouble keeping a straight face.

"He was a nice bloke," Mum commented, as the Lube man repacked his tools.

"Yeah, not as slippery as I expected," I said.

The joke was still lost on her, but Gill was delighted when she walked around the front of the van to admire the graphic of a fist clutching a rather phallic spanner.

"Tony, you've got to see this!" she called.

I went to investigate, walking past the dubiously-worded advert on the side (Dial 13-30-32 for Lube!) – and on the front was the coup de grâce.

'The Mechanic That Comes To You' it said across the bonnet.

"The mechanic that comes all over you!" Gill paraphrased.

"It could be worse," I said. "The mechanic that just pops in…"

Once Rusty's radiator was fixed (again), we decided to risk driving him north to explore Sydney's Blue Mountains. We found a company that ran a caving experience, booked ourselves in, and crawled Rusty at twenty miles an hour around the narrowest ledge of a mountain road. Every meeting with an oncoming vehicle was life-or-death, and it took a good two hours to make the journey.

Once there, we encountered another amusing wardrobe issue; caving is another activity performed in overalls, though these were heavy, mud-stained canvas boiler-suits rather than the high-tech prison-wear we'd sported for the bridge climb.

Mum found a suit to fit, rolled up the legs and sleeves again, and donned a pair of rubber wellies. It was only then that we calculated the following equation:

Gnome + Overalls = Oompa Loompa.

It took great strength of will to avoid humming songs from Charlie and the Chocolate Factory as we headed down into the depths.

We'd all done a bit of caving before in various parts of the world, but there's still something so exciting to me about being underground. The strange stillness to the air; the cool, even temperature and omnipresent, dripping moisture; and the calmness, the sense of millions of years of patient, geological history, surrounding and engulfing me in complete darkness.

I find it oddly comforting.

We did a series of abseils, and clambered over boulders and around tunnels of varying sizes. Then it came time to put ourselves through a 'squeeze'. This is caving terminology for a tight gap or narrow crevice, that you generally have to do a bit of contortion to get through. This one was nearly vertical, meaning you went head-and-hands-first into an opening in the ground, emerging in a chamber below from which you could quickly climb back around to the main area.

Mum chose to watch as we took turns going through the squeeze, before finally summoning up the courage to give it a go.

When she felt ready she knelt on the sandy cave floor, put her arms up above her head, bent forwards, and slithered into the hole.

And stuck there.

Something that we hadn't really considered is that Mum, though short, is somewhat egg-shaped – meaning, she is tiny at the head, with a child-like face, and substantially... um, *wider*, at the bottom end.

And it was by the bottom end that she was stuck; suspended through the hole, with her head and arms sticking out the ceiling of the chamber below.

"Quick! Push!" I shouted.

"NOO!" yelled Mum. "I'll fall!"

"Right! Grab a leg each, and pull!"

"NO! I'll smack my head on the rocks!"

"Well okay then, we'll just leave you there. We can send someone down every few days with some more food and a new book…"

"Don't. Make. Me. Laugh." she pleaded.

Which, as we all know, is secretly a plea to be tickled.

"Sorry, did you say you wanted tickling?" I asked. Just to be sure.

"You tickle me, you die," she said, but she was chuckling while she said it so I didn't take the threat too seriously.

"Hey, if I put my foot on your arse and lean heavily enough on it, maybe you'll pop out like a cork?"

Mum was in full hysterics by this time, her stumpy, protruding legs quivering in time with her laughter.

"H-H-Help meee!" she chortled.

"Can't you wriggle a bit?"

"No! I'm wedged in tight!"

I checked it out.

"That's amazing! Your ass has completely conformed to the shape of the hole! I couldn't even slide a credit card into the gap."

"No way!" Gill exclaimed. "That happened to me in America! So it is genetic!"

"Eh? What happened in America?"

"Oh, we were climbing up this little waterfall, and I tried to hoist myself up backwards. When I planted my bum in the gully, it dammed the waterfall, and a mini-lake started building up behind me! The tour guide said 'Woah lady, that is one malleable ass.' I never forgot it!"

"No, I'm not surprised."

Then Mum spoke up. "Uh, I know it's fun to reminisce, but could we possibly leave it until a time when I'm not stuck upside-down, hanging by my arse half a mile underground?"

"Oh yeah, sorry Mum! Shall we push?"

"NOOO!"

We pushed anyway.

Roo scooted down into the lower chamber to take her arms, and proceeded to catch her when Gill and I finally put enough pressure on her buttocks to squeeze them through.

She was still giggling when Roo helped her back up, prompting a round of applause from our guide and the rest of our tour group.

After that, we wisely decided to head back to the surface.

Mum's holiday was over far too quickly, and her departure brought us to the brink of another series of changes. Roo had decided that as only a year had passed since losing her own mum, she owed it to her family to spend the holiday with them. She'd booked a flight back to Perth, and would be leaving at the start of December, only days after our Mum flew home. This left a Roo-shaped hole in Gill's and my plans, as all the hostels around Sydney were already fully booked over Christmas. We scoured our new favourite website, a collection of backpackers' classified ads called 'the Gumtree', looking for somewhere to rent – and this time we struck it lucky. A science student called Leo was taking a trip to Europe over the holidays, and was looking for someone to rent his flat while he was away. We jumped at the opportunity, sending him a whopping great pile of cash ($600!) as a deposit, so desperate we were to secure some accommodation.

"I hope you did the right thing, trusting that guy," Roo said.

Until she mentioned it, I hadn't even thought about it.

And yet again Gill and I found ourselves alone together, in an unfamiliar city, living in a hostel with Christmas just around the corner.

It was starting to become a habit.

Mum; Addendum

The day after Mum arrived home, we got an email from her. It seems things hadn't been quite as dull as expected in England, while she was away. One night, Dad had received a phone call from the Welsh police, demanding that he come in to the Cardiff city police station. When he'd protested that it was 2am, they'd replied that either he could come straight away – or they'd come and get him. With handcuffs.

My Dad is the most mild-mannered individual you could ever wish to meet. He calmly ushered the dog into the car, and drove for two hours through the night to Cardiff. There, the local constables confronted him. They wanted to know what kind of business he was into, and what kind of 'game' he was playing.

He didn't have a clue what they were on about, and said as much – so they took him up the valley in a paddy-wagon, stopping at one of the houses we'd bought and renovated a couple of years back.

They led him inside, and his jaw hit the floor.

The entire house had been converted into a cannabis factory.

Bless him, my Dad is about as clueless as a person can be when it comes to the evils of this world. I mean, he doesn't even drink.

The cops escorting him took one look at his face and set him free. "If you're reaction had been anything else, you'd be sleeping in a cell tonight," one told him.

Apparently they'd seen his genuine shock, and realised he had nothing to do with it.

Dad then spent a while wandering through the house, staring in disbelief at the damage done. Holes had been cut in the floors and ceilings to run vents through. Thousands of pounds worth of lights had been hung from every surface, beaming down infra-red radiation on both floors – all of which were covered in a foot of top soil. Hundreds and hundreds of plants were being bagged up by a forensic team, while a police electrician tackled the deadly mess our tenants had left by the front door – all the grow lights had been wired directly into the mains, bypassing the electricity meter. Bundle upon bundle of cables snaked off up the stairs, branching out into every room; even though they'd been off for hours, the house at 4am was hotter than a summer's day in the garden.

"That's how we spotted them, too," a young copper informed him, "they were using the attic. A helicopter passing overhead with a heat sensor saw your roof lit up like a Christmas tree!"

"Oh," said my Dad.

"It happens all the time. In most cases, the landlord is in on it, turning a blind eye in exchange for a cut of the profits. But I could tell you weren't involved. I guess because you live so far away, they thought they could get away with it."

"But they were the best tenants we've ever had!" Dad told the cop. "They paid the rent by Direct Debit – always there on the first of the month, and never a peep out of them."

"I'm not surprised. They didn't want you coming down here and seeing all of this!"

"But… why?" my Dad asked.

"Whaddaya mean?" said the cop.

"Why… why have they done all this?"

"To grow the drugs, of course."

"Drugs?"

"Cannabis."

"Oh…"

"You do know what cannabis is, don't you sir?"

"I think so. Um… actually, no."

The cop sighed. He pointed across the room. "*That*, Mr Slater, is cannabis."

"Oh! Right."

"So, you understand now, the seriousness of this situation?"

"Yes officer, I do. It's funny though, only the other day I was wishing all our other tenants were like these ones."

"Other tenants you say? How many houses do you rent out around here?"

"Six, at the moment…"

"Right then, we'll go and have a look, shall we?"

It was a very, very long night for him.

Mum, when she got back, had been unable to resist calling us with a blow-by-blow account.

"It could only happen to your Dad," she concluded, "I'm away for a few weeks, and he nearly gets arrested for running a drug lab!"

"I bet he'd have made a bigger profit than he does on the

houses," I said.

"The cops did tell him, the stuff they found in the house was worth about a quarter of a million pounds. So your Dad asked if he got to keep some of it, in lieu of the damage! I don't think that went down too well with the police."

"Oh my God! No way!"

"Yes, and that's not the best bit. Tell Tony what you told the cops!"

And my Dad poked his head into the Skype window and said a cheery "Hello!"

"Tell him what you said," Mum demanded.

Dad complied. "Oh, well, the police seemed to think it was a good job I hadn't gone round that house to do any rent inspections or anything like that. They probably weren't very nice people living in there, you see, and they might have been annoyed if I'd called in and seen the mess they'd made."

"Yeah, no shit! They could have had guns and stuff!"

"Yes, well, this *is* South Wales. I doubt they have guns. They barely have motor cars. But we'd had a couple of complaints from some of the neighbours, about the state of the garden. Apparently these guys weren't bothering to look after it, and it had gone a bit wild. So in a couple of weeks I was planning on taking our lawnmower round – and asking them if I could cut their grass..."

Student Digs

Saying goodbye to Roo was even harder this time than it had been before. I knew she'd be back, and I completely understood that she had to go and spend Christmas with her family. It was the right thing to do, and she missed them every bit as much as Gill and I missed ours. But still… it made me incredibly sad, to think of spending the next month without her. In the entire time we'd been going out, we'd hardly spent a moment apart. Some people might call that unhealthy, and a year ago I'd have been one of them. But you know, there was just something about Roo that made her… hard to let go of.

There's a word for that, but I think it gets overused a lot in books like this. So for now we'll go with Gill's phrase to describe it: '*a pathetically-needy-limpit-like-inability-to-prise-yourselves-off-one-another-for-more-than-ten-seconds*'.

It's possible that she was a little jealous.

Nevertheless, our first job was to find our new digs and pay for them, before the bloke that had offered them to us changed his mind. Leo and his girlfriend were both postgrad students, in Genetics and Art respectively. We'd been lucky as hell to snag their place, and I'd promised Leo faithfully that we'd look after it. Now we had to meet up with him, learn how to feed his fish, and part with a sum of money so staggering that I was sleeping with it inside my underpants in case our hostel burned down in the middle of the night.

Leo had seemed like a good bloke in our brief phone conversations, and he was clearly a clever chap, so I had high hopes that his flat would be clean and tidy. I know the two things don't always go together, especially considering that he was a student, but I'd been reading and re-reading *The Secret* for weeks now, and I was determined to put that whole 'Law of Attraction' thing into practise. For anyone that doesn't know, it's a souped-up version of the power of positive thinking – basically, what you believe in strongly enough, comes to you.

I was believing as hard as I could that Leo's flat would be worth the money.

And you know what?

It was.

In fact Leo's apartment was amazing. Incredible. There are buckets of these words (called 'superlatives', apparently) that I could use to describe it, but – actually, that's just what it was. Superlative.

I'd seen a grainy photo of his bedroom on the advert, but my first real hint of what lay in store was when we found what we thought was Leo's building. Our entire knowledge of the area extended to a name – Surry Hills – and the fact that our hostel manager thought it was "a very nice neighbourhood". So when my astounding map-reading abilities led us to a sleek new apartment building with a video-intercom by the doors, we thought we'd hit the jackpot.

A remote-control conversation with a confused Indian gentleman followed, the outcome of which was that this was not the right address. We were instructed to go around the corner and down the street for a block, where we would find "the expensive-looking building".

This made me quite excited. And a little nervous.

It also made Gill question my map-reading skills again.

But our second attempt was much more successful.

And the building we were looking for? It *did* look rather nice.

The foyer was clad entirely in marble. Leo buzzed us in, but had to come down to meet us because the lift was activated by a wireless plastic doofer on his key ring. The lobby doors were, too, if there was no-one above to buzz you in.

Cool.

We rode the lift all the way to the top, and I joked that we'd arrived at the penthouse.

"Yep," said Leo. "My parents own the building, so…"

And he opened the door to the kind of room you see on the cover of *Grand Designs* magazine. It was wide, open plan, mostly white, and scattered with artfully staged props. The pictures on the wall had *their own frikkin' lights*, for gawd's sake! That is how posh this place was. The cushions all matched, and there were so many of them on the sofa there was hardly any room for my bum.

A telescope big enough to fit a small dog inside poised elegantly in one corner.

But it contained no dog.

A gleaming black granite kitchen dominated one end of the

room, while at the other end sliding glass doors gave out onto a wide balcony overlooking the Sydney Harbour skyline.

Ho. Lee. Shit.

So, let me show you the room," Leo said.

I had to pick Gill up off the floor first. "Get my jaw while you're down there," I told her.

Leo's bedroom was the master suite of the penthouse apartment. There was another bedroom which he rented out to a friend, who was conveniently also out of town – otherwise, he'd probably be on house-sitting duties, and Gill and I would be sleeping on the street over Christmas.

One wall of the bedroom was lined with matching his n' hers study desks, festooned with computery gubbins. The opposite wall was lined with mirrors, which concealed the walk-in wardrobes. Again, his n' hers (by which I mean, one was noticeably bigger and filled with shoes). There was an en-suite bathroom in grey marble, with a double-headed shower big enough to practise yoga in, and the piece de la resistance: the wall opposite the enormous double bed. It was all glass, and Leo led us through it, out onto a patio area that covered the entire floor-plan of the apartment below. It was stunning. Sweeping, two-hundred-and-seventy degree views (I calculated that) took in the whole of Surry Hills behind us, and everything up to – and including – the Opera House and Harbour Bridge.

My first thought was '*Party!*'

My second was '*No! BAD Tony!*'

Then I noticed outdoor speakers mounted above the glass doors, and a shiny steel barbeque tucked away to one side. *Party it is.*

Or it would be, if I had any friends.

I tuned back into the conversation. Leo was telling us that it was the perfect spot to watch the New Year's Eve firework display.

"But apart from that, we never really come out here. It's too windy to play badminton."

"Big enough though?" I asked.

"Oh, yes."

"You should try tennis. Only, you don't want to get your balls out up here."

"Sorry?"

"Your balls. Don't want to get them out up here."

"I... sorry, what?"

"Well, you'd have to go down in the lift to fetch them. Unless you put a big net up around the whole place..."

"Ah, right, I get you."

Gill was giving me that look that means 'please stop talking'.

She uses that look a lot.

But it works. Sometimes.

Notably absent from the flat was a TV, but Leo seemed like the type who might be above such mundane concerns. I've often wished I could be classy enough to tell people, "I don't watch television," – thereby subtly suggesting that my time is too valuable and too important to be frittered away so frivolously. But I'm not cut from that quality of cloth. Blame my generation, if you like. I love telly.

I decided not to mention this lack though, because I already felt dramatically out of place. That was one step up from asking him, "dude, can my band crash on the couch?"

But I needn't have worried. Leo led us in from the bright sunshine of his balcony, and closed both the doors and the curtains behind us. Then he plucked a remote from the wall above the bed, clicked a switch, and a giant projector screen lowered itself from the ceiling.

"This is how you operate the projector," he said, in a matter-of-fact way that suggested everybody had one. I was expecting James Bond to bust in at any moment and start shooting henchmen.

"Sound is wired through the walls, so keep the bass down or things start to fall off them."

Gill and I mumbled our agreement to keep the bass down.

Leo pushed a few more buttons, and the screen rolled itself up again, vanishing into a hidden cavity in the roof. He waved the remote at us, then returned it to its wall socket.

"Right! You got all that?"

We nodded.

"Great. Let's go see the pool."

Ever hear that phrase 'how the other half live'? Well, now I knew. This was how they live – and for the next month, it was how I would be living!

The basement of Leo's building contained a 15 metre heated swimming pool, a separate Jacuzzi/hot tub, a fairly decent gym, and a sauna. Our plastic dongle gave us access to the lot – and it was available 24/7. The rest of the basement was an underground car park, which sadly we couldn't use for Rusty as Leo was leaving his own car there. Then again, the place was full of BMW's and gleaming 4x4s; Rusty wouldn't last a day down here before someone called the cops and had him towed. Poor Rusty! Somehow we kept him going, but I had a feeling his end was near. And it wouldn't be pretty.

Back upstairs, we thanked Leo for his hospitality and tried not to act overawed by the place. We'd have it all to ourselves until January the 2nd, when Leo and his girlfriend would be returning from Europe.

I did a quick calculation in my head as we handed over the money. We were paying Leo's half of the rent – at $300 per week. So together with his flat mate, they were paying $600. And this was only because his parents let him rent the place at 'cost price'…

Ouch.

My hand shook as I let go of the wad of bank notes, and not without good reason.

Leo was being incredibly generous, letting us stay here for the same price he'd have been paying, especially over the holiday season, when accommodation prices in the city went absolutely nuts.

But none of this changed the fact that we couldn't afford it.

That six-hundred bucks I'd given him, on top of the deposit I'd sent him earlier, had cleaned us both out.

Gill and I were practically penniless.

Which meant we had two weeks to come up with another $600 to pay the other half of the rent…

Or we'd still be sleeping on the street over Christmas.

As I explained to Gill while we packed our stuff in the hostel, we didn't have to worry about a thing. It would all work out.

We just have to believe in it, I reminded her.

No pressure.

A Christmas Miracle

You'd think that with such a potent incentive hanging over our heads, the very first thing we'd do would be to pound the pavement looking for jobs.

That certainly would have been the most sensible move.

But neither Gill nor I have ever been accused of being sensible.

So instead we signed up for a month-long, full-time kung fu course.

The thought process behind this decision went something like this: 'lalalalalalalalalalalalalalalalalalala'

Looking back, I'd say we were deep in denial – and I don't mean the river in Egypt.

Kung fu was something we'd both studied at different times, but never had the chance to practice together. One of the few downsides of travelling is the difficulty of keeping up any sort of regular training, and by this point all forms of physical exercise had long since fallen by the wayside. Now, with free access to our own private gym and swimming pool, we finally had both the time and the opportunity to get in shape – so we took it.

I won't say it was the cleverest decision I've ever made, but I've always felt that something was guiding me – some shadowy hand of fate that moves me from place to place, and beckons me into the actions I choose.

Of course, it could just be that I'm an idiot.

But anyway, the kung fu school gave us an amazing deal!

It was such good value that more than half the students there had no interest in kung fu whatsoever. For a foreigner to meet the conditions of their student visa, they had to be enrolled in a course of full-time education, at a registered and recognised school. The traditional way to achieve this was with any one of dozens of English language schools, many of which had sprung up to cater specifically to visa-seekers. Learning English was, after all, why most of these people were here. The only trouble was, these English schools knew their market, and they'd been slowly ratcheting up the prices. Now, suddenly, there was a new player in town – the kung fu school, wanting to expand their clientele, had registered for visa-granting status. And they were *way* cheaper than the language schools…

And so Gill and I came to spend most of our afternoons trading punches with a wide variety of Asian students – none of whom knew kung fu, and none of whom really wanted to. But they couldn't really complain about it to us, as none of them spoke English either.

And they could take a good beating, so we all enjoyed ourselves royally.

One day, on the long walk home from training, we broached the topic of work.

"We'll have to find some eventually," I said, "or we literally won't be able to afford Christmas. As in, we won't be able to eat."

"I know," said Gill, "but I've been scouring the Gumtree website. There's nothing around, and I keep getting emails back saying that all the Christmas recruitment was done in September. I hate to say it, but…"

"Don't say it! We'll manage. We always do, remember?"

"True enough."

"Imagine this; a year ago we were in Margaret River, living in a pair of tents, and getting up at 5am to pick grapes. Bloody hell! I can hardly believe we got here, struggling across the Nullarbor with Rusty boiling up every ten miles, but we made it. And now… well, we'll do it again. God only knows how, but we always come out on top."

"You're right!" Gill brightened visibly. "It's our positive attitude, and our belief that everything will work out. That's what makes everything… work out. And so long as we keep believing in ourselves, it always will."

"You know what? We should write a book about this! Something motivational."

"As bloody if! You've been working on That Frigging Bear That Ate Whatever The Hell It Ate for how long now, three years?"

"About that, yeah."

"I'll be married and have grandkids before you write a book about this!"

And you know what? As I sit here writing this, I've just come back from visiting a certain someone. I don't want to spoil any of what's to come, so all I'll say is this: I spent an awful lot of time changing nappies while I was there.

And I wasn't even wearing one.

So, you're weren't *quite* right Gill, but then you weren't entirely wrong, either!

For the next couple of days, we compromised our incredible lifestyle and headed to Sydney's backpacker district of Kings Cross to look for work. The first day was a complete bust – seeking out noticeboards in youth hostels, we crossed and then criss-crossed town, becoming more and more cheesed off with each successive failure. There wasn't anything advertised in the few places that even allowed us in to look at their noticeboards, and the newspapers we picked up carried only the usual adverts for commission-based telesales positions, and hookers.

Bored, tired and miserable, we came home to a dinner of leftovers that we'd been eking out for more days than was probably healthy.

"It'll all work out," I reminded Gill – though even to my own ears, it sounded a bit feeble.

The next day, however, I had a change of tune. I woke up in a mood so positive I could have drowned a unicorn in it. I tried to explain this to Gill, as we packed a bag with stacks of CVs and certificates.

"You know," I told her, "I've got one of those feelings."

"Oh hell! It wasn't the furry sausages was it? I told you they were too far gone."

"NO! Dude, for once I am not talking about my bowel movements."

"Oh!" She seemed genuinely surprised for a second. "Sorry – carry on then!"

"Okay, so I have this feeling…"

"If you're about to burst into song, I think you should warn me."

"Gill!"

"Sorry!"

"Right, well I've been thinking. This is a sweet gig we've got going on here. It's *too good* for us to waste. I mean, here we are, penniless backpackers, and we're living in the penthouse. Training kung fu six days a week just for the hell of it, swimming in our private pool, and living life to the max in this incredible apartment."

"True enough."

"So, what I'm thinking, is that maybe we weren't *meant* to get jobs! Imagine what a pity it would be, to live in a place like this and yet to have to drag ourselves out of bed every day and go to work in some crappy backpacker-y type job."

That caught her interest. "So what do you think we should do?"

"Well, I think we should go out looking for jobs, just like we were going to. It's the right thing to do, because we have to at least make an effort. But I also don't think we're going to find any jobs. It doesn't feel right – it's like, I can tell that there isn't anything out there for us. Why would there be? And, to be honest, would we want there to be?"

"So what do we do?" she repeated.

"We look for jobs. But we won't get them. But something is going to happen to help us out of this situation. I know it. Not jobs – at least, I don't think so. Something *else* is going to happen, and it's going to solve all our problems, and leave us free to enjoy ourselves this Christmas. I can feel it."

"Fair enough," Gill said. "I trust you."

And she did, which was an amazing thing all by itself. After all the dramas I'd put that poor girl through, she still believed in me – even when I came out with something that made it sound like I was losing touch with reality.

You know what? Honestly, I think she felt it too.

But there was no point in both of us sounding like lunatics, so she chose to keep quiet.

For the second day of our doomed quest, we headed once more to Sydney's backpacker area (and, coincidentally, the red light district. It worries the backpacker part of me, just how often those two things go together). It was a good hour's hike from the apartment, which gave us plenty of chance to chat about what we expected to find. Gill is the only person I know who can convincingly carry on a conversation for over an hour on the topic of 'nothing'.

This time we started at the opposite end of the Kings Cross strip, hitting up the places we'd been too disillusioned to try the previous day. Our heads revolved like radar dishes, eyes peeled for flyers on walls and in windows. 'Flat wanted,' 'Flat Wanted,' 'FLAT WANTED!' read the messages we saw.

Predictably, every hostel was rammed solid over the Christmas period.

Equally predictably, they were all charging outrageous prices for even the most basic accommodation.

The net result of this was a city bursting at the seams with backpackers – all of whom were frantically chasing the slightest glimmer of a job opportunity.

And most of them had a double-jump on me and Gill; they not

only had a head start, but they were all living right in the area where any jobs to be found, would be found.

When Gill and I called it a day, and made the long, hungry trek back to Leo's, we had to recognise the facts: there weren't any jobs. And if there were, we wouldn't be the ones to get them. And, if we were perfectly honest, we didn't really want to be. The kind of crappy employment prospects the other backpackers would be fighting over risked a serious cramping of our style.

"And anyway," I told Gill as we headed for home, "something will happen. Don't worry. *I just know it.*"

That evening, taking advantage of Leo's breathtakingly-fast broadband connection, I checked my email. There was a message sitting there from Leo himself, which was as expected; our second rent cheque was now due.

I turned the screen towards Gill, and asked her if she'd like to help me write the reply. If nothing else, I figured I could beg Leo to keep the bond we'd paid him, to use that to cover the rent we owed and to promise him that if anything was damaged when he got back, we'd sort it out with him then. I didn't plan on breaking anything worth six-hundred dollars, but in a place like this it was hard to tell – I'd broken three or four things already just by being me, and any one of them could have turned out to be valuable. Rich people almost never fill their apartments with cheap crap for me to break.

Gill sat next to me on the bed, and I took a deep breath, sighed it out – and clicked on Leo's email.

'Hi Tony and Gill,' it said.

'Thanks so much for paying the second instalment of your rent. The money went into my account this morning, so we're all good. Please find attached your receipt for $600. I hope you both have a great Christmas, and I'll see you when I get back.

All the best,

Leo'

We stared at the message in silence long enough for galaxies to be formed.

"But, we didn't...?" she said finally. "Is that... what you expected?"

"I dunno. I guess so," I said.

And to this day, neither of us has any clue as to how that happened.

Miscounting of funds? By a mathematician and geneticist?

Bank error in our favour?

What are the odds of that?

Trust to Fate, I told myself, and I've told myself the same thing every single day since that moment.

It always works out.

Trust to Fate.

Separation Anxiety

I fulfilled a long-held wish that year; I got to have pizza for Christmas dinner. In fact we had pizza for dinner three days either side of Christmas too, as it was on mega-cheap special offer at the supermarket. Gill and I had developed a habit; every evening we'd rock up just before closing time, and scour the shelves for all the food that had been reduced for quick sale.

We'd brandish our discoveries at each other, calling things like, "DUDE! Cottage cheese for ninety-nine cents!" across the shop. Then, cackling madly in triumph, we'd head towards the check-out chicks, and watch them sigh as we approached. Every item in our baskets would be heavily discounted, they knew. And that meant most of them wouldn't scan properly. I could actually see them slowing down whilst serving their next customers, in the hope of keeping their queue so long we'd move to the next register over.

The walk back from the shop, heavily laden, felt like victory; up in Leo's flat, we'd assemble and admire our purchases, swapping them around like puzzle pieces until we decided what combinations would make the most interesting meals.

Thus was born devilled-pasta salad on toast, sausage-and-meatball-kebabs, and Medley of Special-Offer Soups. Gill has always been somewhat creative when it comes to food (pie-and-mushy-pea-sandwiches being a particular favourite of hers) – and over years of extended travel I have developed the ability to eat absolutely anything. To me, a sell-by-date three weeks past is just a number; better than that, it's a challenge. 'This will make you sick if you eat it,' some food technician or scientist somewhere has decreed – to which I can't help but reply 'Wanna bet?'

For the record I'd like to say, I was not sick once over Christmas.

And the only thing I ate that was within its sell-by-date was the pizza.

Which was rubbish.

Plans for a Christmas party had been scaled back repeatedly until one day, walking home tired but satisfied, having pummelled a whole bunch of Asians, Gill went to check her bank balance.

And discovered it was $10.

My own account had been empty since our first payment to Leo.

Desperate times call for desperate measures, and the impending horror of a Christmas without any kind of alcohol – not to mention food – drove Gill to a sudden act of vandalism.

She grabbed Christmas cards from the pile we'd received, and started tearing them open. "Come on," she encouraged me, "these ones are from Mum and Dad!"

And then it dawned on me.

My parents, bless them, are from a different generation. While my sister and I feel content to swan around the world, expecting it to somehow provide for us, our parents know better. They've worked hard – damn hard – their entire lives, and they've done most of it to support Gillian and I.

Every year, wherever we are, at birthdays and holidays they send us a bit of money – and right now, that money was going to be our salvation.

Thanks, guys!

And parents, if you are reading this, and you are the kind that gives money to your children – on their behalf, I'd like to say THANK-YOU! We really appreciate it. Yes I know, ideally we should be working hard to build a stable career, pursuing realistic goals and a sensible relationship, putting in those 9-5 hours and working our way up the corporate ladde… ZNORG? Eh? Oh, sorry, I fell asleep writing that last sentence.

But you know that, deep down, you really want us to follow our dreams, right?

I'm sure I speak for all your offspring when I say: donations to this cause are very gratefully received!

And now, we return to our scheduled programming…

Oh yes. It was around this time that we got a parking ticket for Rusty – not because he was in the wrong place, but because we'd parked him facing the *wrong direction!* We couldn't believe it, but Roo later confirmed it; in Australia, the law says you have to park facing the appropriate direction of travel. Supposedly, this is because in order to park the other way around, you must have done some illegal manoeuvring on the wrong side of the road. Incredible.

Apparently it's the law in some other places too, but where the hell do they actually *enforce* that shit?

Sydney, that's where.

That was one little piece of the bad karma that was balancing out our good fortune, I guess. A much bigger part was the general feeling of loneliness we were experiencing. Gill and I have always had a great time hanging out together, but now Christmas Day was upon us yet again. It made us painfully aware that we were alone, adrift in a strange country, with all our family and friends literally on the other side of the world. This is one aspect of travel which I've always struggled with – this feeling that somewhere back at home, people I care deeply about are living happy, contented lives – and I'm not involved in any way. My usual antidote to this is to find something crazy to do, go off on a trip, or, failing that, get heavily drunk. But I had to be responsible now, as the figurative head of our little family unit. I had to look after Gill, and make sure she was safe, and that she was happy, too.

And anyway, we couldn't afford vodka.

Most of all, I missed Roo.

Gill missed her too of course – the three of us had been together for so long, through so many ridiculous adventures, that we'd bonded to an almost unhealthy degree. But I'm going to go out on a limb here, and say that I missed Roo more than Gill did. Certainly in more different way*s*, than Gill did.

Or so I hoped!

And I also hoped, as she relaxed in Perth with her Dad and her sisters, that she missed me too.

Roo flying back in was one of the happiest moments of my life up to that point.

I wasn't sure if I'd been harbouring lingering doubts about our relationship – specifically about the likelihood of her deciding to remain in Perth with her family – but all that was blown away when she stepped out of the Arrivals gate in Sydney airport.

Rusty was delighted to see her too – the old van had hardly turned a wheel in the month since he'd dropped her off at the same airport, and he was on his best behaviour. I think he was worried about being left behind when we headed off on the next leg of our grand adventure…

To Melbourne!

We'd been discussing our next move over Skype and email ever since Christmas, as Roo's return meant we only had a few days left in Leo's flat.

With no real prospects in Sydney, we'd decided to try our luck further afield – and Melbourne fit that bill perfectly.

That night Roo moved into the master bedroom, and poor Gill was relocated to the couch. I really did feel sorry for her – but not enough to stop me doing it!

This cut right to the heart of a situation I'd been worrying over in the back of my mind, ever since it had first occurred to me in the middle of the Bibbulmun Track.

Gill and me together were great.

Gill and Roo together were great.

Roo and me together were more than great – off the charts great in fact, and somehow managing to get greater all the time.

Gill, Roo and me – that was fun. It had been great. But more and more, I was starting to feel that it wasn't healthy – and that it wasn't fair.

On Gill.

I came out to sit with her after Roo went to sleep that night, and we had a glass of wine from a rapidly diminishing box of *goon*.

"So, Roo's back," I started.

"She is," Gill agreed.

"I feel a bit bad about how this has all worked out for you," I explained. "I'm aware that I kind of…"

"Stole her."

"Yes. I kind of stole her…"

"No, you *actually* stole her. She was mine – now she's yours. That's stealing."

"Okay, fair point."

"Thank-you."

"Right well, I think I've figured out a way to make it up to you."

"Oh?"

"Yes. I'm kicking you out. Here, in Sydney. When me and Roo carry on to Melbourne, we're going to leave you here."

"WHAT?? Are you fucking kidding me? What the hell do you mean, staying here? What the hell would I do in Sydney?"

"Well, you've said yourself – you don't want to leave kung fu. You like it here."

"Of course I do, but that doesn't mean I want to stay! Not on my own!"

"Ah, I see. Oh well – you haven't got a choice. Roo and I need some time alone. And you need… well, you need to meet people. To have some fun without us for a change. Make some new friends – and maybe even a boyfriend? You need to see what adventures you can get up to when we're not around to cramp your style."

I won't write what she said next. Not because I'm a stranger to swear-words, but because I've never heard quite so many of them overlapping each other. Her tirade continued at some length. I don't know why, but I got the feeling that Gill wasn't too pleased with my decision.

So I gave her some space to think it over.

I'm sensitive like that.

Melbourne Bound

Secretly I knew I'd cave – if Gill really did want to come to Melbourne with us, there was no way I was going to stop her.

But I hoped that by hard-lining it, I'd tricked her into thinking about it on a much more serious level than she'd have bothered with otherwise. We talked about it almost exclusively for the next few days. The downsides, which Gill was good at enumerating, were obvious; she'd have to start completely from scratch, in terms of... well, everything. Work. Home. Friends. Life.

But the benefits? They were less tangible, nebulous possibilities with the potential to be transformational – but also, as Gill loved to point out, a load of pointless bollocks. Why did she need to find new friends, when she had us right there? She wasn't desperately seeking a life partner at the moment, but felt she could handle that particular hurdle when she came to it. As for 'increased confidence, self-reliance and personal fulfilment?' Pah. It was easy to see why she usually won these arguments.

Leo came back from his sojourn overseas, and presented us with the exact same bundle of banknotes we'd given to him. So Gill and I were both in funds, albeit temporarily. No mention was made of what Gill and I had come to call our Christmas miracle, so we graciously took our money and left. We moved back to the same hostel we'd been staying in with Mum, and even ended up in the same pair of rooms.

We took a few long walks into the city, marvelling at how ceaselessly busy it was, how the floods of tourists and floods of locals all blended seamlessly on the streets, creating an atmosphere so vibrant it was palpable. We watched buskers with violins, and performance artists with chainsaws and unicycles, and saw the gleaming white hulls of the yachts ranked tightly in the harbour. Sydney was a great place, with a far stronger backpacker vibe than we'd experienced in Perth. It was closer to what a real capital city should feel like: massive and scary, but crazy and exciting with it. Here lives were being lived to their maximum potential, at high speed; thousands of coffees were being drank, and books read in parks, and bicycles ridden, and text messages sent from crowded commuter trains full of people who wished they could be doing exactly what we were doing; which was nothing.

And so it came to pass that the morning before we were due to set off for Melbourne, Gill came to me with a decision.

"I'm going to stay," she told me. Bravely.

Instantly, my fear that she would become old and grey still travelling with us, and never branch out to find someone of her very own, vanished – and was replaced by terror.

What was she going to do? How was she going to cope? What about money, about jobs, about a place to live? What if she didn't meet anyone – or what if she did, and they weren't right for her? What if something went drastically wrong?

These fears, of course, were the same ones that Gill was feeling – the same ones she'd wrestled with late into the night, every night, since I'd first made the 'suggestion' that had led her down this path.

Poor girl, she must have been shitting herself.

But she did it anyway.

The next day was a blur.

Gill and I toured every hostel in the city, settling on one that had old railway carriages as dorm rooms, and was considerably closer both to town, and to the kung fu school.

Then she packed her backpack, trying to squeeze a year-plus of accumulated possessions a third the size of a van into something she could carry on her back.

Every time she shook her head sadly at something too big to take, and replaced it in Rusty, my heart quailed. *I'm doing this to her,* I thought. *Even though it's for her own good.*

And I firmly believed that. I still do.

Gill was – and is – one of the people I love most on the entire planet.

I would never have intentionally caused her pain (well, let's just forget about the infamous bean-bag incident, and the log I dropped on her head, shall we?) – but there was no two ways about it; this was going to hurt.

For both of us.

We posed for a last photo, the three of us and Rusty, with Roo's camera set on timer perched on the wall outside Gill's new home.

We exchanged the longest group hug I think you're allowed to have in a public place. Then Roo retreated into Rusty, to give Gill and me a last moment together.

"Well, this is it," I told her. "It's been a great two years, dude."

"It has. The best."

"Take care of yourself."

"And you. Drive safely."

"We will. You… ah, walk safely! And call us if you need *anything*."

"I will." Gill sniffed, on the brink of tears. "Now bugger off before I change my mind!"

"Okay then. See you soon."

I climbed into Rusty's passenger seat and gave Gill a last thumbs-up through the windscreen.

"You're right you know," she called to me, "you do cramp my style!"

And with that, we were gone.

This is one of those moments where Roo's account of the story differs somewhat from mine. I distinctly remember giving a cheerful wave, and setting forth on our journey like the emboldened explorer I was becoming. Whereas Roo says I wept like a little girl for the next two hours straight. I'm man enough to admit, in hindsight, that the truth probably lies somewhere between the two.

I do remember being in a supermarket some time later, feeling fairly miserable, and being quite surprised when a burly, leather-clad biker came up to me in the cereal aisle and asked if I was okay. Roo covered for me, telling the biker that I was upset because I'd just thrown my sister out of the van. I'm not sure he took the right meaning from that, but he certainly kept his distance when he reached for a packet of Crunchy Nut Corn Flakes.

Letting Gill go had been one of the hardest decisions of my life.

Convincing her to go… Well, let's just say I still had both testicles, so I'd got away easier than expected.

The scars were all on the inside…

Because only Roo could now drive Rusty, and because this was the first time the two of us had been properly alone together, we stopped often on our way to Melbourne. The land between Australia's two greatest cities was much greener and more appealing than the harsh north-west of the country, with vast stretches of woodland accompanying the road on several occasions. We found plenty of secluded groves, well away from the prying eyes of other travellers, to park Rusty in so we could…

Well, you know.

It took us three days to do little over six-hundred miles, free camping in the woods every night and feeling like we were pioneering explorers from another age.

We also felt, almost for the first time, like we were a *proper couple*.

It also helped to nurse Rusty, as he was up to his old tricks again; boiling up frequently, regardless of traffic or weather. Whatever was wrong with the old van, it was clearly serious – and more than likely, terminal.

"Just get us to Melbourne," we routinely asked him, "then you can rest."

But it looked worrying like it would be rest of the eternal kind.

For ourselves though, we were happy – deliriously so, apart from occasional moments when one or the other, or both of us, would suddenly miss Gill so hard it was like a stab in the chest.

But at the risk of sounding trite, what doesn't kill you, makes you stronger. Unless it's some kind of crippling, wasting disease, but no-one ever talks about those.

Whatever we were feeling, no doubt Gill was feeling doubly.

And every time she managed to shrug that feeling off, and go out to meet new friends in the bar, she'd be growing as a person. Gaining in strength and self-belief every day that she was on her own.

Or so I hoped.

Inflatable Love

We coasted Rusty into a Big Four campsite in Frankston, on the outskirts of Melbourne, and pitched our tiny tent in the shade of two giant Winnebagos and a bus conversion the size of a 747.

And there we stayed for the next three months.

To say that we were deliriously happy, Roo and I, is actually an understatement.

There were spectres on the horizon of course; we were broke, and getting broker; jobs proved considerably more elusive than they ever had been in the west; and Gill, bless her, was still coming to terms with being out there all alone – she was struggling with the same issues we were, namely finances, employment, and finding a place to live. I felt terrible for her, but this was the teething part of solo world travel, and the chances were it was going to get worse before it got better.

I sent her a multitude of supportive emails, full of phrases like 'Of course it won't get worse before it gets better,' and 'Who needs money when you've got… well, everything that you've got,' and 'No, you cannot come to Melbourne and stay with us.'

Deep down I knew that Gill was a strong, confident, savvy world traveller; she was just hiding it under the guise of crying herself to sleep every night.

She was a caterpillar on the verge of becoming a butterfly – except that I'd kicked her out of her cocoon and buggered off to Melbourne in it.

One day she'd thank me.

I hoped.

It's fair to say though, that for Roo and I, those months were blissful. We tried as hard as we could be bothered to secure work and accommodation, but not so hard that we were ever in danger of, you know, *finding* any.

Instead we eked out our paltry savings – which were, in fact, Roo's paltry savings – yes, I am that sponging, layabout boyfriend your mother warned you of! We lived cheap, buying all the reduced-price food from a wide range of supermarkets, and cooking it in the camp kitchen. We had early nights and late mornings, and did precious little in-between. Every waking moment was spent together, and as many of them as possible were spent in each other's arms. At night, when the temperature plummeted, we snuggled up together under a pile of blankets, and let the rest of the world do whatever it wanted to. It was, in a word, glorious.

Oh, and I should probably mention the Giant Jumping Pillow.

You'll recall the no-nonsense Aussie attitude towards naming things? Good. So it shouldn't be too hard to extrapolate what I'm talking about here: it was a pillow, for jumping on – and it was giant. Y'see how that works?

This brightly-coloured, stripy inflatable was like the bottom half of a bouncy castle – only it was the size of a tennis court. I re-learned the fabled Art Of Bouncing with the help of a series of tutors, the oldest of whom was about twelve. It's possible that the pillow was placed there for children, but there were no rules against adults using it – the people in the office just shrugged when I asked them, as though it had never come up. So I carried right on, whilst taking extra care not to crush anyone.

Between 10am, when the heat in the tent became unbearable, until about seven in the evening, when the pillow closed for the night, I was more often than not to be found on it or by it – either bouncing around like a maniac, or recovering from injuries sustained in this manner. As is often the case, the kids were disgustingly good at it; I asked a few how they'd learnt their tricks, and they all replied "Oh, we got a trampoline in the back yard." As though it was the most normal thing in the world. Because of course, it is in Australia – everyone's got 'em. Big things too, of the kind I was lucky enough to see at the fair once a year.

Just one more thing that Australians have got right, in their quest to embrace the great outdoors.

Want your kids to play in the garden more? Worried that they're spending too much time on the Xbox?

GIVE THEM A TRAMPOLINE!

My parents are the most loving, caring people in the world, but I will never forgive them for not digging up our entire back garden and turning it into a trampoline.

Or a swimming pool.

But anyway, for the purposes of this book, all you need to know is that I performed my first ever back-flips, somersaults, back-somersaults, hand-springs and assorted combinations of the above, on that giant jumping pillow in Frankston.

I gave Roo a nightly display of my achievements, which amongst other things, stopped me getting fat on a diet of marked-down sausages and burgers.

Roo was suitably impressed by my developing skill, and took it upon herself to be supportive of my endeavour. Every afternoon she would sit there with a book, applauding my efforts in between chapters, and shouting things like, "Very nice, dear," and "Who's a clever boy then?" and "Come in Tony, your dinner's ready!"

I was quite proud of myself. I'd gained a skill that meshed neatly with almost every other skill I posses, in that it is absolutely, completely and utterly useless.

But *so* much fun!

All good things must come to an end, or so they say. Frankston, though idyllic (for us – I'm sure that's not a common perception of the place), was a damn long way from the city. Like most satellite suburbs, it had its own shopping centres, banks, supermarkets and so on – but Melbourne is a massive place, with the population of any other big city contrasted with a significantly lower population density. In other words, it sprawls – so from our little campsite it was a full two-hour journey, first by Rusty, then by train, to get into the city centre. This got old very quickly, especially once the backpacker job agency I'd signed up with began to throw me odd days of work. It was fairly brainless stuff, laying carpet floor tiles for upcoming exhibitions, but it was the missing piece of the puzzle – an income. So we crammed our tent, mattresses, heater and lights, bedding and chairs, pots, pans, crockery, books, backpacks, clothes and shoes, Esky and food – not to mention one giant bag of SCUBA diving gear – back into Rusty, and drove him parallel to the train tracks, right into the heart of Melbourne.

To the amusingly-named suburb of Balaclava, where I was disappointed to see not a ski mask in sight.

I bought one from an op-shop though, so I could have my photo taken underneath the sign on the station platform. This was much more amusing to me than it is to you (you'll just have to take my word for it), because whilst trying (and failing) to become a world-famous actor, I became heavily involved in making a low-budget movie. Strictly speaking it was a no-budget movie, but we all did our best – most of my kung fu class showed up to be extras, all being given a balaclava from a box and a toy machine gun, and being told they were 'the baddies'. There was no plot as such – just an endless orgy of violence, which saw the demise of dozens, nay hundreds of balaclava-clad minions – the vast majority of whom were played by yours truly and a couple of mates. To keep it fresh, we'd swap odd bits of gear – and balaclavas – each time we were killed on film.

So my first action in this strange new town was to send a copy of that photo to my friend and mentor, Mark Strange, who had masterminded the production of that movie.

And, because he's half decent at that shit, he now *is* an actor.

Damn it.

But anyway, it's hard to be bitter when you're living in Melbourne instead of Manchester. Although our accommodation wouldn't suit everyone...

Roo and I rented a room, based on an advert in the ever-useful Gumtree website. As far as we knew, we had a double room – and this part turned out to be right. The room was basic, but after living in a tent for three months, so were our needs. There were two other bedrooms in that house. One had four people in bunk beds, and one sleeping on the floor; the other had four bunk beds and no-one on the floor, because there was barely enough room to stand up between the beds let alone sleep there. The lounge had two mismatched sofas, obviously rescued from the side of the road at some point, and both of these were occupied as well. And occasionally, there would be a couple of house-guests crashing on the living room floor.

It made for quite a friendly little community, with anywhere from twelve to fifteen people living there at any one time. There was one tiny kitchen, which we all managed to share amicably, and one bathroom, which was about the size of an under-stairs cupboard. There was a queue for the toilet twenty-four hours a day, which grew dramatically every time anyone took a shower. It was... remarkably cosy, actually.

The house was owned by an Israeli couple, and several of the tenants were friends and family of theirs from back home. Two of the guys cultivated a healthy cannabis plant in the shed, which they lined with egg boxes and newspaper to keep in the heat. They brought the plant out every day for a bit of sunshine, and in all respects treated it like a pet. They talked to it; they pruned it with a pair of nail scissors, and sprayed it with water from a misting bottle. One of them even played his guitar and sang to it when he thought no-one else was around.

But despite the harmonious relationship we developed with our enclave of housemates, we got sick of late-night toilet visits, which generally involved getting fully dressed and legging it to the public loos in the car park across the road.

Balaclava had only ever been a temporary measure, and as the work became more regular, we found another advert on the Gumtree, and moved in with a lady called Kat, in Yarraville.

At the risk of spoiling the surprise of the next chapter, we would come to call her The Crazy Kat Lady.

And no – she didn't own a single cat.

Kraziness

The room Kat had to let was unfurnished, but that didn't faze us; we strolled down to St. Vincent De Paul's op shop (otherwise known as 'Vinnies'), and bought a second-hand, queen-sized mattress, which we fervently hoped would fit in Rusty.

We hadn't dared drive the van this far, for fear he'd break down on the wrong side of a major junction – so we lifted the mattress onto our heads, with Roo at the front because she was more observant than me (and more stable in every sense of the word), and me bringing up the rear so that I could watch her rear as we walked.

Everyone's a winner!

And we hiked the two miles back home to Balaclava with a queen-sized mattress on our heads. But everyone's had to do that at some point, right?

We crammed the mattress in on top of all the other crap in Rusty, and made the drive to Kat's place at 4am, to ensure we met no traffic. Even so, Rusty barely made the twenty minute journey, and as Roo parked him outside our new home steam was bubbling out of him; I had serious doubts he'd be making another trip anytime soon. Maybe never.

At first we thought we'd struck it lucky; a mix-up of place names had us assuming we were moving to South Yarra, a thriving suburb full of trendy cafés and funky boutique shops. Yarraville was something else entirely; a quiet, rather down-at-heel suburb full of dilapidated period houses in overgrown gardens. It was starting to become popular with developers because the train from Yarraville's single platform to the colossal Victorian edifice of Flinders Street Station in central Melbourne took less than fifteen minutes.

Kat told us that she had only just moved in (a year ago). Apparently she'd bought the hundred-year-old wooden house as a fixer-upper, and she was renovating it at a speed that made evolution look fast. So far she'd succeeding in removing a breakfast-bar, leaving a giant raised concrete plinth in the middle of the kitchen – and that was about it. Tins of paint, brushes and rollers, tarps and tools, lay in piles in a wooden lean-to she grandly labelled the 'sun room'.

In the lounge there was a hard wooden bench with a green vinyl-covered foam cushion, which she mistakenly referred to as a sofa. I could practically see the struggle going on inside her, as she decided whether to tell us we could use it or not. It looked so uninviting, I didn't care either way, but it seemed like a peculiar issue to encounter at the beginning of our lease.

There was only one other piece of furniture in the lounge; a book case filled with shelf upon shelf of fancy tea-cups and saucers. Some of them were quite beautiful, with ornate handles, paintings of birds and flowers on them, and matching saucers with gold-leaf edges. It was the kind of collection that would take pride of place in your Grandma's china cabinet.

Oh, and there was a TV, but it wasn't plugged in and had no aerial. Kat really was one of those 'don't watch TV' type people – which of course meant that from then on, we didn't either.

But we didn't care about any of that. The rent was cheap, it was close to the city, and on the other side of the train tracks there was a take-away called *Weird Pizza*. Oh yes! Their banana-curry pizza was a masterpiece. Not quite as good as the sour-cream-chilli-nachos pizza, but way better than the prickly-pear-and-goat's-cheese.

(As an aside, I got chatting with the owner one day and asked him how he'd come up with the idea. He told me he'd been heavily stoned one day, when his mate said, "Dude, we should totally sell pizzas with really weird shit on them!" And that was that. You had to respect that kind of vision.)

No, there was nothing wrong with Yarraville's selection of pizza.

It was Kat herself, who was the problem.

On our first evening in the house, we heard a knock at our door – and then it opened without waiting for an answer. Kat poked her head around it. "Hi, I just wanted to let you know that I'm back from work! And I noticed you'd put your trash out…" she held up a scrap of card from the back of a battery packet, and a plastic bottle top. "…and these are recyclable, you know? Is that okay?"

"Ah…" There really isn't much you can say when faced with that sort of thing. "Yes, that's fine."

"Okay!" And she scurried off, all smiles now that her lesson had been imparted.

"Woah," said Roo, when the door was safely shut, "she went

through our rubbish! Even though we put out our recycling separately. That woman is bat-shit crazy!"

The house had central-heating, a rarity for Australia, but Kat refused to turn it on. "It's a waste of money," she explained, conveniently ignoring the fact that it was our money she was choosing not to waste. Instead, as the evenings and early mornings became chillier, she resorted to wearing a bobble hat, duffle coat and ski gloves inside the house. Roo and I snuggled up together on our mattress on the floor from about 8pm onwards – wearing jumpers – and shivered through the night.

Ever the eco-warrior, Kat continued to go through our rubbish – even sneaking into our room when we were out, to go through our bins before we emptied them. She'd leave the evidence next to my pillow, with little Post-it notes saying, "Hi! Just popped in to check on something, and found these in your bin. Don't forget to recycle!"

It wasn't a horse's head, but it was pretty fucking close.

In the evenings, she'd follow us around flicking out the lights as we moved from room to room. Quite often Roo would nip to the toilet, leaving something cooking on the stove, and come back to find the kitchen in darkness – and a stern reminder from Kat, written on a Post-it note stuck to the light switch, that she needed to remember to turn things off when she wasn't using them.

"She's timing me in the shower," Roo confided to me one night. "And she goes in after me, to check I used that bucket to catch the 'excess water'. If I forget, I have to fill it up from the taps, or she'll barge in here while I'm naked to remind me about it."

"Wow. Bat-shit crazy is putting it mildly!"

"Quiet!" she hissed. "That bat-shit crazy woman has bat-like hearing too. In fact she might actually be a bat."

"I wonder if she hangs upside down in her room at night?"

"She probably has to – she doesn't own any furniture! Let's not get close enough to find out though. She may bite. And if she does, she probably has rabies."

By this point, the backpacker job agency had found me a semi-regular gig with a company called InstallEx. They built exhibitions, transforming giant empty spaces into display-packed halls, laying thousands of carpet tiles and assembling hundreds of stalls and booths with a quick-lock post and rail system and a judicious amount of swearing. I excelled at the job, and got to see – and decorate – the insides of such iconic buildings as the Melbourne Cricket Ground, the

Crown Casino, the Convention Centre and Flemington Racecourse.

When we were tasked with setting up for the Building Expo, the bosses of InstallEx were on high alert. They wanted a show of force, to prove that they were players in the construction industry – which they weren't, but apparently the Big Boss really, *really* wanted to be. He was there himself in fact, which is where I met him.

Although I didn't know it at the time, because he was in a scissor-lift.

He was in the cage on top of it, inspecting something, and I was walking past the bottom.

"Hey, you!" he called down to me.

"Hello!" I responded cheerfully.

"Listen, I need you to move this thing about two meters over there," he pointed to a huge sign, which he was obviously intent on inspecting.

"Ah… I've never used one of these before, I'm afraid."

"That's alright lad, it's not rocket science. Just steer it with the joystick and press GO."

"Okay… but aren't you supposed to come down first?"

"We're only going a couple of meters."

"Okay. Give me a sec." I studied the controls. They looked simple enough, but I had that feeling of dread in my stomach – the one that knows Sod's Law by heart: 'What Can Go Wrong, Will Go Wrong' – in my life to date, it has held truer than any other law except gravity.

I pushed the joystick, and the scissor life leapt forward. Shocked, I let go of the lever, and it lurched to a halt. There were cries of "WOAH!" from above.

"I'm not too sure about this, maybe you should come down and show me how?"

"Bloody hell, just drive us over there. It's not that difficult!"

So I pushed the lever again. The lift lurched into life once more, covering the couple of metres far quicker than I expected.

"STOP!"

I stopped. In very nearly the right place, it seemed.

"Right – just spin us around."

I looked at the controls, and started to twist the stick, but the lift gave an alarming wobble as it shifted, accompanied by a few yells from above.

"I think it might tip over if I try to turn it anymore," I called to the boss. "The floor down here is a bit uneven."

He swore under his breath, in the way that bosses do when their minions prove unspeakably incompetent, and said, "Alright, bring us down."

Happy to comply, I pushed the 'lower' button – and was rewarded with a screech of steel and a hideous ripping sound.

"SHIT!" I stopped lowering, but it was too late – the far corner of the lift platform had caught the top of the huge sign as it descended, and with thousands of pounds of pressure per square inch, had torn the thing in two.

When the boss got down, courtesy of someone who actually had their Scissor Lift Operator's License, he was so red in the face I thought he would explode like a tomato in a microwave.

So I fled. It wasn't like there was anything I could do – the sign would have to be re-ordered, and the boss would have to shoulder the cost, seeing as how he was risking a huge fine from the Health and Safety Executive for breaking pretty much every rule in the book when it comes to scissor lifts.

I went back to the crew I'd been working with, building a series of small, enclosed rooms at the furthest end of the hall. There I hid, and dwelled on my most recent cock-up while I fitted plastic wall panels into tracks on the steel framework.

An hour later we completed the rooms by fitting a series of locking doors into the last openings. I led the crew inside the first one to tighten the bolts holding it together.

Suddenly, with the door shut, all became peaceful. It was a little haven from the frenetic atmosphere outside.

"You know, it's crazy," I said, "but no-one would ever think of looking for us in here. There's so many staff out there hanging around, doing sod all… we'd never even be missed!"

"Ha! Yeah. Just chill in here, like, till it's all over!" someone agreed.

"I could even stretch out like this – Zzzz…" I lay full length on the floor with my hands behind my head, and closed my eyes in mock sleep. "No-one would ever—"

And that's when the door opened.

"I thought I heard voices…" the boss tailed off, as he was presented with probably the most blatant evidence of skiving he'd ever seen.

We all stood up, trying not to look too busted – difficult, really, because Katie Price isn't as busted as we were in that moment.

The figure in the doorway was *the* boss. Not just of InstallEx, but of the gigantic parent company, Morton.

I recognised him, because an hour ago I'd inadvertently helped

him demolish a five-hundred dollar sign.
I didn't work much for InstallEx, after that.

InstallEx

But you know what? The other bosses at InstallEx were decent people. After the dust settled – and settled some more – and when they were desperate – I got the call again.

Perhaps because, unlikely as it may seem, I was *good* at this!

The steel framing system used on most of their jobs was like Lego – and who doesn't love Lego?

I also discovered I was pretty good at organising the other backpackers, mostly because no-one else seemed to give a shit about it. The bosses had their work cut out just dealing with the endless stream of complaints about lack of tools, or slight injuries, or missed break-times. Without direct supervision more than half the workforce would quite happily just stand there, staring blankly about them, as though they were being remote controlled and the signal had been cut off. I took it on myself, out of frustration more than anything else, to point out the rather obvious contributions they could be making towards getting us all out of there.

"Why don't you start another row of floor tiles?" I'd say.

"Uh? Yeah. Might as well." And off they'd go. Empty handed. So I'd send another lad after them with a trolley full of floor tiles, and another with some helpful reminders about how far from the wall to start placing them, and then another with the missing tape measure that he'd just discovered in his pocket.

When Paul the manager came back, his keen eye for the job must have noticed that something was different. He was a friendly chap – tall, thin, and bald as an egg, presumably from the frustration of running a business reliant on backpacker labour. He soon started seeking me out, asking how work was progressing, who was doing what, and if I had any suggestions on how to divide the labour for the tasks ahead. His instructions to me graduated from, "Take this floor tile. Put it there," to, "Take this map. Grab a few guys, and see if you can build fifty cubicles in the south-west corner."

Without even noticing how it happened, I was promoted from

mindless labour to supervising a team. Whether laying flooring or assembling exhibition stands, I was the one giving out jobs, making the measurements, explaining how to build the railing system into recognisable, three-dimensional booths, and strategizing with Paul about how to get everything done on the typically frantic schedule.

I worked on all their big jobs, building hundreds of individual stalls and displays for international-scale exhibitions – flower shows, future homes expos, computer fairs – you name it, if it came to Melbourne, we built it.

And two, three or sometimes four days later, we pulled the whole thing down again. Packed every steel rail, locking nut and bolt, partition, plinth, sign and carpet tile, back into their appropriate containers and shipped them back to warehouses all over the city.

On the one hand, it was ridiculous; the sheer quantity of labour that went into erecting some of the displays was monumental, not to mention the thousands of dollars that had been spent crafting the individual pieces of signage, and bespoke booths and counters, that we spent dozens of frustrating hours struggling to assemble. This titanic expenditure of cash and effort produced something amazing, time after time – every show was unique, and all of them looked *incredible*. Staggeringly impressive, almost as though hundreds of people had sweated for thousands of man-hours to perfect every little detail across two acres of show-floor…

Which they had.

Ripping it all down again less than a week later was every bit as demoralising as it was satisfying.

And lucrative, of course!

And so for the next couple of months, we did quite well. Roo worked alongside me whenever they called in a big backpacker crew, and later on she got a job counting people on trains (no, seriously!). I worked ridiculous shifts, anywhere from ten to eighteen hours, often getting less than eight hours off before I was needed back again. I earned a reputation for never saying no to a job, for always being reliable, and for remaining relentless cheerful even when it was 5am, twelve hours into a fourteen-hour job that was going to take at least six more hours to finish. The backpackers dropped like flies under such conditions, or called in sick ahead of them; rarely was the crew the same from night to night, as heavy drinking and an inability to cope with long shifts culled the less dedicated workers on a daily basis.

We got to explore the city a bit, braving Melbourne's infamously fickle weather to visit the hippie district of St. Kilda (where the op-shops were so trendy that the clothes in them cost more than they did brand new!). We spent hours forging our way up and down Flinders Street, the city's main thoroughfare, because the foot traffic was so dense it was impossible to do it any quicker. It was a great street though, exemplifying the best things about Melbourne. It was busy and cosmopolitan, seeming much more like a major US city in this regard than Perth. The people thronging the streets were all stylishly dressed, and everything that was old, from pre-loved clothing to the archaic tram system to the buildings themselves, were well-preserved and proudly displaying their vintage status. The modern, from sharp suits to sports cars to the steel-and-glass behemoth looming over Federation Square, were crisp and clean and cutting-edge. Nothing looked broken or run-down or unintentional. Designer shops fought for space with sushi bars and bistros, spilling into narrow laneways either side of the main street and even underground; the redevelopment of the train stations had involved burying them beneath the city, along with scores of shops, food courts and plazas.

Roo and I both loved Melbourne.

Even the bridges were more like art installations, from ancient stone to plate-steel industrial to whimsical latticework – I can't even begin to describe them all, so I'm going to take the coward's way out, and direct you to Google.

It was a city of the future, high-tech and affluent, whilst still acknowledging its heritage with buildings like St Paul's Cathedral and the gigantic Victorian edifice of Flinders Street Station taking pride of place. It's a beaut, that station – the oldest in Australia, and one of the biggest – and more than a hundred-thousand people pass through it every single day!

Most days, I was one of them.

I commonly left for work at some ungodly hour, braving the chill fog with my oversized Balinese leather jacket wrapped tightly around me; lunch would be spent basking in the sun, and the journey home would be made in torrential rain. Four seasons in one day, they call it, and I've never found a place where this was more true. I even have two photos of Roo, taken a few hours apart on the same day off – in one she is sunbathing in Kat's backyard, and in the second she is scooping up hailstones from it!

After three months on the job, Paul took me aside and said he was rewarding me with a brief stint as a carpenter's assistant on a multi-storey office block building site. It was a Union job, he explained, which meant a significantly higher rate of pay – *thirty-two dollars an hour*, which was a hell of a jump from the already impressive nineteen dollars I was currently earning.

And all this time, Rusty sat rusting outside Crazy Kat's house in Yarraville.

I'd become an expert in Melbourne's public transport system (which is, as it should be, world class). I felt a bit sorry for Rusty, as he sat unmoving through everything the sky could throw at him. He never complained, of course, but the old van seemed lonely and decrepit. I started to wonder if he'd ever leave that spot again – if he'd even be able to, after so long without turning a wheel.

As the weather grew steadily colder, we bought a little electric fan-heater for our room. We had to wait until Kat was out to smuggle it in, and could only use it when we had music playing to mask its distinctive noise. Occasionally she would surprise us with a knock on the door, and we'd leap around like maniacs shoving stuff in front of the thing so she wouldn't see it when she opened the door. Which she always did whether or not we answered, usually two heartbeats after knocking, rather than allowing us the leisure of doing it ourselves. Looking back, I'm sure she knew that *something* was going on – probably because she was paranoid. And spying on us. And she was determined to catch us in the act of whatever it was we were doing.

She came damn close to catching us in a different act on a number of occasions, but to be honest I don't think she'd have recognised that one.

No way someone that uptight has ever been laid.

So yet again, we'd built a life for ourselves. It certainly had its quirks, but we were starting to get comfortable with them. And, as always happens at that point, our feet began to itch...

State of The Union

There's a phrase: money for old rope. Well this was money for old wood – *literally*, as I was being paid an additional fifty cents an hour purely because I was working with second-hand timber! Danger money, you see, because that shit'll kill you in a heartbeat.

Or maybe not. But that was just the beginning.

Working on any level above the third floor: an extra 50c.

Working with power tools? Another dollar.

It went crazy after that, with compensations for working on upper floors increasing with their distance from the ground, and all sorts of ridiculous extras. As a rule of thumb, if you needed some kind of protective gear – like a pair of gloves, say, or a dust-mask – then chances were, you'd be getting paid more for it.

And let's not forget: my starting rate for this job was thirty-two bucks an hour!

Overtime was unbelievable. Time-and-a-half for the first two hours – and then double-time for everything after that! When they needed volunteers to work the weekend, you can bet my hand went straight up.

All in all, that week I earned almost two-thousand dollars.

And I paid nearly eight-hundred bucks in tax for the privilege.

I didn't mind one bit. For one thing, I could claim most of that money back; as a backpacker, I'd earned so little this year that I fell way under the threshold for even the lowest tax bracket. But more importantly, I had enough wages left over after rent, food and bills had come out of them, to buy two economy class tickets to New Zealand.

So that's exactly what I did.

Roo was so excited she could hardly sit still. After months of a fairly mundane existence, we'd come up with the ultimate antidote for our boredom; it was time for a sea change.

No, screw that – it was time for a snow change…

I rang Gill in Sydney straight away. "Dude! How do you feel about going to New Zealand and learning to snowboard…?"

I hardly needed to make the call. We'd both dreamed about snowboarding, ever since the richer kids from our school got to go on an organised skiing trip. We'd cultivated a forced disinterest in snow sports from that point on, because it was clearly something that only rich people did – and we were perfectly-happy-without-being-rich-thank-you-very-much. Skiing was not something people like us should aspire to.

But snowboarding… well, that was a different matter.

I believe I mentioned my first attempt to become a snowboarder in my last book, but for those of you that haven't read that one it went something like this:

Went to France.

Was molested by a French pensioner.

Arrived to find the resort closed.

Got a job sanding every inch of a giant wooden ski chalet.

Spent two months doing it.

And then got scammed out of most of my wages.

Went home.

And that was only after I escaped a fiery death in the furnace of a gypsy-killing prune farmer…

It hadn't really been my proudest moment.

A string of my least-proud moments in fact.

This time, I vowed, it would be different.

Or else I'd be *really* pissed off.

With the cash already spent, I seriously considered framing my latest pay slip. It was the most money I'd ever earned in my life, and only Air New Zealand's carry-on policy dissuaded me.

Apparently they discourage travelling with breakable glass nowadays.

The only real doubt I had about leaving Australia, was about how good the country had been to me. It had provided me with plenty of adventures, an adoring (and adorable) girlfriend – and not always, but when I needed it most – a cold, hard, pile of cash. I was going to miss that.

While we're on the subject of cash, if you're reading this in the future then you can FUCK RIGHT OFF with your hover-boards, because WE WERE SUPPOSED TO HAVE THOSE BY NOW! And you probably don't understand what the Global Financial Crisis was, because you don't have money anymore. Or trees. In fact the chances are you're either made entirely of nanobots, in which case you only speak binary, or you're mind-controlled by crab-clawed alien overlords, in which case you only speak space-mollusc. Either way, I'm wasting my breath.

But to bring it back to the not-so-distant future, the Aussie economy is only getting stronger. Twice this year, one of our dollars bought one of America's with change. And that insanely high minimum wage (\$18 per hour!) *even applies to people who work in McDonalds!*

So, you know, think about it.

Anyway, around this time it occurred to me that if we were planning on working in New Zealand's ski industry, we should probably apply for some jobs there.

So I applied for all of them.

Three times.

Once for Gill, once for Roo, and once for myself. It was neater that way.

The first place to get back to me was a company called Ruapehu Alpine Lifts, who ran the only two ski-fields in New Zealand's North Island – they were back-to-back, on either side of a mountain called Mount Ruapehu. Of the two, I'd selected jobs on the 'Turoa' side, purely because the other side was called 'Whakapapa' – a Maori word, used to refer to their tribal hierarchy and genealogical structure. And in Maori, 'WH' is pronounced 'F'.

I didn't think I'd be able to keep a straight face if I ended up working there.

The employment people at Turoa agreed to give us a Skype call by way of an interview – me for the role of 'Ski-Lift Operator/Attendant', because that seemed to me like the whole point of being there; Roo as 'Road Crew', because the job description said it mainly involved parking cars, and she said "I can do that!" – and for Gill, I'd gone for 'Ticket Checker/Customer Services' – because if anyone could talk to customers – talk them into the ground, in fact – it was Gill.

They called me a fortnight later.

The interview went something like this:

So, Mr Slater, you've applied to be a liftie with us."

"I have?"

"Yes. A ski-lift operator."

"Oh, right. Yes, that's me."

"So let's talk a bit about your experience."

"Um, I haven't got any."

"Oh! Okay then, let's talk a bit about your background in snow sports."

"I haven't got any of that, either."

"Alright then, that's okay. So what's your reason for seeking employment in the snow-sport industry?"

"Ahhh… is 'being cool' an acceptable answer?"

"Ha ha! A joker. Great, we like the jokers!"

I thought that sounded fairly positive.

For the rest of the interview, I was grilled on my mechanical knowledge (none), driving ability (none), other sporting background (none), and education (none – okay, so I have a degree in Acting, but I'm pretty sure that counts as 'none').

I was asked if I had any previous work references, and I agonised over this for a good few minutes. InstallEx still didn't know I was leaving, because if I didn't get this job, there was a good chance I wasn't. Beyond that, my most recent job had been for Trevor. Given that I'd had to threaten Trevor with reporting him to the government just to get paid, he didn't seem like the ideal source of a work-related reference. Previous to that I'd been working for Goldie… I seriously doubted he could read or write, and anyway he only knew me as Andy… and prior to that, I'd single-handedly depopulated a Sandalwood plantation one tree at a time. Then there was my stint at The Underground, where I failed miserably to make a bar fail miserably… and a handful of days cleaning toilets for the City of Canning.

It didn't look good.

In the end I asked Lindsey of Buildcraft, figuring that even though I'd left abruptly, I'd been good at what I did for him. Brick paving was about as irrelevant to the winter sports industry as its possible to get (short of, say, volunteering with exotic animals in a sub-tropical climate) – but my options were fairly limited.

Roo's interview was conducted a couple of hours later.

She'd sat listening to my call, so she was prepared for the first few questions.

"So, Miss Reynen, you've applied to be a roadie here at Mount Ruapehu?"

"Yes, but I'm afraid I have no real experience in the winter sports environment. Because I'm from Australia. I'm very enthusiastic though!"

"Well that's good to hear. So what makes you want to come and work for us?"

"I've never seen snow before!"

In the silence that followed, I could almost hear the interviewer's head hitting his desk.

When I called Gill in Sydney to see how her interview had gone, she was (as always) relentlessly positive about it. "They only asked me a couple of questions," she explained.

"Oh? We got a proper grilling."

"No, I had a really nice lady. She asked if I'd been skiing before, so I told her I'd had some ice skating lessons, and she asked if I had any customer service experience, and I said a little bit. Then she asked how I was at talking to people, and that was it."

"Really? Our interviews were half an hour long!"

"So was mine."

"But what..? What else did she ask you?"

"Nothing. We just got chatting. She's always wanted a horse."

"I...? What? Bloody hell Gill, you were supposed to be telling her why you'd be good at the job!"

"Yeah... we kind of ran out of time for that. But she was very friendly. I told her all about Camp America, and driving around in Rusty. She loved the idea of doing a road trip around Oz."

"Oh. My. God."

Gill got the job straight away.

And a week later, amongst many feelings of anxiousness and indecision, both Roo and I were offered the positions we'd applied for. I can only think, it must have been a slow year for applications; we were seriously bottom-of-the-barrel stuff. But no matter! Roo was going to get her wish – she was going to the land of Hobbits, to see snow for the first time in her life.

And I was going to have to tell InstallEx that I was leaving.

Tricky Situations

I didn't get chance to mention my imminent departure, because work on the Union Job dried up after the first week – not for me, but for everyone else on the entire building site.

I still maintain that this wasn't my fault.

I spent a day bouncing back and forth between angry meetings, fielding evasive calls from the big boss of my company and threatening ones from the big boss of theirs.

The trouble was, I was not a member of the Union.

And every other worker on the site was. There was a subtle clue to this fact in the title 'Union Job.'

Now it turns out, this Builder's Union is big deal in Australia. By uniting workers across all the construction trades, they'd used their collective bargaining power to create a list of demands, mostly about rates of pay and working conditions. It was for this reason I'd been paid so handsomely, for doing so little – the almighty Union had made it so, and for that they were heavily rewarded. Membership of the union didn't require any special skills – it just required a yearly payment of six-hundred and fifty dollars.

Obviously, I didn't have that kind of cash stuffed under my mattress. Hell, I barely had a mattress. Technically my employers, as in InstallEx, should have supplied a Union-appointed labourer to the site, or else turned the job down. Now, after a flash credential inspection revealed me to be non-Union labourer, two things happened: first I was suspended, pending a round of discussions with my boss; and second, the entire job site was shut down. Lock, stock, and bearded carpenter – to a man, the Union members downed tools at the behest of their official representative, and refused to move another muscle until all the non-Union labour was expelled from site.

It was, for want of a better word, *awkward.*

It was also a shame, because I'd been getting on quite well. The tradies on the site all seemed to like me. As usual, my enthusiasm outstripped my ability somewhat, and I'd managed to accidentally chop up a series of ceiling-cladding tiles that were due to be installed that day. But one thing those guys understood was that mistakes were for the making, and no-one got through a career in construction without making a few of them – so they were happy enough to cover them up and carry on.

Unless the mistake is not belonging to the correct organisation, in which case summary execution is the only permitted response.

I'd quite enjoyed working on the site, money notwithstanding, and I considered ending the dispute by telling my boss I'd use my credit card to join the Union on the spot – only, I knew I was leaving soon. Six-hundred and fifty bucks would take one hell of a bite out of my salary, with no guarantee of me being allowed back here to earn more.

My boss wouldn't back down, because he stood to risk his sizable commission for supplying me to the job, and the Union officials wouldn't back down, because... well, because not backing down was pretty much their entire purpose.

It was stalemate, until finally all parties agreed to let me work out the rest of the day – on my own – and recall the rest of the workers tomorrow.

Without me.

And to be honest, since I was only there as a carpenter's labourer, to hold the wood while he cut it, there wasn't a lot for me to do on a ten-storey office-block building site on my own. So I just sort of stood there, surrounded by tools, trying to look inconspicuous.

Awkward had just reached a whole new level.

For the rest of the week I was back on the regular InstallEx jobs, building stands and booths in the gigantic Melbourne Exhibition Centre. Paul, by way of apology, invited me to a little get-together he was having in the pub. The other managers would be there, along with a select few hand-picked workers; it was a free-booze affair, and they weren't about to throw open their bar tab to the backpackers of all nations (they'd have been bankrupt in about half an hour if they did).

I went to the party, but my customary excitement for such an event was lacking.

There was something I had to tell Paul, and this seemed like the perfect opportunity to do it – but inside, I was dreading it.

I hate letting people down.

I'd been there for an hour, chatting with the other four non-management level staff who'd been invited and nursing a pint of ice-cold cider, when Paul stood up to make a speech. He turned to address our little table of workers.

"Okay, you all know you're here for something special, so I won't keep you in suspense any longer. As I've said, you guys are my A-Team."

There were a few cheers, but on the whole the mood was tense and restrained. All the lads were craning forward, as though moving their heads closer to Paul would enable them to hear the news first. Meanwhile, I slouched back on my chair, drink in hand. It didn't matter what came next; not for me, anyway. My decision had already been made.

"So," Paul said, "here it is. We're going to put you five on permanent contracts. Those of you that need it, we'll be sponsoring you to become Australian residents."

My jaw dropped. Just a little.

"We're going to get you all your own set of tools, and we're talking to a fleet hire firm about company vehicles. We'll be sending you out, sometimes individually, to our top jobs. You'll be managing small teams of the regular guys, or doing one-off specials for us. And this means you'll be on contract rates, too – so more money, more bonuses, paid holidays, health care, the whole shebudle."

There was stunned silence around the table. I don't think any of us could believe it. I had to check my watch to make sure it wasn't April 1st.

"Well? What do you think?"

And then the roaring began. Everyone was on their feet, yelling in triumph, shaking hands and doling out high-fives. I carried on with the rest of them, but I was still shell-shocked from the announcement. I mean, I'd never really wanted a *real* job – it didn't really go hand-in-hand with the life of reckless adventure I had planned – but as far as incentives go, this was a biggie. It really was the whole package.

"Tony?"

"Oh, yes! Sorry Paul." He was beckoning me aside. *This is it*, I thought. *This is where I tell him.* Somehow he knew – maybe he'd read my body language, could tell my heart wasn't really in the party that was going on all around me. Paul was a very perceptive bloke, but I guess you didn't get to manage a successful business relying largely on backpackers without picking up a Jedi mind trick or two.

I moved across to an alcove, and Paul edged around his celebrating work force to meet me.

Oh, man. I hated doing this.

"So, Tony, what do you think mate?"

"It's great Paul. Really great, for you to do this—"

"Listen. What I wanted to talk to you about is this. That building site job? We're going to send you back until it's finished. We'll pay for your Union membership. It'll be a good hard slog – maybe, five months of work? And lots of overtime. But you'll do well out of it. You've earned it."

"I… I…" As anyone who knows me can attest, it's not often that I'm lost for words.

But I had to find them sooner or later.

"Paul, I'm so sorry! I've been meaning to tell you. I've decided to leave InstallEx – to leave Australia. I'm going to New Zealand in two weeks time."

"Oh?" he was, understandably, a bit surprised.

"I can't believe what you've just offered me, and I'm really, really grateful. But I can't take it. I'm sure one of the other lads will be over the moon, though."

"Erm, yeah. I guess they will."

And that was that. I sculled my drink (an Aussie slang word for pouring the whole thing down my neck without stopping), and left.

For some reason, I wasn't in a party mood.

I thought about nothing else, on the train home to Yarraville. What would I tell Roo? How would she react? After all this time, being so worried about money, finally it was right there for the taking. But then… much as I wanted to experience being well-off for a change – to be able to buy food that was still within its sell-by date, to wear clothes and read books that hadn't come from an op-shop, to be able to take Roo out on a date and *not* eat in McDonalds – I still really, *really* wanted to go to New Zealand.

Snowboarding…

It was the pinnacle of my life's ambition. From when I'd first understood the meaning of a certain word, I'd wanted nothing as much. All through school, through college, through university and my abortive attempt at world-fame as an actor, and ever since, I'd had this desperate urge. And now, somehow, despite all the odds that were against it, in New Zealand I finally had a chance of becoming *cool*.

Round and round it went in my head. Would Roo be disappointed? I felt keenly the need to be her provider, to take responsibility for making enough money to keep our lives comfortable and enjoyable. Because what kind of man would I be, if I couldn't even look after my woman properly? Roo would still love me, of this I was sure. But would her respect for me be diminished? Even just a little? *Maybe I should have taken the job,* I thought. *Blew off the damn flights. Who's cooler, the penniless backpacker who can ride a plank of wood down a mountain, or the honest, hard-working bloke who puts the needs of his family first?*

There was no contest, really.

Maybe I wasn't cut out to be cool after all.

But it wasn't too late. I could still ring Paul. Tell him I'd changed my mind.

Holy shit! Why is it always so damn difficult?

I felt like my mind was being pulled apart by the decision. Back and forth, my thoughts flitted, stacking up benefits and bonuses against hopes and dreams – until finally it hit me: this was as much Roo's decision as it was mine!

And realising that helped a little – it lifted the burden from me, and allowed me to fling it squarely onto Roo's shoulders. This did not seem at all cowardly at the time. I was empowering her with control over our future! Well, that was how I justified it.

I'll let Roo decide.

Coward.

"You're back early," said Roo.

I threw my bag down and scooped her up in the fiercest hug I could muster. I felt like I needed to absorb a bit of her strength, along with the warmth, before I could lay this one out for her.

"Is everything okay?" she asked.

And so I told her.

"Bloody hell!" she said, when I'd finished. "They really did want you to stay!"

"Yup. I guess so."

"But you still told them no, though, didn't you?"

"I did."

"Oh, thank God for that!"

And just like that, the decision was made.

"So you don't want us to stay then? Even with the extra money I'd be earning?"

Roo looked at me like I had three heads.

"What? Hell no! I wanna go to New Zealand, baby! I wanna see SNOW!"

And that was yet another reason why I loved Roo so much. Not just because she always knew the right thing to say to make me feel better, or because she valued craziness and adventure over posh shoes and a big pile of cash, or even because she was so content to come with me, on some ridiculous joy-ride into completely unknown territory.

It was because, just like me, inside she was still only eight years old.

The End Of An Era

There was one last millstone around our necks.

Rusty.

Like an old friend of the family – hell, he *was* one of the family – we'd be incredibly sad to be parted from him. But there was no two ways about it; our relationship, with all its ups and downs, trials and tribulations – and almost enough heart-ache to write a book about – was over.

Rusty had to go.

But how?

"Here's the thing," said Roo. "We can't just leave him. He's still registered to me, and there's a massive fine for abandoning a vehicle. So we've either got to wreck him, or sell him."

We both cast a lingering glance through the living room window, at the dishevelled van parked outside. Neither of us spoke for a few seconds; it was almost like an agreed moment of silence for the old car. A mark of respect.

I loved that van.

"Me too," said Roo. I hadn't even realised I'd spoken aloud.

"We could at least take him to that garage round the corner. We should be able to make it that far, and we can wait there for him to cool down before... driving on to the wreckers, I guess, if there's no joy."

"Yes, I think that's it. We'll ask if there's anything at all they can do, absolutely anything just to make him saleable. He's carried us so far... I can't bear to scrap him."

So we climbed back inside for what could potentially be our last ever ride.

Following the mechanic's instructions, we parked Rusty outside the garage.

"I'll see what I can do," he said, and for once there was no trace of condescension.

We left feeling upbeat, in spite of the potentially crippling repair bill looming over us. We had less than a week to get Rusty fixed, advertised and sold – or we'd be sending him to the great car graveyard in the sky…

Via the great car graveyard on Lloyd Street.

It was a nervous wait. When the call came, the mechanic's assistant couldn't even give us a quote. He simply said we'd better come in for a chat…

It didn't bode well. Unsurprisingly.

The mechanic himself was in a jolly mood, though. Expecting to attend an execution, we started clutching at straws of hope as he described the battery of tests he'd put Rusty through.

"And I couldn't figure out what the hell was going on," he concluded. "No reason at all why he should be boiling up like that."

"Mm." It was more or less what we'd expected.

"But then!" the mechanic held up a finger to magnify the suspense, "I thought to look at *this*. He reached into Rusty's engine bay and twisted off the radiator cap. "See that?" he held it up for our inspection. "The rubber's all perished. I'd guess that this is the original radiator cap, so it'll be, what, twenty-odd years old?"

"Sounds quite likely."

"Well then! There's your problem. No seal on the cap, so your radiator water is being pushed out by the pressure! So by the time you've done a couple of miles, the steam will have been spraying out – but it's invisible, and the engine's underneath you anyway – so there's no water left and you boil up!"

"What? I don't… are you trying to tell me that this… this *radiator cap*, is the problem?"

"I'd say so."

"And if we replace it, the van should be fine?"

"Tip top. Nothing else wrong with him. Other than being a bit Rusty…"

"Where can we get one of these things? How much are they?"

My heart was racing now. I was half expecting to wake up at any moment.

"Should sell 'em right there." He pointed behind us. Opposite his garage was a branch of Super Cheap Auto. "Should cost about ten bucks."

"No. Freaking. Way."

"What do we owe you?" Roo asked him.

"Ah, that's alright. Just feels good, to have found the problem.

Bit of a puzzle, I can tell you!"

"Really? You're sure?"

"Yeah, no worries. Just bring him back here if you have any more problems."

So we hustled into the shop. I don't think anyone has ever been breathless with excitement over buying a radiator cap before – the staff treated us warily, as though we might have just escaped from a mental asylum.

"YES!" I shrieked, when the register clocked up $12.75.

"Bloody car bills," Roo quipped. "They're ALWAYS more than the original quote."

We fitted the cap to Rusty, and went for an exploratory drive.

And we drove. And we drove.

And Rusty, bless his little petrol-powered heart, was as good as new.

That night, Roo advertised him on The Gumtree for $1500. We had five calls in the first three minutes – on the Skype phone which Roo had also advertised for $80. It was still new, but the Skype function wouldn't work in New Zealand. The cash from selling it would go towards buying a lesser phone for each of us, so we could stay in touch if we were working different shifts in the ski fields.

Everyone who called about Rusty agreed to buy him before they put the phone down. I'd actually got to choose who to call back, as we wanted to be sure he would go to a good home.

We settled on a young surfer-dude called Sam, who said he'd let us know when his mechanic friend was available to come and check him out.

We waited for them to call with baited breath. We didn't move without the phone. We took it to the shop with us when we went to buy dinner.

We took it to the kitchen with us while we cooked dinner.

For two nights, we slept with it between our pillows, though Roo had made me promise that when the time came, I would answer it.

So I was sitting in the lounge, watching TV after my last shift with InstallEx, when I heard a loud "SHIT!" from the direction of the bathroom.

Roo came running in, shaking something in her hand.

"Shit! It's the phone!"

"What? Is it ringing?"

"NO! Oh my God, Tony – I dropped it down the toilet!"

"What? How is that even possible?"

"I don't know! It was in my back pocket, and when I pulled my pants down…"

She held the phone out to me. It had a certain… *moistness* to it.

"EEeew! It's still dripping! Did you pee on it?"

"I HAD NO CHOICE."

"Oh crap. So, that's knackered then."

"But we *need* that phone! Shit! *It's been bought for eighty dollars!*"

"Well, I doubt they'll want it now. Unless, you know, some people pay extra for that sort of thing…"

"NOOOOO! What about the guys who want to buy Rusty! How are they going to call us now?"

"Ah. Um… I don't know."

"I can't believe it! All we had to do was look after that phone, and I dropped it down the frigging toilet!"

"And peed on it."

"AND PEED ON IT!"

"Okay. Let's think about this. Give me the phone. How did you get it out of the toilet?"

She glared at me.

"Oh. Okay, well, you go and wash your hands."

I took the phone very gingerly, and carried it into the kitchen, where I laid it to rest on a tea towel. The display was blank, and there was a bit of liquid behind it. No response to my pushing the power button. I cracked open the back of the phone, and unleashed a mini tsunami along with the battery.

Roo came up behind me to look over my shoulder. "Is it dead then?"

"Well, it's definitely off the market."

Roo felt terrible, so I tried not to take the piss out of her too much. After all, the phone had already done that. It possessed remarkably sponge-like qualities, for a phone.

She blurted out solutions as fast as I could shoot them down.

"Can't you borrow Kat's phone?"

"And do what?"

"Call them!"

"Nope."

"What not?"

"Because their phone number is in that phone."

"SHIT!"

We passed a nervous evening, until Roo heard something jingling from my work bag. "Oh my God! Your old phone! I must have put both numbers on the advert!"

In a mad scrabble, we got to it and answered it before it rung off.

It was Sam, exactly the bloke we'd been waiting for.

And he still wanted Rusty.

"I can't interest you in a phone that my girlfriend has pissed all over, can I?" I asked.

"Nooo!" Roo hissed.

But I'd already hung up. It was just a bit of toilet humour.

I'd arranged to meet Sam and his mate the following afternoon, which happened to be our last full day in Australia.

This was cutting it a bit finer that I'd intended. If they decided they didn't want to buy the van…

Well, we were screwed.

I had one more job to do that evening.

I had to contact our buyer and explain that our Skype phone had been withdrawn from sale.

Due to water damage.

To say we were nervous about meeting Rusty's future owners, is an understatement akin to saying the Bible caused some controversy.

They both seemed keen though, and stood in awe of the van's fading paint job.

"It's AWESOME!" Sam exclaimed.

They jumped straight in for a test drive, and looped the block several times, while Roo and I took turns in apologising for each of Rusty's idiosyncrasies.

Character traits, we called them.

And after the test drive, the mechanic friend (who I'd been picturing as a human-sized clockwork robot) crawled underneath to look at… well, whatever the hell it is knowledgeable people look at under there. Could be a doorway to Narnia, for all I know.

He seemed satisfied. "One last run?" he requested.

"Alright," Sam said, "and then we'll go and talk cash."

So they got back in, and Roo and I watched as they did donuts around the junction, screeching the tyres and burning some rubber. It was much harsher treatment than we'd ever subjected Rusty to, and I cringed, half expecting him to topple over. But no – he passed that test with flying colours too.

They pulled up, and turned off.

On a whim, the mechanic turned the key again, performing one last test-start, just to be sure.

There was a click – and then silence.

And for all I know, Rusty may never have moved again.

We apologised profusely over pizza at a nearby restaurant.

It had to be the immobiliser – we'd never had a problem with it before, but the symptoms matched. The timing was unbelievable. All I could think was the rough driving had shaken a wire loose somewhere. And now…

We stared into our pizza boxes and waited for the verdict.

"I was going to offer you $1300," Sam said. "Because he needs a bit of work, and the roof rails are rusted through, so I'll need to replace them to carry my surfboard rack."

"Mmm," I agreed.

Sam was silent and thoughtful for a long while. Then he spoke again. Roo and I braced ourselves for the worst.

"And you know what? I'm still going to offer you $1300."

"What? Really!"

"Yeah. I've got a mate who'll come and reset the immobiliser. I'm sure that's what it is."

"That's incredible! Thank-you so much!"

"No worries. It is an awesome van."

"You are *so* right!"

The money changed hands – cash on the spot – and we filled out the paperwork over the last slice of pizza. Roo and I shook hands with the two guys, and we all went our separate ways. On foot.

"I can't believe it," said Sam, as he left, "I just bought a car – and yet I'm going home on the train!"

Roo and I walked home slowly, alternately laughing at what had just happened, and shedding tears about never seeing Rusty again. It probably sounds daft, to be crying over a car, but for all his idiosyncrasies Rusty had always been there for us. Together, we'd racked up well over thirty thousand kilometres.

My relationship with Roo had started out on those cramped and awkward back seats.

Hell, we'd racked up a few miles of our own in there…

But we'd decided not to mention that during our sales pitch.

I'd like to think Rusty is still out there somewhere, shuttling a bunch of gnarly surfing dudes to the beach at five in the morning to shred some waves. It would be a fitting retirement for a van of his experience. If he is out there, to his current owners – I salute you! And to Rusty –

thanks for everything. You were a star.

New Zealand

Does anyone know where the hell Old Zealand is? Well, unless it's amazing, the New version is way better.

Okay, I just found out: it's in Holland.

Which is a lovely country, but rather *flat*, and so not an ideal place to take up snowboarding.

Conversely, New Zealand is perfect for it.

Before leaving Australia, we'd scoured the op-shops for cold-weather gear.

Roo had bought a pair of near-new snowboarding pants from eBay. They were pristine, glacier-white, sexy as hell and a great bargain. They were also far too small – she could only fasten them whilst holding her breath, lost the ability to bend at the waist once they were on, and the last four inches of her ankles stuck out of the bottoms. But apart from that, they were great.

"I'll lose weight when we start snowboarding every day," she pointed out, ignoring the fact that she was already borderline skeletal.

"And you'll lose height…?"

"Big socks."

So that was settled, then.

Our flights passed without a hitch, and almost before we knew it, there we were – on the bus from the North Island capital of Auckland, en route to the tiny ski-town of Ohakune.

We certainly knew about the bus ride, though. It took six and a half hours, and has gone on record as the only bus journey in my life that I wished would last longer.

The scenery we passed through was incredible. New Zealand is much, much bigger than most people think – bigger than the whole of the UK, in fact.

And less people live there than live in London.

Result? An endless expanse of raw, untamed, natural beauty.

Miles and miles of rolling hills, snaking rivers, lush green forests – and always, on the edge of the horizon, the mountains. After the harsh, dry wilderness in the centre of Australia, seeing New Zealand for the first time was like a cool breeze of familiarity. We could have been driving through the most picturesque spots of England, Scotland and Wales – except that, we kept on driving. And the beauty, unspoiled and empty, didn't end. The entire country was like this – a handful of pocket-sized cities with well-groomed, miniature suburbs – and nothing in between them but green, verdant paradise.

I loved it.

Roo loved it.

Our eyes were glued to the windows of the bus, and we kept shouting "Ooh! Look at the river!" or "Wow, you can see the edge of the mountains…"

I could write a whole book about how beautiful that landscape was.

But it'd be a bloody boring read, so I'll stop right there.

We came to Ohakune just in time; the yearly rush on temporary accommodation was about to begin, when employees of the ski-field would fight tooth and nail over every room, loft, garage and out-house in town. Put simply, there wasn't nearly enough of it; Ohakune was tiny, and for more than half the year less than a thousand people lived there. Around the beginning of June, the hordes descended; first the ski workers, desperate for affordable digs, and then the punters, who had no choice but to spend big in the hotel, the motel, the lodge – or the backpackers, which had the cheapest beds in town at around $80 per night.

We struck it lucky, because we had an agent in town; her name was Gill, and by some amazing quirk of fate, her Australian visa had run out exactly three months before mine.

Consequently, she'd been here for some time.

It was a joyful reunion. I'd kicked Gill out hoping it was in her best interests; I'd hoped (and prayed) that she would spread her wings and soar, freed from my shadow and from having her every move determined by a three-way vote.

And, after a slightly rocky start, she had done just that.

She told us now about the fling she'd had in Adelaide with a travelling entrepreneur; she talked about the friends she'd made, blokes she'd met, and the Great Ocean Road trip she'd undertaken with a girl she knew from high school; she chattered on unstoppably about the

Sting concert she'd worked on, the Chinese family she'd been adopted into and the bizarre turn of events which saw her representing an international designer at a fashion festival in Sydney.

In short, Gill had transformed. She was still the kindest, friendliest, happiest individual on the planet – but now she had something else, too.

She had confidence. She had the ability to rely entirely on herself. And she had a love-life.

But that was none of my business, so I tried not to pry.

Well, not much.

Gill had found us a place to live for the ski-season, and had already signed a lease on our behalf. She knew we'd love it, she said – and she was right.

A lovely old couple called Dave and Diane, living ten minutes walk from the staff bus depot, had a 'sleep-out' to rent. I guess we'd call it a granny flat, or a self-contained apartment. Loads of houses in New Zealand had them, presumably because it's so far between towns – you can't visit anywhere on a day trip.

Roo and I were delighted with the tiny, bright yellow room, just big enough for the double bed and a chest of drawers, on which rested the essentials; a kettle, a toaster and a microwave. Our landlords, who we referred to as The Hobbits because they were a matched pair at exactly five-feet tall, were generous to a fault. The only bathroom was in the main house, but our snug little abode had everything else we could want – including unfettered access to the hot tub, installed directly outside!

Wow.

Poor Gill had a rather more difficult time finding somewhere to live; three times she assembled groups of new arrivals, all keen to rent a place together. All three times the rest of the group signed into a place without her, after meeting other people or finding smaller houses.

Two weeks in, with work long overdue to start, she was still living at the backpackers. They were going to raise their prices from 'off-season' to 'on-season' at any time – and from then on, she would be homeless.

But, being Gill, she managed to stay positive.

A week later we woke up to our first white morning. Work still hadn't started, so we lazed around in bed and nearly missed it – but when Roo opened the door to the sleep-out, she instantly became five years old.

"TONY! Tony Tony Tony! It's SNOWING! Can we go out in

it? Can we? Come on, get up, I WANNA GO OUT IN IT RIGHT NOW!"

So we did. We spent the rest of the day introducing Roo to all the things I'd loved about Christmas as a kid.

Starting with a snowball fight! Well, she didn't realise it was a snowball fight for the first ten minutes, because my aim is so bad it took me that long before I hit her. And then she just thought I was being mean.

"It's so *wet!* And *cold!*"

"Yeah, I know! Shall we go back in then?"

"ARE YOU CRAZY?"

So we spent the rest of the day romping around town, flinging ourselves into snowdrifts, trying to catch snowflakes, and laying in the middle of the road to make snow angels.

By the time Gill found us, there was really only one thing left to do.

We found a bench outside the local supermarket (which must have been the smallest shop ever to be granted that title), and we set to work building Roo's first ever snowman.

Gill and I were veterans at this, owing to the fact that neither of us have ever really grown up. We scooped fresh snow from the thick blanket all around us, and piled it up on the bench. A sitting snowman, it was decided, would give us the greatest chance to be artistic.

While Roo worked away defining one arm, Gill was in charge of the head. She gave him her trademark big smiley face, with bottle tops for eyes. He looked very friendly. I'd been sculpting his left arm, and for a bit of variety I'd laid his hand in his lap. Then, for a bit more variety, I carved it into a rough approximation of a fist, and rolled a small snowball into sausage-roll-sized stump, which I added jutting out of the top.

Finally, we all stood back to admire our efforts. Roo was the first one to notice something was amiss.

"Is he... masturbating?"

"I dunno," I said, "but he certainly looks like he's enjoying himself! Look at that grin!"

Gill turned an exasperated look on me (it's one she's had plenty of practice with). "Tony, did you just give that snowman a snow-boner?"

"I did! I figured, he's all on his own, so he might as well play with himself..."

"Oh God! We can't take you anywhere."

Just then a gaggle of customers pushed their way through the supermarket doors.

"Shit!" said Gill. "No time to do anything – leg it!"

So we beat a hasty retreat down the road, and stopped to chuckle in the shade of the video rental shop.

"Did you have to desecrate Roo's first ever snowman experience?" Gill asked me.

"Ssshhh!" Roo hissed. She was peering back down the road, listening intently. "They've found it!"

All ears focused back towards the supermarket, where we could hear a woman saying, "Yes, he's a very happy snowman, isn't he?"

"Mama, can I sit next to the snowman?"

"Of course dear! Would you like me to take your picture with him?"

"Ooh yes! Tell me when to smile, mama!"

"Smile!"

"Mama, why's the snowman holding his pee-pee?"

"OH DEAR GOD! Come away from there!"

Our pornographic snowman lasted most of the week – penis and all – because the temperature in town was perfect for it, and the local kids must have found him amusing enough to leave him be.

And because, even for the sake of decency, who's going to touch a snowman's pee-pee?

Ruapehu Alpine Lifts

Our first day of work was the source of much trepidation.

As far as we knew, most of the staff did this all the time – some even followed winter around the world, moving from here to Japan, from there to Canada or the US, and from there to Europe. It was a way of life; working hard, partying harder, and hitting the slopes hardest of all.

There was a lot to recommend it.

But the job, predictably, wasn't one of them.

We showed up for the Staff Induction, all three of us together again. It was like old times, and as we were all 'outdoor' staff, we stayed together through the presentation about Mount Ruapehu's history (it was used as Mount Doom in the Lord of the Rings films), and that pointless slideshow they always show you at the start of these jobs, where they tell you about every different job there is. Presumably to rub our faces in the fact that we'd picked the worst ones...

Then we sat through the Q&A, and that's where I got the first inkling of just how foreign a field we had stepped onto.

Because everyone around us was asking questions – I didn't understand one of them.

"What about the rules on hot-laps?"

"What's the back-country policy?"

"How deep is the base?"

"How much snow do you make?"

"How often do you bomb?"

A-R-G-H.

I was clearly in over my head. Again. This time in snow, which gave the appearance of being softer – but which, as any hardened snow-sports addict will tell you, was considerably more dangerous than it looked.

Here then, for the uninitiated, are the answers to those questions:

Hot-laps were banned for the first few weeks. It turns out, this is a clever trick used mainly by lifties, whereby they take it in turns to actually run the lift they're working on – each person doing two people's jobs, while their partner takes the lift to the top and skis or snowboards back down again. Then they take over running the lift while the first guy goes up. It's a great way to get a sneaky bit of extra riding in, and is generally overlooked by bosses – so long as each person manning the lift is capable of running it on their own.

I was not.

Back-country was everything outside the boundaries of the ski-area; it was not to be trifled with, for fear of avalanches. The base (snow-depth) was two metres, but by the time we'd been there a while it rose to four (requiring much digging-out of cars and buildings in the process); snow was 'made' every single night, to supplement the snow that fell naturally – there were gigantic cannons stationed all over the mountain for this purpose, each capable of shooting tonnes of misted water skywards. The resulting snow was granular rather than powdery, but meant the mountain could be open for skiing whether it snowed overnight or not. And the bombs? These were exactly what they sounded like. Explosives, detonated by the expert ski-patrollers, to set off potential avalanches in a controlled manner.

Whew! There was a lot to learn.

Not about the job though.

Our Lift Supervisor, who told us all to call him 'Boob', took us up, down and around every lift in the ski-field. We followed him like a string of ducklings, waddling through the knee-deep snow, until by some minor miracle we found ourselves back at the base – a wet, sparsely furnished staff building called 'Tor One'.

"So now you know the lifts," he informed us. "Bet you can't wait to get started, eh? See you all tomorrow! And don't drink too much tonight!"

And that was it – just like that, training was over.

I'd never pushed a button. I had only the flimsiest concept of how a ski lift even worked, much less how to fix one if something went wrong.

I didn't know radio etiquette.

I didn't know my job description.

I didn't know how many things I didn't know – but one thing was for sure; there were plenty of them.

"So, what do we actually *do*?" I asked the bloke sitting next to me on the staff bus taking us back down the mountain.

"Search me," he said, "I'm new here. I'm Keith."

We shook hands.

"I'm Tony, nice to meet you. This is shaping up to be an interesting week!"

The first part of the job was something I could understand – if not quite believe. The next morning we assembled in our staff room, did a quick roll call, then armed ourselves for combat and headed straight out again.

Our opponents were the lift chairs, which overnight had turned into fantastic frozen sculptures. The relentless weather, coupled with dramatically sub-zero temperatures, transformed the humble steel and wooden frames into a series of massive ice-monoliths, layered and carved by snow and wind into intricate abstract shapes.

They were breathtakingly beautiful.

They were also a pain in the arse.

Every chair was filled with ice, taking up the space where three or four paying customers would need to sit. Foot-long icicles hung in thick rows from every surface, sometimes melding together into trunks the size of a human leg. The steel cables groaned under the weight of it all, thousands of kilos of ice outweighing even the hundreds of customers who thronged the lift on a daily basis

Our mission was to remove all this ice from the chairs – by beating the shit out of them with baseball bats!

The bats were known as 'yeti sticks' – presumably because, in the instance of a mass-invasion by abominable snowmen, they would be our weapon of choice. What good they'd be against an eight-foot-tall science-defying monster was beyond me, but they worked a treat for their primary purpose, which was wilful destruction of company property.

It was great fun, although knackering – exertion at altitude is more difficult, and one-on-one combat with a suspended steel chair is about as hard-core an exercise as you can get. At first I would pound away at a chair, making little visible difference no matter how hard I smacked the damn thing. I was aiming at the ice, you see, assuming it to be brittle. But the ice wasn't the right target.

After a few days I learned to find the sweet spots on the chair's superstructure, where a precise hit could set up a chain reaction that would destroy the Death Star! Okay, what it really did was vibrate the frame violently enough to shake large quantities of ice loose in one gigantic avalanche. It was incredibly satisfying to see an iceberg approach, to time it just right, aim and swing – and see a hundred kilos of ice crash to the ground, revealing the shivering form of the chair within. Then, a few good whacks from the next liftie in line would clear the debris, and by the time the chair had completed its run around the base pylon and was heading back up, it was largely frost-free. In theory.

There were variations to this scenario, all of which I demonstrated admirably in my first two weeks on the job.

There was the mis-hit; fractionally off, usually due to bad footing, it produced an embarrassingly loud CLANG! from the chair, but achieved nothing more dramatic that the redistribution of a few snowflakes.

Then there was the flat-hit, when either the angle or the grip-tension was too great; this sent a shock-wave of equal and opposite force back up the arm, typically causing me to drop the bat, fall backwards into the snow, and shout "ARGH! MUTHERFUCKER!"

And there was the one-in-a-million shot, where powerful contact with unyielding metal sheared the tip of the bat off, and sent it spinning into Keith's face.

Yeti sticks broke all the time doing this job, and there was a fairly high turnover of them – but only once did someone require stitches as a direct result of it.

By the second week, a few minor mishaps aside, I felt I was getting the hang of it. I turned it into a game, competing against the others on a chair-by-chair basis – or, I would have done, if anyone else had cared enough to play along. Most of them just stood there looking bored, giving each chair a lazy clout as it went past. Pah! Not me. I was *dedicated* to this job, man!

So I competed against myself, narrating my private game internally (and sometimes externally, when the excitement took me).

"Chair one-seven-nine approaches, looking heavy… he sights for the sweet-spot… he swings!"

Only, it was the dreaded mis-hit. *NOOooo!*

I swung again – too hastily because the chair was now too close, well within the arc required for optimal power. My bat smacked into the ice with a wet thud, making nothing more than a dent.

Rookie mistake.

The mistimed shot had also robbed me of the chance to take another big swing – if I'd waited until the chair was past, I'd have had the perfect angle on it again, only from behind. But now it was gone, pulled out of reach on its chain, full of ice, ready to taunt me all the way back up the mountain.

No.

There was only one thing for it.

Show that chair who's boss.

As the other lifties turned their attention to the next chair in line, I brandished my yeti stick like a samurai sword, screamed "BONSAI!" at the top of my lungs, and charged off through the piles of crushed ice after the one that got away.

I scored another whack as it swung around the supporting pylon, and was gaining on the chair as it began its long trip uphill.

The accepted wisdom was that the chair would come around again, and until then there were plenty more of them to focus on – but I took it personally that an inanimate object could escape my wrath so easily.

Learning from my earlier mistake, I concentrated on catching up to the chair rather than swiping ineffectually at it from a distance. A couple more strides and I was on it. I brought my yeti stick down as I came alongside, and was rewarded with a shower of collapsing icicles. Only a few remained, frozen solid around the top of the frame.

Two more steps…

One final leap, coupled with a mighty downswing, smashed free the last chunks of ice, and they rained down on me as the chair was swept up, up and away.

I landed in a crouch, not unlike a triumphant ninja.

"YES! I GOT IT!" I bellowed, announcing my victory to everyone in earshot.

But there was danger in this tactic. As with all potentially game-winning strategies, there were risks – and in this case, that risk was the next chair in line, which had swung around the pylon and followed me inexorably up the hill. As I turned to bask in the admiration of my peers, there was a cry of "Look out!"

And the next chair ploughed into me at penis-height, folding me double around its frigid steel bars, and carrying me with it on its prescribed path.

"Shit! It's got Tony!" I heard from the control booth.

"No worries!" I yelled back, as the lift swept me higher. My feet swung free in the fresh, chilly air as the ground fell away beneath me.

"JUMP!" someone shouted, followed immediately by someone else shouting "DON'T JUMP!"

But my hands wouldn't hold on forever. As amusing as the thought was, of being carried the whole way to the top of the lift, it was a fifteen-minute journey. And my fingers were very, very cold. I braced myself for an heroic plunge, but there was a sudden clunk, and I felt the lift slowing to a halt. One of the others had slapped the emergency stop button.

I dropped a couple of body-lengths into the snow below me,

which was plenty deep enough to absorb my impact. I was still floundering around when Boob reached me, thrust an arm down, and hauled me out of the Tony-shaped hole I'd created.

"You didn't have to stop it," I greeted him. "It wasn't an *emergency.*"

"It bloody well was! In another thirty seconds, you'd have been twenty metres up! Dangling by your bloody hands!" He shook his head in disbelief. "And that's the third time this week. You've got to stop doing this!"

Dirty Jobs

There was no two ways about it; being a liftie was a damn hard job.

Especially for those of us who took it seriously. I was consciously trying to make up for my complete lack of experience and knowledge with enthusiasm and good customer service – two things that absolutely no-one else in my job gave a flying shit about.

In the morning, after an hour or so spent beating chairs with sticks, I'd ride up to my assigned lift and start assembling my queue gates. This was a typically low-tech method of organising a queuing system; it consisted of a series of plastic pipes, which I had to drive into the compacted snow with my yeti stick. They were connected by bungee cords, and I had to position them so they formed narrow lanes, one skier wide, and led away from the lift in switchbacks. I'd been doing this by hand for weeks before I discovered RAL possessed a metre-long steel drilling tool called an auger, fitted to an electric drill, for just this purpose. One of the lifties spent his morning skiing around with it slung across his chest like some kind of James Bond villain, helping everyone but me by drilling holes for their queue gates. Apparently at some stage one of the others had watched me attack my plastic pipes with such vigour that they'd decided it was way more amusing than letting me borrow the drill.

The bastards!

The rest of the day was spent greeting the guests, and helping them on (or off) the lifts. Mostly this went well, as customers had generally done this thousands of times, but beginners would always struggle, especially if they were five years old. So in the ten seconds between lift chairs, I took it upon myself to greet each row of customers with a cheery, "Hey folks, how's it going?" and decide if any of them looked like they were about to wet themselves through sheer terror.

If so, I would reassure them, pull the lever to slow the lift, ring an electronic bell to alert the liftie at the top that the lift was about to slow down, and try to get back in time to help them.

Fifty percent of the time, the lift chair simply mowed them down where they stood.

This required a sprint back to the control booth to stop the lift (and a double-bell signal to alert the top), back to the child/beginner to help them up and convince them to stop crying, then back over to start the lift up again (with appropriate bell signals). This time I would have to take a more active role in helping them – usually by picking them up and dumping them on the chair, then throwing myself flat to get out of its way before it took off up the hill.

It was draining.

And all the while, my liftie partner would stand there with a 'don't talk to me, I'm so over this,' expression on their face. They rarely, if ever, spoke a word to the customers, and most of them seemed to take the opinion that anyone dumb enough to screw up getting on the lift, shouldn't be on it – and consequently, wasn't worth their assistance.

And, for the most part, neither was I.

In between customers we also had to maintain our entry (or exit) ramps. These were carved (by us) from packed snow and ice, and degraded throughout the day as customers rode over them and the relentless weather either turned them to puddles or piled them high with fresh powder. Either way, it meant that shovelling snow was a constant effort, and thankfully that was one area in which the other lifties deigned to help. Technically, I guess that was our job; keep the lift area safe, and keep the lift running smoothly. Calming crying infants and providing individual greetings and lift-riding instruction probably wasn't in our job description – but I always read between the lines, and I was determined to do something right.

And at this point, it wasn't likely to be snowboarding.

Because two weeks into the job, I still hadn't dared try it.

Roo's experience was somewhat different.

All the other roadies loved her, treating her almost like a mascot – and because of this I was afforded the rare honour of being allowed into their staff room. Other lifties wouldn't dare enter the stronghold of their rivals; they'd claim not to care what went on in there, but the truth was, they were scared. There were only six roadies, but three of them were the size of at least two regular people; towering mountains of Maori muscle, who were every bit as friendly and easy-going as they were intimidating.

The roadies had it tough; one of the reasons they'd scored such a lush staff room, despite their low numbers. All their gear was in good shape and *all* their radios worked. This was because the bosses knew that, of all the gigs on the mountain, the road crew had it toughest.

Sure, it got cold up top, and when the weather closed in I'd be sat shivering in my tiny control booth; but rarely did I spare a thought for the discomfort of the roadies, deployed halfway up the mountain road where there was no shelter at all. It was their short-straw job; squatting in a lay-by just below the snowline, wearing no gloves because they "just got in the way," fitting icy metal chains to frigid car tyres with their bare hands. They usually did it two days each per week.

They had fun jobs too of course. In her first week Roo was taught several different ways of breaking into cars with various tools, because every day at least half a dozen customers managed to lock their keys inside.

They rarely got to do 'hot laps', as it took way too long to get up the mountain from the base, where they were stationed, but they had their fun. When the protective padding from the base of a ski-lift pylon blew off and disappeared over the side of the ski area, the roadies were sent to retrieve it. Then they declared it MIA, called a staff meeting at the furthest edge of the car park, and spent an hour trying to ride the thing down the sheer ice-cliff separating the two parking levels. Roo went first, of course, and survived the experiment by the narrowest of margins; which is just another reason why they loved her.

While we lifties were grousing about how hard it was to maintain our snow-ramps, the roadies were calmly getting on with one of their biggest tasks; clearing three feet of snow off the main car park. All of it. With shovels.

Roo, wrapped in so many layers she was nearly as wide as a regular woman, worked as hard as any of them – only there was one small addition to her outfit. Unable to resist the role of mascot, she regularly went to work wearing her tutu – and a pair of wings she'd found in an op shop and brought all the way from Oz "because you never know". Well, she knew all right – and within her first couple of weeks (around the time I was earning the reputation for being a cheerful idiot) – Roo was officially nick-named The Parking Fairy.

And that's why, when the roadies held their staff party, I was the only liftie they grudgingly invited. Because, as one of them said to me, "it can't be all blokes."

There were stacks of other jobs on the mountain, both indoor and outdoor; regularly I found myself fantasising about what life would be like for the restaurant staff, or someone who worked inside the ski rental building.

I was taking a rare break in the staff room when Mary, a friendly, blonde, English girl who was working as a cleaner, pushed her mop bucket into the room.

"I should be a cleaner," I told her. "I've done loads of cleaning, back in Oz. It's got to be easier than what I'm doing now."

Perhaps this was the wrong thing to say to someone currently employed as a cleaner, but I felt that Mary would understand. Her boyfriend had done time as both a roadie and a liftie. She must have known how hard we had it.

"Come with me," she said. Her tone revealed nothing. She walked through to the toilets, and paused outside the Ladies. "In here."

I was intrigued – as, I believe, most blokes would be. Secretly. The ladies' loos are one of the last bastions of entirely female-controlled territory on the planet. I've seen every kind of public convenience in my travels, from ones that played soft music at me to poo-stained holes in the ground. Yet I've always suspected that, as a bloke, I'm being short-changed; if only I knew what it was like on the other side of that partition! There could be anything. Carpeted floors, delicately fragranced air, soft, fluffy towels, free toiletries, slippers, Champagne – sofas for crying out loud! It could be a wonderland, a haven, a place of light and joyous contemplation. With cookies. But, like most blokes, I would never know about it.

Or would I?

This could be my chance. Purely to put my curiosity to rest.

"Is there anyone in there? What if someone comes?"

"It's closed," she said. "I closed it."

"So we're going in?"

"It's my next job."

Mary pushed open the door – it didn't creak *even a little bit*, I noticed – and beckoned me into that forbidden interior.

I glanced around furtively, in the harsh glare of the fluorescent strip-light. It was... disappointing. And absolutely identical to the men's loos.

Except for one thing.

In the middle of the third hand basin was a gigantic fresh turd.

It glistened wetly against the stark white enamel of the basin.

"It's been going on for a while now," Mary said. She sounded tired. "No-one knows who it is, but they keep doing it. It must be the latest joke."

I stared in disbelief at the turd. Obviously human. And whoever had given birth to this behemoth clearly ate a lot of corn.

"What the... who the... what the hell are you going to do with it?"

In response, she pulled a pair of rubber gloves from her belt. "Would you like to help?"

"Um, no thanks."

"Would you like to watch?"

"Um, no thanks."

"Then maybe you should just stick with being a liftie, eh?"

"Ahhh… yeah. Good idea."

So I left her to it. After all, she had shit to do.

Uneasy Rider

My first proper snowboarding lesson was a bit of a surprise.

I'd been ordered to do it by Boob (and yes, that sentence looks every bit as weird to me, writing it, as it does to you reading it).

Boob was my boss, remember; he'd noticed me turning up for work in the $200, fur-lined snow boots we'd been ordered to buy on day one, and asked me where my snowboard boots and board were.

"I don't have any," I told him.

"Why not?" he asked.

"Because I don't know how to use them."

It wasn't my proudest moment, admitting to the boss of the lifties that I'd never even been on a board.

"How the hell do you get home when I station you at the Giant return, then?"

"I walk."

The 'return' was the top of the lift, where a single liftie would be posted to help people get off; and The Giant, as its name suggests, was one of the biggest lifts on the mountain. Walking down from there took forever, although I'd been sneakily begging an illicit ride down on the Movenpick, the next biggest lift which went all the way back down to base.

In response to this new information about me, Boob did two things (well, three things if you count calling me a 'bloody lunatic'); he booked me (and Roo) onto the first available snowboarding lesson, and he began stationing me exclusively on the beginners slope.

Standing on a snowboard for the first time was not at all like I expected. If you've ever tried to get onto a skateboard, only to have it shoot out from under you, you have some inkling of this – except that a snowboard can shoot out from under you *in any direction it chooses*.

And as I had one leg fastened to it at the time, this produced the first completely successful front-splits I've ever done. I was braced for the damn thing to shoot forwards, landing me on my ass – so when it shot backwards – and my free leg remained firmly where I'd planted it – I landed on my testicles instead.

Which hasn't happened since I was a was a very small boy, and was running too fast around the top of a climbing frame.

And it hurts even more than I remember, because frankly, my legs aren't supposed to bend that way.

Take two.

A snowboard on snow is like a bar of soap in the shower, in that if you stand on it there's a strong likelihood that hospitalization will ensue. Suffice to say, takes three through eighty-seven were spectacularly unsuccessful too.

Eventually I figured it out; *leaning* was the way to control this slippery beast, as it went in whatever direction my weight was pointed. And as I got better, I also learnt that it went wherever I was looking, which made staring at Roo's backside a rather more hazardous activity than usual.

But having achieved what must have been the very lowest echelon of snowboarding skill, Roo and I decided we'd earned a reward; it was time to trade in our rental gear for something more serious.

Possibly the worst place in the world to buy ski wear is a ski resort; every item on offer is ridiculously over-priced, even when compared with the ridiculously over-priced version you could buy in any major city. Because of this, both Roo and I invested plenty of time in browsing online auction sites, and our hard work was rewarded when we both bought our dream snowboards for less than a quarter of the price of the cheapest board for sale in Ohakune.

When they arrived we were ecstatic; Roo's board was a pale purple, with a dragon curling around it, and mine was black and red and featured a shadowy knight brandishing his sword. Apparently some people choose their snowboard based on totally irrelevant details – like if it's the right size for them, or designed for their level of expertise, or made by a reputable company – but we knew that what really mattered was the pretty picture on top of it.

Gill went one better than us in this regard; she bought a bright red snowboard that had obviously been a prize in a Bacardi competition. It was almost as tall as she was, and she stubbornly refused to ride it the right way around – because that would mean that the Bacardi logo on the bottom would be the wrong way up!

Roo and I just wanted one thing that looked good, as our ski-wear was… well, most of it was hiking-wear that we'd last worn on the

Bibbulmun Track.

Our ski-pants were the exception; Roo's tight white pants oozed sex-appeal. She could only get one leg into them at once, but again, it's not about the clothes that fit, and are practical – it's about the *look* of it. Everyone knows that.

My ski pants had cost me $8 in a Melbourne op shop. They were a solid, battleship-grey, with no branding or logo of any kind. They were also rather tight in certain places, which I suspect was the fashion for ski-wear circa 1982. Perhaps the strangest thing about them though, given they were sold as ski-pants, was that they weren't actually waterproof. It must be a recent advance in materiel technology that allows those designer GORE-TEX garments to stay as fresh as a daisy, despite the realities of the winter sports environment. Thus, the major limitation of being a snowboarder versus being a skier became more obvious; when we get to the top of a lift, before we go anywhere, we snowboarders have to sit down to fasten our free leg back onto the board. Skiers generally take this opportunity to flip us the bird, as they glide past on both skis, and shoot off down the slope without pause.

But we don't care, because we know we're much cooler than they will ever be.

Or, we would be, except that my trousers absorbed a goodly amount of water whilst I sat fiddling with my bindings. They kept my arse nice and warm, but it was that very warmth, specifically its snow-melting properties, that was the culprit. And I had no idea, until I'd been riding down the mountain at every opportunity for several weeks. And then one day a fellow liftie swished up to me and said, "So, you've given the top run a go, have you?"

"I have," I said, battling to keep the pride from my voice. "I've been doing it for *ages* now."

"Oh, right," he said. "So, how come you're still pissing your pants?"

And he swerved away down the slope.

Only then did I realise that every single run I'd made had been done with a huge, very obvious, circular wet patch, reaching from the seat of my pants to midway down the back of both thighs.

With my improved snowboarding ability came improved working conditions; I was finally sent back up the mountain, to brave the weather at the top of the various lifts. These were positions of high responsibility, as being alone up there meant I had to anticipate and solve all the problems, from people falling off the lift and being run over to angry parents refusing to believe I wasn't allowed to let their terrified child ride the lift back down again. I had to shape and maintain my own ramp, stop and restart the lift in case of emergencies, and I tried to do all of it whilst maintaining a cheerful and polite demeanour.

It wasn't always possible.

When the rain, snow and sleet closed in, high up on the exposed return stations was the worst place to be on the mountain. Ramps still had to be groomed, snow drifts continually removed, and every customer watched like a hawk for fear they'd baulk at the crummy conditions and try to stay on the chair as it ran around the great cogwheel and back down to base.

Only in the very worst conditions were we allowed to cower in our tiny control booths.

That's what I was doing at the top of the Movenpick on a particularly foul afternoon, when the phone rang. This was unusual, in the middle of a shift, but not unheard of. With shit-awful weather flaying the outside of my booth and hardly a skier in sight, I had the sudden hope that this call could mean an early closure.

"Hello, Movenpick return."

"Is that Mr Tony Slater?"

"It is."

"Hello, Mr Slater. Your name has been put forward to us for possible sponsorship. We're looking to sponsor a number of up-and-coming young snowboarders for the rest of this season."

"Oh? Right! Well, I'm, ah, not very good, I'm afraid."

"Nonsense! We sponsor mostly new faces, and we've heard good things about you from one of our members."

"Oh. Who is that, if you don't mind me asking?"

"It's Mr Jenkins who recommended you."

"I see." I had absolutely no idea who this was, but I only knew most of the Turoa staff by their nick-names. "Well that's very nice of him, but really I am just a beginner."

"That's quite alright. Beginners are the future."

"Well, true enough."

"So, are you interested?"

"I don't know. What does it involve?"

"We'll be sponsoring you to ride for us in upcoming events. We'll pay your entry fee, and you'll ride in our gear."

"Okay! That sounds great!"

"And our gear is all branded: Snowboarders For Christ."

"I... what? Oh."

"It's very important that we spread the message of Jesus Christ to the new generation, and snowboarding is the way we've chosen to do it."

"Ah. I see."

"Do you accept Jesus Christ as your saviour, Mr Slater?"

"Um, well, I guess so. I don't have to do anything for that, do I?"

"Just remember to give thanks to God and Jesus if you win anything."

"Right…"

"How do you feel about wearing a loincloth and a crown of thorns?"

It was at this point I detected a hint of familiarity in the voice on the other end.

"Keith? Is that you?"

This was met with hysterical laughter.

"Keith, you bastard!"

The laughter carried on until I hung up on him.

Evidently it was a slow day at the bottom of the lift, too.

The Great Storm

There has been much debate about The Great Storm – specifically, about which storm this title pertains to. For me, there will only ever be one Great Storm – not to be confused with the rather disappointing Great Perth Storm in 2011, which I also lived through (and which, despite a series of panic-inducing warnings from the government, caused nothing more damaging than widespread rearrangement of plastic patio furniture).

The thing is, when you work a ski season, the weather forecast goes from being that completely irrelevant bit at the end of the news that only your mum wants to watch, to being a vital piece of information. It's not uncommon to find groups of people huddled together like kids in a playground, debating the three-day outlook as though it was the finals of the EUFA Cup. Put simply; weather *matters*.

Because we had to get up so early, it was rare for anyone other than the company to have up to date information. As we stamped and shivered, waiting for the staff bus in the tin-roofed shack that served as a depot, we were treated to an endless stream of people walking up to read the forecast pinned to the noticeboard, and either punching the air jubilantly, or muttering curse words under their breath.

You see, there were always three distinct categories of people waiting for that bus, and they all wanted different things. If the weather was perfect, then anyone working inside would be mightily pissed off – because not only would they be forced to watch everyone else having a great time outside, they would also be rushed off their feet by the influx of customers. Those working outside got to appreciate it more, because they were in it – and might even get chance to sneak off for a couple of hot-laps and *really* appreciate it. Of course, they would also feel the effects of a mountain full of punters, but it meant that they (which means me!) could mock the indoors-types for their cosy, and ultimately less rewarding, existence. The third group was generally the happiest, because they were the people on their day off, who were catching the bus up the mountain purely for recreational purposes.

No-one liked them.

Now, if the weather was bad – or even, really, really bad – it was a complete reversal of fortunes. The lucky buggers working inside would be safe and warm, and bored enough to risk nipping out for a ride in the long gaps between customers. I, on the other hand, would be stuck outside, piss wet through and freezing my ass off, and inwardly pleading with the five die-hard teenagers circling my lift to give it up and go home before I was forced to hurt them.

The poor bastards who had a day off got the shittiest end of the stick, and would generally be stuck up the mountain until they could bum a lift back down again.

They'd suffered, got nothing to show for it, and worst of all, they'd missed the chance to have a nice lie-in.

But no-one had any sympathy for them.

Weather forecasting, however, is not an exact science. Even with all the technology at our disposal these days, mother nature is a tricky old bird, and has a nasty habit of switching her plays at the last minute. So when I headed up the mountain on a blustery grey day, with more severe weather expected in the evening, I was cautiously optimistic. It wasn't actually raining, but the threat of it would keep the lift queues light. I was pretty well wind-proofed in my outfit, up to five layers deep in places, so I hoped I could stay dry, and take advantage of a slow day to get some practice in.

It was not to be.

By mid-morning, conditions were going downhill rapidly. Rumour had it that the storm was moving up quicker than expected, and might even hit before close of business. From where I stood, halfway up the mountain on a slope called the Winter Garden, it was surprising that we hadn't closed already. Wind was raging, buffeting chairs and customers alike, and a slushy drizzle was slowly working its way through my layers.

When a liftie called Con rode up on his knackered board to cover my break, I asked if he thought we should bother; it must have been truly miserable up top by then. But Con was an old hand; he knew the score. "Nah way they'll close her now! Gotta wait till after lunch, then they don't have to give out any refunds!"

Of course! The crafty buggers. If the mountain closed early, half the ticket price would be refunded to anyone that asked; by staying open a little later, even though the conditions were horrible, they were still offering the chance to ski, even if no-one in their right minds would want to. Thus, no refunds had to be issued. It seemed a bit harsh at the time, and was a reminder that although we were there to have fun and muck about, for the bosses of the company this was all about profit.

And decisions made purely for profit, in my experience, are rarely good ones.

It took seconds to ride down to base for my break, but it was a real battle to get back up afterwards. I managed, soaked and frozen stiff, and toughed out another pointless hour before I got the call to close down the Winter Garden. I hadn't had a customer in over half that time, so the call was long overdue, but no matter. Everything above me was already shut. All I wanted to do was get all my queue gates packed away, and get the hell off that mountain.

By the time I was ready to go, another call had come in; the whole ski field was closed, and customers were being directed by the ski patrollers to get down as quickly as they could. Which is exactly what I did.

I didn't know this at the time, but conditions at base were already quite bad. Roo, working with her fellow roadies, had been tasked with escorting customers to their cars; it wasn't safe to send them out alone, as the wind was threatening to blow people clear across the car park and over the edge of the cliff. Roo struggled a bit, being as how she weighed less than most of our customers, but she bravely battled on, hauling car doors open with all her strength and using her body to stop them filling up with snow. She half-carried a woman with a broken leg, freshly wrapped by the medics, and even loaned the woman her ski gloves.

One of the last people on the mountain, I skidded down to base in a full blizzard. I could see absolutely nothing, but I'd learnt the terrain well enough to get most of the way down on feel.

Base, when I got there, was in barely organised chaos. Roo had just been sent out on another trip; two ski patrollers were with her, hauling four members (and three generations) of the same family between them. It was now considered too dangerous even for staff members to go out alone. Roo was inching her way across the car park, arms linked with a ten-year-old boy, when the full force of the storm hit.

I was last to board the staff bus, which thankfully had waited for me; I felt terrible about leaving Roo in the middle of all this, but so far it was still just a particularly shitty burst of bad weather. She'd be on the next bus, along with all the managers and the rest of the road crew, and I'd make our tiny room nice and warm for her when she got home.

Or so I thought.

The bus crawled out of the car park and started down the road, but it was a total white-out. The huge windscreen filled with snow much faster than the wipers could clear it, so Keith stepped into the breach; he jumped off the bus and walked in front of it, one gloved hand on the windscreen, directing the driver one frozen footstep at a time.

We still crashed.

There was a ravine on one side of us, a sheer cliff face that fell hundreds of feet down the mountainside. I guess I should be glad we didn't crash in that direction! Instead we crunched into the uphill side of the mountain, and stuck there.

As gusts of wind revealed and concealed the road ahead, we could suddenly see that there was no further to go; only a few metres ahead of us, a 4x4 had crashed into the back of an ambulance (which presumably had Roo's broken leg patient inside it). The ambulance seemed to have crashed into whatever was in front of it, and this slow-motion pile-up had blocked the narrow road completely. Drifts of snow were blowing in, filling the gaps between the vehicles. Our driver got on the radio and reported our situation – and that was that.

We waited.

Rescue

Two hours passed.

The bus had no heating, so we were glad of our work-wear. Well, those of us that had work-wear were glad of it. I'd long since surrendered my jacket to a girl who worked in the restaurant, and had been sitting there in a shirt and trousers, but I still had two layers of fleece to protect me. Even so, sitting there, cooling our heels so to speak, we began to get very cold indeed.

Then there was a knock on the door (which shocked the hell out of me, because I'd been half asleep for the last hour).

Two ski patrollers hauled themselves inside, having crawled all the way here from base. The reason? Why, to bring us Mars Bars, of course! They flung handfuls of chocolate bars down the length of the bus, and told us not to worry – that help was on the way. Honest!

And then they were gone, back into the howling gale, to take chocolate to everyone else in the pile-up. It might sound silly, but these were emergency rations. Being trapped for hours in a freezing snow-drift was more than just uncomfortable, especially for people on their own in a car. Staying warm when you can't move anywhere is difficult at the best of times. The ski patrollers, fully equipped with their rescue gear, took everyone they could find in the cars in front of us to safety, by the simple expedient of tying them all together.

We considered fighting our way back through the storm, but not everyone was equipped for it. Some of the indoors staff had thick waterproof jackets on, but no suitable footwear. It was all-or-nothing – either we all stay, or we all go. So we stayed.

Another two hours passed.

I was half asleep when the radio crackled with the news that the snow plough had opened the way behind us. The driver gunned the engine, put the bus in reverse, and, with the help of several spotters outside, negotiated the route backwards all the way back to base.

Gratefully we flooded off the bus and through the double doors to our staff room, noting as we did so that the foyer was waist-deep in snow.

That was where I found Roo – battered and traumatised, but otherwise intact.

When the wind peaked at just over 200kmph, it had been too much for her. The boy she was linked to had been torn from his father's grip, and the pair of them – Roo plus boy – had been bowled over. Relentless gusts sent them sliding downhill, faster and faster over the rain-slicked ice. Roo knew where that slide ended; the cliff edge, and a brutal plunge down the side of the mountain – but luckily there had been a car in the way. She'd slammed into it head-first, and managed to stick there, still clutching the young lad. The ski patrollers had fought their way down to her one step at a time, reaching them and hauling them a few metres back to where the family's car sat half buried in snow.

"How the hell can you stand up in this?" Roo had asked one patroller, shouting into his ear from an inch away.

"We've got crampons on," he replied, looking puzzled. "You haven't?"

Not long after this the decision had been made to stop ferrying the customers to their cars. After all, it wasn't like they could go anywhere. Shortly after that, the decision had been made to go and find the customers now stranded in their cars, and bring them all back to Tor One. See what I mean? Chaos.

By the time we arrived, Tor One was rammed out with customers. Possibly the worst news was this: the buggers had drunk all the coffee in the vending machine!

For this reason (probably amongst others), it was decided to try to transfer the customers to the restaurant. Until now there hadn't been enough staff to make such an attempt, but a whole bus full of frozen lifties was exactly what was needed.

The plan was for all the outdoors staff to link arms into a human chain, stretching from Tor One, along the driveway, up a flight of steps, across the courtyard, and into the restaurant. We would then pass the customers along the chain – or, to be more precise, they would have to climb us.

It went well.

We did it in small bursts, as staying outside for any length of time was incredibly dangerous – not to mention unpleasant. The raging winds tore at us, with sudden gusts capable of throwing us around like rag dolls. Plus, we were all thoroughly soaked and freezing cold; the last thing we needed was an entire crew with hypothermia.

Most of us had to work tomorrow.

After being part of the first few chains I started to gain confidence, and was trying to be more helpful. Stationing myself on the steps, which were the worst place – concrete covered with ice, offered absolutely no purchase – I clung to the railings with one hand, and helped people over the trickiest part of the route. I only dared let go of the railings once, to pass a nervous customer up to the next person in line – when a ferocious blast took my feet from under me. I literally flew halfway down the stairs, and had time enough to wonder if I'd be rolled all the way across the car park to the precipice at the far edge – when a gloved hand shot out and latched onto my arm, swinging me back into the railings with some force. I grabbed on, as tight as I could with numb fingers, got my feet back under me, and quietly shit myself.

Yet again a Ski Patroller had saved the day. These lads were made of real hero stuff, make no mistake; in spite of the cold, his grip on my arm was like iron.

"Careful mate!" he shouted, sounding considerably more cheerful than I felt, "it's a bit windy out!" And he turned to help the next customer in line.

In the restaurant, there was space to spread out, and it was heated. Some customers had been trapped there since the mountain closed, and were overjoyed to be reunited with friends and family they thought were missing. We spent the rest of the evening trying to keep the crowd in a positive mood, as we listened on the walkie-talkies for news. The series of events we heard unfolding were actually quite amusing, to those of us not directly involved in them. It was a classic cascade of cock-ups, which you really had to be there to fully appreciate.

First up, the snow plough that had liberated our bus had pushed onwards down the mountain, finding a path around the damaged vehicles and making it as far as the first bend in the road. There it had met its match in snow, and had become bogged.

Not to be deterred, the bosses sent out our monstrous John Deere tractor. This was a titanic machine, with rear-wheels taller than me. Its mission: to pull the snow plough out of the snow-drift. What could possibly go wrong with this?

The tractor had made it halfway to the stranded snow plough when it had run out of gas. Whilst trying to figure out what was wrong, the tractor driver had gone to get out for a look – only to have the door torn off by the wind as soon as he opened it!

"Fucking idiots!" was heard over the radio, presumably directed at whoever's job it was to keep the tractor full of fuel. Then there came a somewhat weaker addendum: "Ah, can someone come and help me? The cab is filling up with snow…"

So it was the idiot's turn to save the day. They piled into a ute and, with tyres wrapped in snow chains and a few gallons of petrol in the back, they charged off to the rescue.

At least until a flying chunk of ice shattered their rear windscreen, showering them with glass and snow in equal measure. They drove a bit more slowly after that.

But the chain of bad luck had to break. The ute boys refuelled the tractor, dug out the cab, and in turn it freed the snow plough. Then all the vehicles made a solemn, funeral-procession pace, all the way down the mountain.

It took them three hours.

That was the worst of it, though. We started filling the staff buses with customers, using the same human-chain method, and they set off one at a time to make their slow way downhill. The buses made better time of it than the snow plough – it only took them four hours to make a return trip!

And then, at long last, it was our turn.

As our bus inched its way down the mountain, opinion was yet again divided into three camps. There were those who viewed the day as a complete disaster; they were pissed off at the managers, annoyed with the customers, and were moaning constantly about how terrible the whole ordeal had been. They were mostly indoors staff.

Then there were the people who thought, like me, that this had been one hell of an adventure! It was the most exciting thing by far that had happened to me on the ski-field. *One day*, I thought, *I might even get to write about this!*

My shift had started that morning at 7am.

I'd clocked off and been sent home at midday.

At 2:45 the following morning, I staggered in through the door, still soaked to the skin, chilled, and exhausted. Roo arrived even later, the six roadies having been the last group to leave the mountain, crammed into the battered ute with no back window. I'll admit, I nearly cried with relief when she clomped in, still covered in snow. Four people died in that storm (which, for New Zealand, represents a significant portion of the population). Luckily for us, none of them were on our mountain; somehow, we'd managed to get everyone down without a single serious injury. We even got a mention on the news for it.

Oh, and the third opinion? Held by a small minority of veteran staff, it was best voiced by a huge, heavily tattooed Maori bloke who was working his seventh consecutive ski season: "Ah, that was nothin' eh?" he said, to anyone who would listen. "Y'se shoulda bin here for the *Great* Storm…"

Gill For The Win

We didn't see much of Gill that season, because having spread her wings at last, she was flapping as hard as she could. Okay, that doesn't paint a very flattering picture… Hm. I'd like to say she was soaring like an eagle, but Gill's a bit stubby to be compared to an eagle. I dunno, is there such a thing as a Stunted Eagle?

Anyway, the point is, she was doing well.

Very well, as it turned out.

She was spending most of her evenings at the Turoa Lodge, a pub frequented almost exclusively by the RAL staff. Pretty much every night there was some kind of staff party held there; pool tournaments, fancy dress nights and staff-only beer offers cropped up so frequently it was no wonder half the lifties showed up to work still hammered from the night before. Unfortunately the Lodge was at the extreme opposite end of town, three-quarters of an hour's fast walk away from where we all lived, down a long, empty road. It was so agonisingly cold at night that I regularly made the walk expecting to come across the frozen corpses of the last few people to leave the pub. All it would take was for someone to be drunk enough to lay down for a nap halfway home… it never happened of course, which given the state of inebriation required to even attempt the walk, had to be a minor miracle.

Gill made the trip often enough to appreciate its rare benefits – it didn't matter how hammered you were when you set out, by the time you got home you were stone-cold sober – and had burnt off all the calories you'd consumed in a night of boozing. It was an extreme endurance event which I rarely felt the need to undertake, as I had everything I needed – which was Roo – right there, in my tiny little hobbit-hole.

Speaking of hobbit-holes, Gill had finally landed on her feet. After accepting a room in a house that was still being renovated, and acknowledging that she'd have to provide 'a few things for the kitchen' – she'd turned up to find those few things included more than just a bunch of pots and pans and a kettle.

There was no kitchen.

There was no furniture of any kind.

There were no carpets.

And there were no doors.

In fact, if you were to replace the phrase 'being renovated' with 'derelict', you'd probably have a more accurate appreciation of the house she'd been offered.

Still, Gill is nothing if not resourceful.

Somehow, in a town the size of Ohakune, she sourced second-hand carpets, a bed, a table and some chairs, and was well on her way to making the place liveable – when the owner admitted he wouldn't be able to install any heating this season.

Or connect the electricity.

Or water.

But he was happy to knock some cash of the rent for these inconveniences…

Ranting about her situation over lunch to a ski-technician called Chris, she'd been amazed when he told her about an available room where he was living.

The girl that had originally rented the room had hooked up with another staff member, and decided to move in with him to save cash.

So, delightedly, Gill abandoned her moth-eaten carpets and took a room at 'The Penguins' – arguably the most sought-after accommodation in all Ohakune.

After serving as a one-woman letting agent, finding places to stay for half the staff in town at the expense of herself, it had a karmic vibe when she moved in; her room was bigger than most lounges, she had a huge bed, central heating, wireless internet and Sky TV. Plus, she was a good twenty minutes closer to the pub.

She was very, very happy there.

And as the weeks turned into months, I couldn't help but notice that Gill was spending more and more time with Chris.

Because he was short – the same height as she was, amazingly enough – and cute (although don't tell him I said that); and he was clever, a geneticist by profession, though he much preferred following winter around the world and fixing skis for a living.

He had blonde hair and blue eyes, which was the icing on the cake as far as Gill was concerned (him having already fulfilled her dream trifecta), and according to all known sources, she spent more time in his room that season than she did in her own.

And it later transpired that he was studying to become a helicopter pilot in his spare time – so I figured I could stop worrying about Gill for a while.

The most time I spent with her was on the staff bus, on the way to work in the mornings. That was where we got to compare notes about our lives, and she would try to convince me that her job was even more ridiculous than mine.

You see, Gill was working as a ticket-checker.

It was her job to make sure that everyone in the ski-area had paid the right amount to be there.

It was a source of endless frustration for the customers; partly because the ticket-checkers were so understaffed that only two of them stood by the main chair lift, so they created a bottleneck right in front of it; and partly because a good few of them had no tickets, and were relying on a bit of confusion to slip through unnoticed.

"The stupidest thing," Gill told me, "is that we've got these super-dooper electronic barcode scanners to check the tickets with. Only they *aren't waterproof!* So half the time the bloody things don't work at all, and I'm supposed to use a pen – *a pen,* for God's sake – to write down the numbers on everyone's tickets! Like I could just nip off for a few hours to run them all through the database, and then come back and catch whoever had invalid ones!"

"Holy shit!"

"Of course, pens don't work in the cold, so that got mentioned to the boss… and then we were issued with – wait for it – *pencils!* So they have this multi-million-dollar ticketing system, all computer-based and designed to be impossible to forge – and it comes down to us, standing in the snow, trying to copy down 13-digit barcodes with pencils. Onto paper, which just disintegrates anyway."

"Okay, you win! Your job is *way* more ridiculous than mine. How the hell do you cope?"

She shrugged. "We don't. It's got to the point where, once the scanner stops working, I just point it at people and say 'beep'."

"No way! And does anyone say anything?"

"Sometimes. Yesterday this bloke said to me 'Did you just point at me and go *beep?* And I said, 'yep'. And he said, 'fair enough'. And that was that. Hell, I might as well make a scanner out of snow and use that!"

And to prove a point, the very next day she did just that.

As the season drew to a close, our contracts came up for renewal. It was left up to each individual staff member, to decide if they wanted to carry on working until the ski-field ran out of snow, or if they wanted to leave to pursue their own agendas. Roo and I fell into the latter category, as we'd saved up a bit of cash and hoped to spend our last few snowbound weeks careening uncontrollably down a different mountain.

There were leaving parties every other night at that point, and much drunkenness as new friends and old got together to celebrate before their ways parted once more.

Roo and I got permission from the Hobbits to hold a party at their place, and the allure of the hot tub drew people we'd hardly seen all season.

It was a typically raucous affair, although I refrained from my trademark act of streaking on the grounds that a) I lived here, and that would just be awkward; and b) I'd streaked at every staff party I'd been to all season, and people were probably getting bored of seeing me run around naked.

Hanging around until the bitter end, Gill and Chris were still nursing their drinks when Roo and I apologised to them and went to bed.

We had to spend the next day packing everything we owned, once again – as the day after that, we'd booked our bus out of there.

Gill and Chris, noticing that the hot tub was finally empty, had taken full advantage of the fact. Despite not having any shorts or swimming costumes with them, they'd climbed in – fully clothed – and sat in there for quite some time.

It must have occurred to them that, as they were now sopping wet, it was going to be a very long, very cold walk home. So they stayed a little longer, finishing off a few other drinks that no longer had owners.

It started to snow as they sat there, luxuriating in the warm water – a bizarre sensation which I'd been lucky enough to experience a few times myself.

Then Chris, whose surname was Robinson, saluted Gill with a glass of wine and started singing, "So here's to you, Mrs Robinson…"

"Ha!" Gill responded, "That's my song!"

"It could be, you know," he told her.

And whatever else they got up to in the hot tub that night, I'm probably better off not knowing. Because I had to clean the thing the next day.

"Did that really just happen?" Gill had asked Chris, as they sloshed their way home at five o'clock in the morning.

It was a while before Gill told me this story, and at first I didn't quite understand what she was getting at. But it seemed very important to her, so I ran the conversation back through my mind a bit more slowly.

That's when it hit me.

"Hang on a minute," I said to her, "does that meant that...?"

"YES!," she said, "it does! Chris proposed to me that night! He and I are engaged!"

Countdown

Leaving Ohakune was a bit of a wrench. It was a stunning, magical place, with the glistening snow-cap of Mount Ruapehu looming tantalisingly above all of it. The town, and the season, had been good to us. Both Roo and I had spent plenty of time moaning about our jobs, but then part of the glue that held the ski community together was moaning about their jobs. Everyone thought they had it hardest – at least until their day off came around, and suddenly it was the best place in the world to work! The other component of the community glue was the booze, of course, and this was an element that Roo and I had largely abstained from. Not because we don't love to party – we'd put in an appearance at every major event – but because the walk to the pub was so damn long and unpleasant, and for the first time in my life I didn't feel the need to be the centre of attention, the craziest of party animals; I had no burning desire to show off and make a fool of myself in front of everyone. I still did though, but mostly by accident.

We had learnt to snowboard.

Neither of us were going to break any records, but neither of us had broken any bones.

Roo, it has to be said, had achieved a far greater measure of cool than I could ever aspire to. It was time to admit it; that ship had sailed. I was clumsier than ten regular people tied together at the ankles, and twice as likely to earn strange looks from passers-by. But that seemed to be my lot in life, and so long as Roo could cope with it, I was starting to think that I could, too.

Most of all, we'd been happy, the pair of us, tucked away in our little Hobbit hole.

But now, new horizons beckoned, and we made our way by bus, ferry and bus again to New Zealand's South Island. Our destination; Mount Hutt, another ski resort, and one at which we planned to grasp the tail-end of the season and cling on to it for all it was worth.

Item one on the agenda: jobs, as our savings from Turoa had

been spent equipping us with passes to the Mount Hutt ski field, and paying the bond on a room in the nearby town of Ashburton.

Or 'AshVegas', as the locals liked to refer to it.

I don't know why, but I got the feeling there was a touch of irony in that nick-name.

Ashburton wasn't much of a place; it had one supermarket, called Countdown, so we headed in there with our CV's and applied for jobs on the shelf-stacking team.

There wasn't much else on offer – it was either that, or McDonalds, and if I worked there and ended up being grossed out by the food, I'd lose about a quarter of my dietary options at a stroke.

It was a tense couple of weeks while we waited for a call from the supermarket manager, but when it came it was good news; we'd both been offered jobs on the night shift, which would leave the days free to snowboard. It couldn't have been more perfect.

They'd hired Roo without a second thought, as being an Aussie she could legally work for them until the day she died (and probably for several months afterwards – what with the smell of the stockroom and the average IQ of the staff, I doubt anyone would have noticed). My UK passport had caused some head-scratching though, until I convinced them that my visa was valid for at least another year, after which I was eligible to be sponsored by them.

Lyndon, the manager, took himself very seriously. Possibly because he looked about sixteen. He'd actually called all our references – most of whom were overseas, and all of whom were fake – and asked them extensive questions about our trustworthiness.

So. Obviously he was satisfied, and we could get to work…

Well, after the inevitable reams of paperwork, mandatory inductions, Health and Safety videos and Job Orientation.

It was laughable, because the job description read like this: 1) Stack shelves with assorted products.

2) Refer to item 1 (see above)

Providing I could avoid decapitating myself with my box knife, and resist the urge to shout "INCOMING!" and hurl five-kilo sacks of rice over the shelves into the next isle, it was pretty much in the bag.

Although we were treated to a fascinating lecture on how to wash our hands.

A whole staffroom full of new employees sat in on this one, again delivered via the magic of corporate training video circa 1987.

It covered every aspect of safe chemical usage, from the

omnipresent dispensers of foaming hand-wash (classified as 'C1'), all the way up to harmful chemicals like industrial bleach (known as 'C10'). This intrigued me. As the tape droned on, I squirmed round in my seat to cast a surreptitious glance at the wall behind me. A series of brightly-coloured posters marched across it, describing in detail the directives associated with each chemical in sequence. And sure enough, there it was: the official, company-approved guidelines for handling C4.

I was laughing about this later that evening, as we watched the intro to a TV show which purported to be an exposé on New Zealand's deadly criminal gangs.

The reporter, using hushed tones, described the horrors facing those foolish enough to stray into gang-controlled territory. There was shot after shot of the teenaged gangsters, all huddled together in their hoodies. I got the impression they were hiding from their parents, rather than the dreaded 5-0. In every shot, a different member of the gang would get up close and personal with the camera, waving a big shiny hunting knife in front of the lens whilst making threatening faces and gestures.

For no immediately apparent reason, the other five of them would be bobbing and weaving in the background, doing overly aggressive hand movements. It looked like they were making a really bad rap video.

I leaned closer to the TV in mock awe, and that's when I noticed – they were all using the same knife! This gang was so bad-ass they must only have one between them, and they were taking it in turns to menace the camera with it. I even recognised the knife; you could 'Buy It Now' on eBay for $15.

The clincher, though, was the final dramatic interview. The reporter had saved this one till last, presumably attempting to build up the tension throughout the show.

Now she spoke in hushed tones with the masked leader of this vicious street gang.

"Have you… done robberies?" she asked.

"Yeah, we done robberies," came the callous answer.

"Have you… done assault?"

"Yeah, we done assault!"

"Have you… done murder?"

"Yeah, we done murder!"

Then a high-pitched voice at the back piped up, "Uh, we ain't done murder…"

The ringleader glanced around, suddenly embarrassed. "Oh yeah, we ain't done murder," he agreed.

I was laughing too hard by that point to hear the wrap-up.

I imagine it was some terrifying message about the out-of-control violence on New Zealand's inner-city streets, and how our lives were in constant danger from this shadowy underworld.

Ha!

I think the most serious criminal activity any of them had been involved in was shoplifting *Mars Bars*. Unless you count Deceiving a Reporter. Or Impersonating N.W.A.

I bet not one of them was late home for his dinner.

I debated the authenticity of the show with a couple of the shelf-fillers at work the following evening.

"It could happen, you know," one of the ladies told me. "Even here! Look."

And she pointed to a section of the staff room walls, which were festooned with information sheets and notices of the kind I presume litter such rooms the world over. Bulletins from Head Office explaining the importance of being polite to customers (and presumably waiting until they're out of earshot before commenting on the size of their tits). A Store Evacuation Plan (Leave by the door. Assemble in the car park. Try not to shout "Shit! Shit! The shop's on fire!"). I half expected to see an alphabet chart, or one of those diagrams on how to tie shoe laces – but she was drawing my attention to a cheerfully laminated poster giving the guidelines for dealing with an armed robbery.

In Ashburton, for Christ's sake! I mean, leaving aside for the moment the fact that acquiring an illegal firearm in small town New Zealand was likely so difficult and expensive you'd have to rob every supermarket in the country just to break even, there was one other mitigating circumstance, making casual armed robbery highly unlikely in Ashburton: the size of the place. Everybody knows everybody else. I doubt more than five people there have ever been to jail. And every one of their mums works at Countdown. I imagined it going down something like this:

Robber: "Everybody FREEZE! This is a robbery!"
    Cashier: "Hey, Fred? Is that you?"
    Fred: [Deeper voice] "No."
    Manager: "What's going on here?"
    Customer: "Fred's robbing the store!"
    Manager: "Oh, hey Fred."

But you had to hand it to them; the top links of the supermarket chain weren't leaving anything to chance. If there was to be a hold-up in one of their stores, well, they'd at least made sure we were all prepared for it.

'The 5 C's of Armed Robbery Response' the poster was titled.

1) Calm - Remain calm at all times (which seemed easier said than done. After all, everyone knows Fred used to pull the legs off of insects as a child. He makes a damn good pot roast though).

2) Cooperate - Do precisely as the offender instructs ("Don't call me Fred!")

3) Communicate - Activate alarm and call police as soon as it is safe to do so.

4) Conserve - Remain calm at all times. (Wait a minute! I think we've had this one?)

5) Complete - Remain calm at all times. (So basically they could only think of 3 C's, but decided to repeat C1 three times because '5 C's' sounded like a much more comprehensive strategy…)

I could see the headline: 'Gunfight narrowly avoided in Ashburton supermarket this morning, as staff remained three times more calm than expected…'

On my next break I pointed out the poster to Ron, a kindly old bloke who'd started working at Countdown at the same time as Roo and me.

"So, Ron, do you know what to say in case of a hold-up?"

"Sure," he replied. "I'd say 'This is a stick-up! Put all your money in this bag!'"

White Out

With all our days free, Roo and I spent every possible opportunity sliding down Mount Hutt on our shiny, yet woefully inappropriate snowboards. We loved the place. It benefitted from a significantly milder climate than Mount Ruapehu, with none of the ice we'd become accustomed to. Consequently, the snowboarding here was as fun and easy as a lazy summer afternoon.

At least until the weather turned to shit.

It was bound to happen one day, and at first we were keen to carry on regardless. Slushy rain was falling from a sky so low we could touch it.

There was no wind, so the freezing rain fell in eerie silence, soaking everything it came into contact with. If I'd been working in Turoa, I'd have been cursing the birth-circumstances of the half-dozen die-hard kids who refused to quit, forcing me to stay at my post long after the will to live had departed. Thankfully, these days I was my own master. Visibility was getting worse, the clouds were threatening, and it looked like an early trip home was on the cards.

There was just the glimmer of a chance that conditions were better up top – with the clouds so low, we'd be passing through them on the lift. Anything could be going on above them, up to and including a perfect summer's day. So.

"You wanna try one more?" I asked Roo. "In case?"

She thought about it. "One more. It's cold, and I'm wet. Unless it's amazing up there, we should probably go."

"Sweet!"

So we jumped on the express lift, taking advantage of the empty queue gates as most of the public had already called it a day.

The chairs carried us through the worst of the blizzard, and then up into the clouds producing it; it was fantastic, a featureless white veil surrounding us, enclosing us, stealing away everything but the wood and steel of the chair we were sat in.

"We're about halfway up," Roo pointed out. "We're going to have to go through this on the way down!"

"Cool," I said.

"Just go slow," she told me, "be careful."

"Always!"

"Yeah, right."

And then we were above it, the rest of the world dropping back into focus around us. As surreal experiences go, it was one of the best – and one of the wettest.

"Bugger this," Roo said. Rain from higher up was already pelting us, only this rain was substantially more frozen. It was like being shot at with a ball-bearing rifle set to fully automatic.

We reached the top, strapped into our boards, and set off. The fresh snow and hail made for a super-slick surface, and I was cruising along quite happily. Roo caught up to me a few times, and I hung back to agree with her that this would be our last run.

Then I noticed the cloud thickening, almost imperceptibly, as I rode. Ahead, the trail faded into impenetrable white mist. I could hear the hiss of Roo's board just behind me, so I craned my neck and gave her a shaky thumbs-up – and the cloud swallowed me whole.

That was the last I saw of her for a while.

A white-out is very hard to describe to someone who hasn't experienced it. It felt like I was floating; the mist enveloped me so completely I could see absolutely nothing. Not the board under my feet, or the gloves on my hands – much less the surrounding terrain. I was flying; with no frame of reference beyond the slight tremor of my board on the smooth snow, I could have been going downwards, upwards, or just standing still. No breath of wind betrayed my passage, which is why I was shocked when my board began to judder, grinding against something hard – ice? Somehow I'd crossed the run from left to right, and was now being forced against the side of it – a near vertical wall of ice reaching up towards a different run. I was obviously travelling much faster than I'd thought, so I swished around to carve what I hoped would be a shallow angle back across the slope.

In this, I was far more successful than I anticipated. I shot right across the width of the track in a handful of heartbeats, and must have whipped through a row of now-invisible warning flags.

I saw the edge of the cliff at exactly the same moment I went over it.

Oh. Shit, my mind said.

Suddenly I was in free-fall, and although it can't have lasted for more than a couple of seconds, it felt like an eternity.

Still the white clouds wrapped me; it was like an out-of-body experience, or that scene in a movie where the main character is suddenly whisked into the presence of God; weightless, drifting in an endless sea of pure white light. It was quite idyllic, apart from the bowel-loosening certainty of serious injury at the end of it.

I landed upside-down on a block of ice with bone-jarring force. Luckily, my head broke my fall. It's the softest part of me after all, and there's nothing in there worth damaging.

In all seriousness though, I probably owe the fact that I'm still walking to the fact that ski areas are, well you know, *pointy*. There aren't many flat bits on them, and this area was no exception. It was an ice-field, too steep and broken to ski on, littered with chunks and boulders of frozen rock and snow. I ploughed through the lot head-first, picking up speed as I careened downhill.

I slid through a patch of clearer air, and thought I could make something out; quite a way below me, clinging for all her worth to an icy outcrop, was a girl.

And I was heading right for her.

I think she noticed it in the same moment I did. Along with realising that I wasn't going to slow down.

There was nothing I could do.

"SORRY!" I called out – and seconds later I cannoned into her, smashing her from her perch and sending her skidding off down the mountain.

As she vanished into the fog below, her ghostly cry wafted back up to me; "That's okay!"

That was the last I saw of her, for a little while, as well.

The impact had transferred all my momentum to the poor woman; now I found myself taking her place, hung up by my board on the outcropping. Face up but head down, the logical part of my brain began considering my next move. Slide, fall or tumble seemed to be the options. Apparently this was quite a popular cliff to ski off today, and there was a reasonable chance that the next person over the precipice would do to me what I'd just done to that rather polite young lady.

So.

What I really needed to do, was get my board under me. The very first thing a beginner learns is the heel-edge descent: a slow, controlled grind where you assume the position of someone stood upright on the flat, letting only the metal rim on the back of your board contact the slope. In my days of working much higher than I could safely get down from, I'd honed this technique to a fine art.

If I could right myself, I could ride my heels all the way down the mountain, if need be.

If only I could get my board under me…

My struggles dislodged me, and I began to slide again. This time I wasn't going too fast, though it was still making a mess of my hair. I seemed to be slowing.

And then I slid to a halt on a rare patch of level ground. Just beyond me was a huge hole in the ice, with a massive steel pylon rising out of it.

From somewhere in the hole, I could hear movement. And cursing.

Aha! That'll be that girl, then.

Owing to her borrowed momentum, she'd shot out into fresh air once again, crashed into the tower, and had ended up in a heap at the bottom of it. After I unstrapped from my board and helped her climb out, I found she didn't blame me at all. Which was nice.

"How the hell do we get home?" was what she was more concerned about.

This was where I got to repay her trust. Knowing the slopes pretty well, I guessed which ski lift was cranking away invisibly above us. And as a general rule of thumb, when you're trying to get off a ski-slope the way to go is *down.* Carrying our boards, we hiked through the rough terrain, supporting each other over ridges and ditches, until we stumbled out onto a stretch of groomed *piste.*

It was the end section of the very lowest run, and we both strapped on our boards for a gentle glide home.

Roo was waiting for me at the finish line, almost an hour since she'd seen me vanish into the mist in front of her.

"I was starting to get worried," she said, her words belying the trembling of her body as she hugged me. "I was about to send out the ski patrollers."

"They wouldn't have found me in this," I said. "How did you get down?"

"Same as always, you know – slow and careful."

"Hm. Maybe that's not such a bad thing after all."

"Ah! So you're going to be more slow and careful in future, are you?"

"Well, no, but it's not a bad thing for you."

"Asshole!"

And yet she was delightfully careful with my bruised body, once we were safely back home.

Ma Homies

Home, incidentally, was a room in a shared house; following an advert on the supermarket noticeboard, we'd moved in with a friendly Kiwi girl called Nikki. A tall, easy-going blonde chick, Nikki got on great with us, especially Roo, as they'd both studied agriculture at college and were both farm girls at heart. Nikki owned a brace of gorgeous horses, which we went to visit a couple of times. Unfortunately, she also suffered with ME, which we only discovered when she walked into the lounge one afternoon and said, "Hey guys, I don't want to worry you, but I'm about to pass out and have a fit. I'll be fine, you don't have to call an ambulance or anything, but you might have to help me back to my room afterwards. Is that okay?"

Roo and I exchanged glances, and said, "Err… okay?"

"Thanks guys, that's great!" said Nikki.

And then she keeled over on the carpet.

It was frightening to me, to find out there was a condition about which so little was known – and which, like PTSD before it became accepted, was widely dismissed by the medical community. With no cure and little sympathy from her doctors, Nikki was left struggling through daily life when just a few years previously she'd been a semi-professional athlete.

Scary stuff.

Our other housemate was rather more unusual. He moved in a few days after we did, having just arrived from America. Halfway around the planet he'd come, to the winter-sports capital of the world – wearing a neatly-pressed shirt, trousers with suspenders, and socks with little suspenders of their own.

To get a job.

But not in the ski industry.

"Any job, really," he said when pressed, "I'm just gonna look around and see what there is."

He was an odd one. There seemed to be something imperceptible *missing* in him. A spark, a sense of humour perhaps, some sign of... sentience.

Slowly, we pieced his story together. It was important not to ask him too many questions, as he got confused quite easily, and also tended to spit further the more excited he got. So to avoid a bath in mucus, the best way of extracting information from him was in small snippets here and there.

So. He'd worked as some kind of manual labourer in Kansas. He'd lost his job, but fortune had shone on him when a friend of a friend told him that there was plenty of work to be had in New Zealand. With no further research, he'd gone to the nearest travel agent, explained his plans, and booked a one-way flight. The travel agents had clearly seen him coming; not only had they let him buy the ticket, itself an act of cruelty bordering on the malicious, but they had also charged him four times the going rate.

And told him that everything would be alright when he got to New Zealand...

It was a wonder the immigration people hadn't picked him up.

He had no work visa. He had no working holiday visa. He had no way to get either, being too old, unskilled, and, well, American.

He'd blown all his savings on the flight over, so he couldn't leave. Hell, he wouldn't leave, studiously ignoring the fact that no-one in the country would risk a fine and imprisonment just to employ his dumb ass.

But for the most part he was happy, and harmless – unless he was playing his violin.

Now, I've seen plenty of people travelling with instruments. It's a great ice-breaker when meeting new people, and everyone loves the bloke who pulls out a battered guitar and starts strumming a few pop songs. I could never be that bloke, because I play the drums.

Badly.

This bloke played the violin badly. Or more accurately, he couldn't play at all – he was the rawest of beginners, and had obviously dragged the thing all the way over here with him solely because – wait for it – *he was planning on starting a new life here!*

Really.

Despite being on a three-month tourist visa.

But the craziest thing about his musical ambitions was not that he preferred to pursue them – violently – in the early hours of the morning; nor that they extended exclusively to religious hymns (only evident because he'd brought a vast quantity of sheet music with him, all of which was for hymns). It was this: he was also travelling *with a folding music stand*. You know the ones – stainless steel, tripod base, adjustable, use them a lot in school, weigh about eight kilos…

I can honestly say, I've never seen anyone travel with anything less practical.

Including the decapitated dog's head I carried across the Gulf of Thailand in a polystyrene box.

Other than that, it was business as usual; we eked out damn near two months there, snowboarding five days a week and working most evenings, before Mount Hutt closed down for the season.

In that time we saw all kinds of dramas unfold in the microcosm of Countdown Ashburton, including the breakdown of at least one marriage; it emerged that the shift supervisor (who was subsequently re-assigned) was sleeping with – and accidentally having a baby with – one of his night-fill girls. This was the sort of gossip that kept us occupied each evening, as we busied our hands with a strange task known as 'facing'.

It was my favourite part of the job, and by far the most ridiculous; for the last full hour of every shift, the entire team would take to the shop floor, working our way down every single aisle – *turning all the tins and packets around so that their labels faced the right direction!*

Oh yes! I couldn't believe it either. But the supermarket management placed such a high value on customers being presented with a uniform wall of correctly-orientated products, that they were willing to spend hundreds of dollars each night paying us to achieve it.

How bizarre.

And so, inevitably, there came the moment when Roo and I had our 'when should we tell them we're leaving?' discussion. The problem has always been the same; no-one wants to hire us short-term, so we always kind of gloss over the fact that we're effectively transients, when we apply. We're both hard workers and fast learners, and we always give 110% to an employer – our motivation dramatically eclipsing the poor sods who really are working there for the rest of their lives.

And in almost every job we've ever done, we get great progress reviews and recommendations for promotion from the management.

Typically around the same time we're thinking of leaving.

So then we have the familiar problem; do we come clean and explain our plans, and spent our last weeks working under a cloud of disappointment? Or do we wait until the last minute, and make up some shock excuse; "Gotta leave – family emergency," or "Sorry – just discovered we become technically illegal in your country in three days time…"

I hate doing this. But having already booked our tickets back to Perth, it seemed like the logical time to tell someone about it.

Geoff, our friendly night-shift supervisor, was the ideal candidate.

I'd have sought him out at work, only he sought me out first.

"There you are Tony," he said, "Guess what? It's time for your progress interview! Step into my office…"

Ooooh bugger, I thought. *Here we go again…*

"So tell me, Tony – how long to you think you'll be here?"

I glanced down at my watch. Today was Wednesday. So… six days? It didn't seem like the kind of answer he'd appreciate.

"I'm not sure, really," I said instead, "my options are open."

"That's good to hear! See, you can have a real future with this company."

"Absolutely!" I lied.

"Where do you see yourself, five years from now?"

The urge welled up within me to say 'not bloody here, mate!' – but I fought it.

"Uh, I dunno," I told him.

"Within five years, you could be a supervisor. In less than ten, you could be running a whole shift. An assistant manager. You could be sitting here *conducting* this interview!"

The mind boggles. Well, mine did. I bit down hard on a sarcastic reply that I could feel forming. He really wasn't making it sound any more enticing.

In the end I went with, "Ah, yeah, that's interesting."

And it was. I'm often fascinated by how many people seem content to settle for so little – a pay rise, an office with a window or some kind of token authority. Or maybe I'm the mad one? Settling for permanent insolvency, with no career, no real property, and less chance of getting either than I have of walking on the moon?

Then again, a couple of years ago I never imagined I could fall in love.

I flashed forward in my mind, wondering idly what I would be doing in five years time. *Beaches,* I thought. *Somewhere hot. With cocktails with umbrellas in them. Maybe I should go to Tahiti. Tahiti sounds exotic. Do some diving, perhaps. And Roo can get a tan.*

I realised Geoff was staring at me, waiting for an answer. I groped around for something suitable. "It's a lot to think about," I settled on.

"I know, it is," Geoff agreed.

And we both sat there, pondering Tahiti for a few more seconds. Well, maybe that was just me.

"Right, I'd better let you get back to your pallets," he said, and stood up to open the office door. "Think about it," he advised, as I edged past him. "I'm putting on your form that I've recommended you for supervisor training!"

"Thanks Geoff," I said, gratefully. He really was a decent fella, and he was doing his best by me. As far as he knew.

It almost made me feel bad that I was leaving for Perth in less than a week.

Full Circle

When Sonja picked us up from Perth airport in her crumbling Morris Minor, the drive back to Roleystone already felt like coming home.

It was bittersweet, moving back into the games room in her dad's house.

I reclaimed the sofa, but this time Gill wasn't sleeping opposite me; she'd stayed in New Zealand, moving in with Chris as they tried to plan for a future together.

Roo returned to the room she'd slept in as a child – but Frieda, of course, was gone as well.

A lot had changed, for all of us, and this was very much on my mind as the last few days ticked down to my third Christmas in Australia. Because as far as change goes, I was about to push the envelope just a little bit further. Or at least, I was going to try to.

As midnight approached on Christmas Eve, I felt strangely detached from the merriment around me. It wasn't that I was unhappy, but I had a job to do, a task to accomplish – and it was one of the scariest situations I had ever found myself in. I paced the corridor leading to the bedrooms, muttering to myself. Paced, and muttered. If anyone had noticed me, they have thought... well, let's face it – they'd have thought it was perfectly normal. For me. I've been seen doing plenty of stranger things in my time.

But no-one saw me, and time was exactly my problem – because it was running out. I had to do this. It was now, or... or some other time? It didn't *have* to be now after all, there was no real reason for it. A silly, self-imposed deadline was all that I'd be breaking, and any rule that I'd come up with was bound to be flawed. *Maybe I should give it up altogether,* I thought, *at least for now...*

No.

This had to be done. And now, before I lost my nerve.

Ha! Who was I kidding? I wasn't even close to having the nerve.

But I have something else in abundance: I have stupidity. So I ignored my screaming instincts, and did it anyway.

I knocked on the door of Gerrit's study, and went in. "Hi!" I said, trying – and failing – to sound casual. "Can I talk to you about something?"

"That sounds serious," he said.

Then I closed the door behind me, and I think that got him really worried.

So I cut right to it. I didn't think he'd appreciate small talk, and I wasn't up to it. I was sweating, visibly trembling; even my voice was shaking. I was, quite plainly, terrified.

"I'd like to ask your permission to marry your daughter," I said. I blurted it out all at once, for fear it would stay inside me forever if I didn't.

Gerrit's face went from concern to shock to delight in less time than it took me to write it – considerably less actually, as I only type with two fingers.

"Yes! Of course! That is great news, mate! I wondered if this was going to happen soon."

"Oh, thank God for that! I was so nervous!"

"Yes, I can tell!"

And that was that. I swore Gerrit to silence, and hugged him – for the first time ever. He'd have to get used to it, I figured, if he was going to be my father-in-law. But I should probably draw the line at calling him daddy.

And then I went back into the family room, where last-minute adjustments were being made to the pile of presents under the tree. Less than an hour remained. I asked Roo if she'd like to come for a quiet stroll, and she said she would. Which was good, or I'd have struggled to get her alone in a house full of her sisters on Christmas Eve.

We walked through a pleasant Roleystone evening, taking advantage of the comparative coolness. We talked, as we usually did, but you know what? I can't remember a single word of it. I can only hope I wasn't babbling like an idiot, as all my focus was on what was about to happen. I'm not a great multi-tasker, it has to be said; if I talk while I walk, I invariably end up lost. If I try to eat at the same time, I end up in hospital. Roo was steering me, as usual, with light pressure on my hand, so this freed me up to spot potential sites. Unfortunately, I was drawing a blank. We'd walked a larger circuit than usual, passing down the hill and back up it from a different direction. We'd passed houses a plenty, and scraggly bits of bush, but this was still a fairly well-developed area; there weren't any hidden spots of woodland, or sudden breath-taking views on offer. It was only the road, and as we walked beside it, closer and closer to her house, I started to get desperate.

"Let's turn up there," I suggested, and pulled Roo off the pavement to follow the road a bit further uphill. Now I could see trees around me, but only enough to shield the surrounding houses from the street. We reached the top of the hill. From there, the way led down – directly to the top of Roo's driveway. We'd taken the long way around, and it had rewarded me with nothing.

I looked around frantically. This was it – last chance. Still nothing presented itself. Except…

"Let's go and stand over there," I said, pointing across the road.

"On the storm drain?" she asked.

"Oh, that's what it is!" I'd noticed the raised platform on the opposite verge, and frankly had no other options. "Yes, it's perfect!"

To her credit, Roo never questioned me on this. I guess we'd been together for quite a while by now, and she knew I was a freak. At least I hoped so, or she might be about to get more than she'd bargained for. I led her over the deserted road, through the coarse, scrubby verge-grass, and onto what turned out to be a large manhole cover, set into a raised square of concrete. We stopped there, and I held her close. "It's beautiful here, isn't it?"

She cast a wary eye back down the hill we'd hiked up. The view was of road, fading into a darkness punctuated by streetlights. On the upside, it was lined with trees; on the downside, they were invisible in the shadows. We were directly under a streetlight, which kind of obliterated most of our surroundings anyway. I figured it was as good as I was likely to get.

"You know how much I love you," I started. I was looking right into her eyes, and she was looking into mine.

"Yes," she said. "Me too!"

"So, I want to ask you something."

I heard her sharp intake of breath as I lowered myself to one knee. I noted in passing that a colony of massive red ants were trooping straight across the steel cover. Ah well – nothing I could do about that. *Just be a man*, I thought.

I looked up. Roo was crying already, faint tear-tracks staining her cheeks, tiny beads glistening on her eyelashes.

"You know how much I love you…"

She sniffed back a sob, and nodded.

"OW!" I shouted at her. "Sorry! It's the ants. They're everywhere, and they bite!"

"That's okay. I love you."

"Right! Well, I know we've been together for a while now, and I was thinking, OW! You little BASTARD!"

"Are you…"

"Sorry! Sorry."

"You can stand up, if you want."

"Thanks, but I want to– ARGH! MotherFUCKER!"

I stood up. "Sorry, that one really hurt." I scratched my knee, where a substantial lump was already blossoming. "Hang on…" I lowered myself into an awkward half-crouch, with one knee vaguely lower than the other. I took hold of her hands, more for support than for romantic emphasis. The only things still touching the ground were my feet, and the ants were swarming all over them.

"I can't stay like this for long," I explained, "so you're going to have to answer this quickly."

There was no response from Roo – she was properly crying now, either with love, or with despair.

I took a deep, shuddering breath.

"I love you with all my heart. I'll love you for as long as we live. I want to spend the rest of my life with you, and be together forever. Will you marry me?"

Roo, drenched in tears, gave a kind of snotty burble.*

"Was that a yes?" I asked.

She was shaking her head – to clear the tears I hoped, as I had hold of both her hands. My attention was ninety-six-point-four percent on her, awaiting some kind of confirmation or reply. The other three-point-six percent of my attention was on the truly impressive bull ant climbing my leg, which had reached my knee and was now headed towards the gaping leg-hole of my shorts.

"Um, I'm afraid I'm going to have to rush you…"

"YES!" she cried. "I said yes!"

And with that I was released, both emotionally and physically. I stood up and wrapped my arms around Roo, pulling her close and sobbing into her hair. "I love you so much!"

"I love you too!" she sobbed back.

"Just think of all the adventures waiting for us… think of all the things we can do together…"

"I know!"

And then I felt a sudden pinch, and sprang back away from her.

"I'm sorry," I said, but it's…"

"I know."

And there she stood, gazing at me with what I like to think of as devotion in her eyes – while I hopped from foot to foot, shrieking and cursing, and punched myself repeatedly in the nuts.

*Roo has asked me to make it known that she has never in her life, in fact, made any noise even remotely resembling a 'snotty burble'. I have chosen to keep the offending statement in however, as there are two sides to every story – and this is mine. ☺

Epilogue

Roo was delighted. Roo's sisters were delighted. Roo's dad was delighted, which was quite a relief for me, I can tell you.

"Frieda would have been delighted too," he told me, which brought a tear to my eye.

There was quite a lot to talk about when I called my parents to wish them Merry Christmas.

Predictably, they were delighted.

Gill and Chris had decided to wait to break their engagement news until Mum came to visit them in New Zealand. Being rather nervous themselves, they ended up waiting until Mum was leaving – actually until she was on the escalator on the way up to airport security, having checked her bags in and everything.

Then Gill shouted the news up to her, as though she'd only just remembered it – and Mum, all five-foot-one-and-three-quarters of her, turned and sprinted back down the 'up' escalator as fast as her stumpy little legs would carry her.

Alas, her somewhat gnomish stature didn't lend itself well to such acrobatics, and after a good few minutes of full-tilt downhill stair climbing, just about keeping pace with the upward speed of the escalator, she gave up and let it carry her to the top, before taking the matching escalator back down.

There, she embraced the happy couple, and whispered a few choice words in Chris's ear, which none of us were to find out about until many months later.

"If you hurt my daughter," she'd said quite cheerfully, "I will kill you."

And then it really was time for her to go, and Gill and Chris were free to announce their engagement to the rest of the world.

Roo and I made our engagement public soon afterwards.

All of which left us with a couple of interesting dilemmas to sort out.

Because Gill and Chris were now living in his mum's house in New

Zealand.

And Roo and I planned to set up shop permanently in Perth.

Most of the families concerned lived thousands of miles away in England – apart from the non-Australian contingent of Roo's relatives, who were Dutch.

We had two weddings to arrange, on one side of the world or the other – or both – and not quite enough money between all of us to pay for the cake.

Oh, and for those of us who were still English, there would be the small matter of emigrating.

"Don't worry love, it will all work out," Roo said.

And deep down in my heart, I knew that she was right.

Somehow, things always did work out for us.

And after all, it was only marriage! How hard could it be?

One thing was for sure – whatever we managed to organise, it was bound to be an epic affair.

Chaotic.

Potentially disastrous.

And, at least from my perspective, utterly terrifying.

I'm not a big fan of responsibility, you see. In fact, I regularly wake up in a cold sweat, having had a nightmare about owning a house and a car, struggling to make mortgage repayments, and holding down a job where they didn't try to pay me in beer vouchers.

And what did this mean for my life of adventures? Was it over?

Was I on the verge of being domesticated?

Nah. Not a chance!

I had finally found the woman of my dreams, and she was very nearly as crazy as I was.

So far she'd seen me at my best (which, I'll grant you, isn't fantastic) and she'd seen me close to my worst; and she'd seen me washed off the side of Australia's national monument, so I like to think she had some inkling of what was in store for her.

"Hey, does this mean we get a honeymoon?" Roo asked. "We could go anywhere in the world! How exciting!"

"Erm… yes, quite," I said.

One more thing to add to the list.

"And maybe you could publish that book you've been writing since before we met…" she added.

Ouch.

And then of course, there was the biggest question of all to answer; because getting married was just a happy speed-bump on the road trip of our lives.

For now, for once, we could see at least that far ahead.

But what was around the corner?

What would happen next?

And you know what? We've just about run out of room here, so I guess I'll have to keep that surprise for the next instalment...

THE END!

Your Free Ebook Is Waiting!

Hi there folks!

For a LIMITED TIME ONLY, I am offering a FREE e-copy of my first book 'That Bear Ate My Pants!' to anyone who signs up to my New Release Mailing List!

The number one question I get asked by readers is: *"When is your next book coming out?"*

Actually, that's a lie. The number one question I get is: *"How are you still alive?"*

But what if I told you there was a way to find out exactly when my next book was coming out? Personally? From me! And what if I told you I would also send you all sorts of cool stuff – *completely free?*

Well, clearly you'd knock me over the head and steal my bus money.

BUT WAIT – there is a way! I have created a special New Release Mailing List, specifically to let people know when my next book is ready to be launched. Not only will the people on it be the first to know, I'll also send (very occasionally) special offers, updates on what I'm up to and what I'm planning next…

Oh, and did I mention: a FREE BOOK?!?!

Yes, I know. I've said enough.

Follow the link below to claim your FREE COPY of the e-book that started it all; the crazy travel-comedy, 'That Bear Ate My Pants!'

You'll also be able to secure a spot on my list, which is VERY GOOD NEWS INDEED. Why? Well, because I said so! But also because I'm working on something special: a compilation of the Missing Chapters from *all* my books (you know, the ones I had to cut out because otherwise they'd be way too long…). When those puppies are ready, the only place they'll be going is to the people on this list.

So. Are you in?

Just type: **www.TonyJamesSlater.com/freebook**
into your web browser.

Hi folks! Tony here…

Thank-you so much for buying and reading Kamikaze Kangaroos! If you're interested in what happened after the end of this book, you'll be pleased to know that the sequel – 'Can I Kiss Her Yet?' – has just been released!

If, however, Kamikaze Kangaroos didn't make any sense at all, it's probably because you haven't read my first two books – in which case, kudos for making it this far!
If you fancy checking them out, you can find them both on Amazon:
'That Bear Ate My Pants!' – the book that started it all, following my stint as a volunteer in an exotic animal refuge in Ecuador.
And:
'Don't Need The Whole Dog!' – the sequel, based partially in the UK, and then following my adventures in Thailand

A fifth book, about our epic, six-month long adventure around Asia, will be out shortly.
Meanwhile, you can always visit my website, which features pictures of Rusty, Roo, Gill, and all our adventures around Australia (as well as pictures from my first two books). It's here:

www.TonyJamesSlater.com

Also, you can find me on Twitter:
> **www.twitter.com/TonyJamesSlater**
or catch me on Facebook:
> **www.facebook.com/TonyJamesSlater**
or if you get the urge, email me:
> **TonyJamesSlater@hotmail.com**
and check out my crazy blog:
> **www.AdventureWithoutEnd.com**

If you enjoyed this book, please consider leaving a review on Amazon – it doesn't have to be long! Even a couple of words can help convince other readers to try it – and word of mouth is the best form of recommendation an author can get. I really appreciate my reviews, and I read every single one. Thanks in advance!

Can I Kiss Her Yet?

Tony James Slater is back!

This time he's got only one thing on his mind:
Getting married.
According to Bill Shakespeare, the path of true love never did run smooth...
And this is Tony; NOTHING ever runs smoothly for him.
So the path of true love is about to beat him around the head with a snow shovel.

It started so well – with a proposal that left bite marks, and Tony selling his body to medical science in exchange for the wedding budget.
But there were bound to be hiccups.
Like his fiancé not being allowed into the country...

Join in the hilarious antics, as Tony and his bride-to-be fend off randy camels, rapacious rodents, and gigantic cardboard underpants – whilst traveling to Spain, the Middle East, and all over England.
This is a story of life, death, love, marriage, and everything in between.
It's also the story of how not to plan a wedding.
And don't get me started on the honeymoon!

Check it out: type *Can I Kiss Her Yet* into the Amazon store of your choice.

And turn the page for a pair of excellent books from my good friends...

'Free Country'
by George Mahood

The plan is simple. George and Ben have three weeks to cycle 1000 miles from the bottom of England to the top of Scotland. There is just one small problem... they have no bikes, no clothes, no food and no money. Setting off in just a pair of Union Jack boxer shorts, they attempt to rely on the generosity of the British public for everything from food to accommodation, clothes to shoes, and bikes to beer.

During the most hilarious adventure, George and Ben encounter some of Great Britain's most eccentric and extraordinary characters and find themselves in the most ridiculous situations. Free Country is guaranteed to make you laugh (you may even shed a tear). It will restore your faith in humanity and leave you with a big smile on your face and a warm feeling inside.

Check out 'Free Country' on Amazon!

'More Ketchup than Salsa'
by Joe Cawley

When Joe and his girlfriend Joy decide to trade in their life on a cold Lancashire fish market to run a bar in the Tenerife sunshine, they anticipate a paradise of sea, sand and siestas. Little did they expect their foreign fantasy to turn out to be about as exotic as Bolton on a wet Monday morning.

A hilarious insight into the wild and wacky characters of an expat community in a familiar holiday destination, More Ketchup than Salsa is a must-read for anybody who has ever dreamed about jetting off to sunnier climes, finding a job abroad, or momentarily flirted with the idea of 'doing a Shirley Valentine' in these trying economic times.

Check out 'More Ketchup Than Salsa' on Amazon!

About the Author

Tony James Slater is a very, very strange man. He believes himself to be indestructible, despite considerable evidence to the contrary. He is often to be found making strange faces whilst pretending to be attacked by inanimate objects. And sometimes – not always, but often enough to be of concern – his testicles hang out of the holes in his trousers.

It is for this reason (amongst others) that he chooses to spend his life far from mainstream civilization, tackling ridiculous challenges and subjecting himself to constant danger. He gets hurt quite a lot.

To see pictures from his adventures, read Tony's blog, or complain about his shameless self promotion, please visit:

www.TonyJamesSlater.com

But BE WARNED! Some of the writing is in red.

Made in the USA
Middletown, DE
26 March 2021

36187209R00227